CULTURAL SUICIDE

CULTURAL SUICIDE

The Colonisation of Britain

THOMAS PAINE

ISBN 978-190964-465-6
Printed and bound in Great Britain.
Published by Thomas Paine Books 2015

CONTENTS

DEDICATED TO THE MEMORY OF

ALL THOSE MEN AND WOMEN

WHO FOUGHT FOR OUR FREEDOM

IN TWO WORLD WARS

INTRODUCTION

OVER THE LAST 50 YEARS I, and many of my native compatriots, have become more and more concerned with the increasingly serious problems thrown up by the transformation of England in particular, and to a lesser degree Britain as a whole, into a so-called 'multicultural society'. In the earlier decades of this period we were bombarded with propaganda from politicians and liberal intellectuals in an effort to convince us that this momentous social experiment would improve our society and by implication make us all happier. We were told that ethnic diversity was culturally stimulating, that immigration was good for the economy as it would bring in much-needed skilled people, and that poor immigrants were needed to do the jobs that the natives were unwilling to do. Leaving aside for the time-being the possibility that these were controversial claims, it was noticeable that, like most propaganda, the presentation was completely one-sided. Indeed the initial attempts by some people to air their scepticism or a contrary view were soon firmly suppressed. It was not long before it was impossible to protest without being labelled a 'racist', 'fascist', Nazi or 'xenophobe'. To my consternation, the long-cherished British freedom of speech, hard-fought for over centuries and considered to be the major bulwark of democracy, was rapidly being snuffed out. Anyone listening to this one-sided 'debate' might well have concluded, despite the obvious emerging social problems, that there was a consensus in favour of the 'multicultural society' and that it was a major aim of all political parties, and by implication of the public, to welcome and enhance this desirable cultural change in every possible way and as soon as possible.

Nevertheless it was obvious to me that very few ordinary citizens had been so grossly unhappy with the relatively homogeneous society which had survived World War II that they were clamouring for the mass immigration of people from many other cultural and racial groups. In other words, our democratic right to live in and sustain a culture of our own making and choosing was being trampled on by our political rulers for their own purposes, and this establishment group seemed determined to squash all opposition, using the full force of the law to achieve its ends. Some initial street-protest marches and objections from Trades Unions soon ceased. So-called 'race riots' by 'extremists' were also quickly suppressed by the use of severe legal penalties. The lone parliamentary protest voice of that highly intelligent and maverick MP, Enoch Powell, was silenced by sending him into the political wilderness of Northern Ireland.

Paradoxically, at the same time that we were constantly being reminded of all the advantages that mass immigration was supposed to be bringing, there was a stream of news stories about the serious problems that this social change was bringing. To mention only a few problems: we witnessed 'race riots' in our major cities, difficulties with integration in schools and housing estates, mass illegal immigration, and an epidemic of crime. It soon became clear that the politicians who had begun the immigration policy had no control of our borders and did not even have an accurate system for counting the numbers of legal immigrants, let alone the illegal ones. In private, many of my friends and acquaintances expressed grave concern at what was happening to the social fabric as a result of the mass immigration, or even a downright hostility to the policy, but which they were afraid to voice in public.

Much of the media discussion was at a very superficial level, and seemed to assume that every decent person must be in favour of the dramatic and uncontrolled social changes that were taking place, and that the many advantages of a 'multicultural society' were self-evident. Those few people who dared to raise objections were labelled with pejorative terms, and usually recanted under a fierce verbal attack, including the few protesting politicians. Even radio presenters adopted this intimidating tactic towards phone-in listeners, and thus discouraged further protesters. The general climate in the broadcast media therefore quickly suppressed any sceptical or opposing viewpoint, and, in private, people complained that free speech was no longer permitted in a country that had long prided itself on this main pillar of democracy.

In the last decade there has been a slight diminution of the liberal message of the advantages of mass immigration. Slowly, an acknowledgment, by some of the intelligentsia and the chattering classes, of the severe stress caused across British society, has replaced this message. This change has resulted in a slightly more open debate, but in the broadcast media this still takes place at a very superficial level, and seldom has there yet been an adequate representation of any contrary view. The debating TV audiences are now often packed with a strong element of the younger immigrant settlers, who not surprisingly are all in favour of the 'multicultural society', and feel that they are entitled to be here and to enjoy all the privileges and rewards of full citizenship. Not surprisingly the native element often disagrees and much mutual hostility is evident.

Britain has for a long time been proud of its history of tolerance, and of welcoming, or at least tolerating, immigration. My strong impression, from day to day conversations soon after the migrant flood began, was that this previous tolerance has quickly run out, and has been replaced by a widespread and deep resentment. In the very early days, the good people of Dover expressed their dismay at the influx through the Channel Tunnel of illegal immigrants, who invaded their town via the ferries from Calais. They complained that some of the immigrants were accommodated by the Local Authority in a building that had been an elderly persons' home, which had been closed down a few months previously for lack of money. In March 2002 we saw the closure of the rail freight service through the Channel Tunnel, because of the failure of the

French authorities to police effectively the Sangatte freight terminal and its approaches. People privately wondered why anyone would want to join the police, who were frequently being accused of being 'racist' whilst trying to control rising street crime, and often had to stand between hostile groups of city 'race rioters' without effective means of defence. Many natives believed that the police were often frightened to arrest immigrants committing petty crimes, for fear of their being accused of being 'racist', and, in effect, there was one (lax) law for the immigrants and another (strict) law for the natives.

A glance across the Western world reveals that these problems are not unique to Britain. I have used the word 'Britain' throughout most of this book, although 'Britain' seems to be changing its meaning in the national sense, with the advent of successful nationalist movements in Scotland and Wales. Nevertheless, it seems likely that much of the subject matter will apply not only to England but also to those increasingly independent nations within the United Kingdom that are beginning to suffer similar problems in common with many of our European neighbours and, of course, America.

The rules of the European Union, to which Britain belongs, include one that requires countries to accept immigrants fleeing from persecution (refugees), and another that requires the country of first entry to be the one that should accept them for settlement. These rules, with a later one granting freedom of movement across borders within the Union[1], predictably resulted in an open invitation for criminals and organised gangs to traffic huge numbers of poor people from Eastern Europe, and as far afield as Africa and the Indian subcontinent. The problem was particularly severe for Britain because it was seen (and still is) as being a generous welfare state that would welcome all comers to share our relatively good

---

1   Wikipedia: European Union: Internal Market: Free movement of goods, capital, services and people.

fortune. Many Western European countries faced with similar problems ignored the rule of settlement in the country of first entry, and were only too anxious to assist the economic and illegal migrants on their way to Britain, the country of first choice for many travellers, because most other European countries were less lavish with their welfare benefits. Hence the protracted problem for us of the Sangatte shelter in Calais, which helped the migrants who were illegally journeying to Dover, on trains through the Channel Tunnel and on lorries using the ferries.

History reveals that mass migrations across the globe have not been confined to recent times. I intend therefore to study this phenomenon in the round, hopefully in as objective fashion as is possible for one who is alarmed at the changes taking place in Britain and the developed Western world, with a view to learning lessons from other situations that may help us to deal more rationally and humanely with a pressing and serious, modern, social problem. This problem seems to have produced complete confusion in the minds of British and Western European politicians as to the benefits, disadvantages and causes of immigration, and consequently they seem to have no idea what they should be doing to deal with it. Indeed, most of their *ad hoc* measures have made the situation worse.

It is my hope therefore that this book will help to stimulate a meaningful and informed debate to help us, in Britain, decide whether we wish to live in a 'multicultural society' or not, and what we must do to fulfil most people's reasonable aim of living in a peaceful and harmonious society. I drafted an initial version of the book in 2002, but in the censorious climate that then prevailed it was rejected by publishers without their even looking at a synopsis or sample chapter, because it was 'too controversial'. Thanks to the wonders of the internet this amended version is being privately published, despite my belief that many of the liberal intelligentsia may wish it could be banned. Whatever its failings,

I think that many people whose views have been suppressed for decades will welcome a serious attempt to analyse the causes of our current social problems, in order to see if a sensible strategy can be devised to remedy the situation.

It is true that many university academics have written about the advantages of 'multiculturalism', and some of these intellectuals have also criticised the phenomenon from various viewpoints. However, the views and opinions of ordinary people have largely remained unheard or ignored – for a number of reasons. The first and most obvious one is that free speech and expression have, until very recently, been systematically suppressed, and even in 2014 free speech on this subject is seldom encouraged by the intellectual and political establishment. The second reason is that political leaders and activists have realised that their parties require the votes of the immigrants in many constituencies and, therefore, they have had to create an attitude of approval and welcome within the political class, and thus opposition and hostility to 'multiculturalism' within that group is (still) discouraged by the party leaders. Thirdly the politicians, the BBC, other broadcasters, and 'liberal' intellectuals have mounted a steady and ubiquitous propaganda campaign to indoctrinate the electorate with their views.

I have attempted to produce, first, a rational analysis of culture and the factors that underpin it, together with an investigation of the phenomena of multiculturalism, mass migration, cultural conflict, and how these threaten our Western democracies. I have followed these analyses by conclusions which I think should provide a guide to planning the urgent solutions needed to mitigate our serious social problems. The strength of this book (if it has any merit), is that it will give voice to a body of opinion that has been almost totally unheard, namely that of the ordinary British man and woman in the street.

I have had to write without recourse to a lot of the research as to the facts and figures that I would have liked to use to validate my assertions and conclusions. However, any scientist, historian or serious journalist knows that it is easy to adduce evidence and to quote references to prove one's point or theory, by carefully selecting source material. For this reason I have proceeded mainly on the basis of my own views, founded on what I hope are reasonable perceptions and conclusions, after discussions with a good many native British people, and after thinking carefully about the information supplied by many books, a host of media reports and the internet. This contribution is therefore based on my own opinion formed on 'facts' derived from the media reports and literature available to all people in Britain interested in politics, rather than on scientifically established facts, with the hope that others will follow with well-based critiques of the ideas and with better arguments. There are, almost certainly, some errors of fact that research by others will reveal, but I doubt whether such errors will destroy my thesis. Certainly, my own experience indicates that many of my opinions, perceptions and conclusions are shared to some degree by a considerable body of ordinary people, whose voice has so far been suppressed.

After all, as has been said in other contexts, perception is everything.

§

CHAPTER ONE
The Importance of Culture

CULTURE IS THE SUM TOTAL of the shared history, beliefs, values, language, art, religion, literature, customs and behaviours characteristic of a (usually) stable human social group. Commonly in the past the members of such a group had similar racial origins and usually occupied a long-established home territory. The importance of culture today is sometimes overlooked or taken for granted, particularly if the group has existed for a long period isolated geographically from other cultural groups. When two different cultural groups have first come into contact in the past the differences have been highlighted, and there has almost always been conflict, especially if one group has suddenly invaded the territory of the other group. Such meetings have usually been disastrous for one of the groups. If one group has been more powerful, more numerous and better armed, it has usually overwhelmed the weaker group and its culture. The invasion of North America by Europeans resulted in the displacement and near annihilation of the American Indians (or Native Americans) and their culture in a very short space of time. Indeed these invaders deliberately starved the natives into submission, stole their long-held territory and obliterated their culture. The Spanish invasions of the Maya, Aztec and Inca territories in Central and South America produced similar results, helped by the inadvertent introduction of European infectious diseases. The invasions of Australia and New Zealand by the British were also examples of this process. Even as I type, the process of cultural obliteration of some indigenous tribes is proceeding in the Amazonian jungle as a result of the actions of logging companies, who are destroying the trees that are an essential part of the ecosystem that the tribes have traditionally relied on for all their necessities.

If a weaker group manages to survive physically by virtue of relatively large numbers or other factors, their culture is nevertheless obliterated or attenuated, and its members usually finish up as an inferior social group, pathetically hanging on to remnants of their original culture on the fringes of the stronger and dominant one. The invasion of Australia by the British in the late 18th Century, which caused the overwhelming of the 40,000-year-old culture of the Aboriginals, is a typical example of this phenomenon. Even if the invaders have no intention of destroying the weaker group, their superior technology, the sheer weight of greater numbers and their economic dominance usually ensures the serious attenuation and submission of the native culture. In addition, contact with invaders from across the globe has often resulted in the transmission of diseases for which the natives have had little immunity, and their numbers have consequently been decimated. The surviving victims may eventually be tolerated at the margins of the dominant, invading culture as an inferior, native, remnant group, often demoralised, prone to alcoholism, chronic unemployment and other severe social ailments.

If two cultural groups first meet on more equal terms, the result has usually been prolonged conflict and mutual attempts at domination, with much distrust and hatred on both sides. Northern Ireland, the former Yugoslavia and Israel/Palestine are all recent examples of this scenario. One notable aspect of this type of cultural conflict is the intense and apparently irremediable hatred that is often maintained for centuries. Another exceedingly disturbing feature is that sometimes the two groups may appear to be living in harmony for a long period of time before some incident, or perhaps merely a rumour of an incident, sparks off mutual violence to a horrifying degree, as happened in 1999 in Indonesia between Christian and Muslim communities.[2] Tens of

---

2   www.frontpagemag.com/archive (25.11.2002): Islamism's Other Victims: The Tragedy of East Timor.

thousands died when Muslim gunmen terrorised Christians who had voted for independence in East Timor. Another example of this seemingly inexplicable and explosive, barbaric behaviour was the violent conflict between Hindus and Muslims at the partition of India in 1947, followed by riots between the two religious groups, which resulted in almost a million deaths. In 1984, following the assassination of Indira Ghandi, India's Prime Minister, by her Sikh bodyguards, several thousand Sikhs were killed in subsequent rioting. In February/March 2002 in the Western India state of Gujarat, fifty-six Hindus were burned alive in a train torched by Muslims and this massacre sparked off communal violence across the state that resulted in seven hundred deaths. Ironically most of this killing took place in Ahmedabad, the capital of Gujarat and the spiritual home of Ghandi, from where he began his campaign of peaceful non-cooperation with the British in the 1920s. Despite this recent, violent history in secular, democratic India, that country is usually thought to have had a relatively good record of social harmony for a diverse post-colonial country.

Clearly we are dealing here with very powerful and universal human emotions, that it would be foolish to ignore. Although these conflicts are often described in racial or religious terms, the more fundamental factor is surely that of culture in general. Of course culture includes religion, and cultural groups may well be distinguished by racial origin, but neither of these two factors is essential to serious cultural conflicts, although they undoubtedly figure frequently. Religion and race (or ethnicity, as the modern attempt at euphemism has it) act as symbolic badges of identity, that are useful in differentiating members of one group from the other, and they strengthen in-group affiliation. It is always helpful in a serious and dangerous conflict to be able easily to recognise one's adversaries from one's friends. Indeed, actual badges of identity, such as uniforms, badges and flags, are recognised by all antagonists to be essential in formal warfare; to be captured during battle, masquerading under the enemy uniform, is to invite summary execution. It is a sad comment on our version of modern 'civilisation' that we have agreed rules of warfare so that the frequent mutual killing process does not (hopefully) overstep the line into 'barbarity', which it usually does.

We need, if violent inter-group human conflict is to be eliminated, to understand why culture is so important, and why an outside threat to one's culture is so disturbing that people easily become intensely motivated by hatred, with resentful and violent feelings, and even commit unspeakable atrocities that seem completely at odds with their previous civilised behaviour. In such circumstances a community is then vulnerable to being led down an unthinkable barbaric path by demagogues who are usually careful to identify and stigmatise the hated group, such as happened in Nazi Germany. It is interesting, in the present context, that the Nazis insisted that a badge (the Star of David) was worn by the Jews and displayed on their shops, so that the German population could easily identify the objects of their hatred.

Above all, we must not think (*whichever cultural group we are affiliated to*) that we will never follow such examples because of some imagined moral or intellectual superiority. We may be civilised, rational humans on the surface, but we are all still emotionally-driven barbarians beneath the skin. Circumstances change, and often human behaviour changes with them. One has only to look at the changed cultural behaviour of the Jews, victims of persecution throughout the ages, since they became Israelis in their own land (again). Some of us, including some of my Jewish friends, think that the Israelis frequently act towards the displaced Palestinian people as did the Nazis to the Jews. They have certainly thrown off their previous victim status, and most of us will applaud them for that. We can also understand their determination to fight for a land of their own and their right to be recognised as a nation. Unfortunately their land is disputed territory and they are surrounded by displaced Palestinians, many of whom do not recognise the Israelis' right to the land, or Israel's right to exist as a national entity.

The origins of culture stem from our nature as *social animals*, reliant on small group living for survival at least as far back as our primate ancestors. Hominids developed over millions of years as animals with ever bigger brains, dependent on their superior intelligence and social organisation for defence or attack, rather than just on physical strength and bodily weapons. The long period of dependency of their young and the accompanying extended developmental period, during which the offspring learnt essential survival skills from their parents, siblings and extended family members, made the need for social interaction with its emotional complement an important part of their psychological makeup. This social interaction involved the learning of the differences between members of their own tribal group and potentially hostile strangers, in competition for scarce resources, and the more subtle differences within the extended tribal group. Thus the early learning of facial features and expressions, signs of emotional states, and behavioural signals (body language) were crucially important for survival, enabling early hominids to distinguish quickly friend from foe. The strong tendency, even now, to examine strangers carefully and suspiciously must have been incorporated into our ancestors' psyche early in our evolutionary history, as were the aggressive tendencies that would be needed to repel threatening intruders. Paradoxically, at the same time, the important tendency to cooperate with family and tribal members would also be incorporated into our psyche, as can be seen not only in modern humans but also in modern primates and other social mammals such as lions and wolves (called 'kin preference' by geneticists). The long period of evolution ensured the selection of these psychological traits, and they therefore became 'hard-wired' into our ancient brains and hormonal systems. Culture, the vital glue of social interaction, consists of subtle, learned patterns of behaviour grafted onto these inherited traits, so that modern humans engage easily (if somewhat paradoxically) in both cooperative and aggressive behaviour, according to perceived circumstances.

Whether this simplified description amounts to a scientifically accurate account, or not, of the evolutionary basis of our habit of examining people we encounter in our daily lives, it is known that the developing infant very early becomes emotionally attached (or bonded) to its nurturing adult carer(s), usually its mother, and initially does not distinguish friend from stranger. However, at about the age of six months it begins to be fearful of strangers and then gradually, during early childhood, develops a hierarchy of relationships so that its attachment or affiliation to parents and other family members is strong, with a widening circle of friends, neighbours and compatriots, with whom there is a gradually diminishing strength of affiliation. In this learning process the child is guided by the example of family members, who also teach it whom it can trust and whom it should treat with caution or suspicion. The admonition to be wary of strangers is a common parental message strongly impressed on children in the current atmosphere of heightened awareness of the dangers of paedophiles and other predatory adults.

Family upbringing is the means by which the prevailing culture, with all its subtle and multifarious manifestations, is initially handed on to our offspring, later supplemented by a common educational system and peer pressure. Each family has its own version of the common culture, as do the neighbourhoods and wider regions of the country. These subcultures are mostly minor variations of the regional and national culture that unites the society, and gives its citizens their feeling of national identity. Of course, some families, and some small groups of people, develop very different subcultures, that will often be perceived by the majority to be eccentric at best and deviant or criminal at worst. If members of these families or groups are sufficiently different from their neighbours they will usually be ignored, ostracised or even hounded out, if they are perceived as being a severe and chronic nuisance, or a threat to the majority.

Some social groups with strong affiliations to their professions, occupations or common activities have their own subcultures, which again reinforce their important subgroup identity. Army regiments, police forces, the learned professions, Trades Unions, commercial companies and sporting clubs all tend to develop subcultures that foster mutual help, pride and achievements, and improve morale. Codes of conduct are formalised, new recruits are often indoctrinated into the mysteries of the group, and symbols such as flags, coats of arms, badges, uniforms, ceremonies and rituals reinforce identity and promote allegiance within the group. These subgroups are a universal phenomenon and arise because of the very strong need for people to have daily social contact with familiar friends, neighbours and colleagues, in the otherwise anonymous crowds in which they exist in our large conurbations. Evolution hard-wired into our brains the tendency to need *a small group* of relatives, colleagues and friends, within which we all feel most comfortable. It is thought by anthropologists that hunter-gatherer groups usually consisted of up to about 150 genetically related members,[3] and we still find that we need that size of social group with whom to socialise. Many of us indeed find smaller groups much more preferable.

The above description implies an ancient background of a relatively stable, peaceful and long-established 'monocultural society'

---

3   Wade, Nicholas (2006) pp.12, 58.

on a small scale. We now live predominately in large conurbations
of recent origin, the change beginning when agriculture was
invented about 10,000 years ago.[4] Since the industrial revolution
in the 18th Century the process accelerated, and now most people
the world over live in large, ever-expanding cities with populations
of millions. We have had to learn to control the behavioural traits
hard-wired into the ancient parts of our brains, by means of rational
and learned behaviour which is mediated by our expanded and
intellectual modern cerebral cortex. Unfortunately, this learned
behaviour has had little time to adapt us to the fast social changes
that are imposed by living in vast groups of anonymous strangers.
Most of the time, most of us who consider ourselves to be civilised
(a word derived from the Latin *civis* meaning 'city'), and try to
act in a polite, considerate and friendly manner, but we cannot
always control our ancient, inbuilt emotions when frustrated or
threatened. Thus we often find ourselves in a conflicted state
of mind and sometimes later regret what we have said or done
under the influence of emotional states that arise spontaneously.
The frustrations of crowded city life often result in outbursts of
violence, such as 'road rage'. Experimental psychology continues
to discover more ways in which our behaviour and choices are
emotionally driven, even when we think that we are making
rational decisions. Our ancient brain still has a profound influence
on our behaviour even though it works unconsciously.

Nevertheless most modern people live more or less happily
with their families, friends and work colleagues in their own
subculture, but are just as happy, more or less, to holiday, to visit
relatives, or to move home to other regions of the country. We
have in effect adapted somewhat to the 'extended family' of the
nation state, especially when many serious conflicts in the nation's
history are now more or less settled, although remembered as part

---

4   Ibid. p.101.

of the common culture developed by our shared ancestors. Of course, much of this history has been embroidered over centuries into a more acceptable narrative, and we take pride in our heroes and their exploits both true and mythological. Less acceptable historical events are often misinterpreted by using current moral standards, especially by the critics amongst us who wish to present themselves as morally superior.

The long-standing state does not need to make much effort to unify the nation because the nation has 'self-unified'. In other words there is a long history of unity and pride in the nation's achievements, its heroes, myths and organisations. This reassuring common culture is therefore taken for granted, and the minor differences amongst the population, especially in different regions of the country, are not perceived as alarming, distressing or threatening. On the contrary, for most citizens these minor subcultural differences are interesting and stimulating, and some people may even come to prefer a different subculture from the one in which they were brought up. It is common nevertheless, for jokes to be circulated about people from different subcultures, based on some subgroup characteristics (often exaggerated to beef up the humour). These jokes seldom cause offence, and indeed, are often told with pride by citizens against themselves, for example Jewish, Irish, Welsh, Scottish and English jokes among the British. The basic national culture binds the major group together so that all members can go about their daily activities in an atmosphere of unconscious and dependable trust. This means that casual meetings with one's compatriots are carried out harmoniously and happily, because the cultural signals are mutually reassuring, and 'mind reading' is easy and spontaneous. The happiest social situations that one can enjoy are usually with people like oneself, and where trust is taken for granted because of the cultural similarities.

However, within the large 'multicultural' cities that house the majority of citizens throughout the modern world, and that are plagued with criminals, one cannot rely on all one's compatriots or neighbours to be trustworthy, friendly and helpful. Not surprisingly therefore even adults, especially vulnerable ones such as the elderly or disabled, have to be very wary of strangers, many of whom are on the lookout for easy economic prey in the 'urban jungle'. This wariness is likely to be exaggerated when encounters occur in unfamiliar territory, and when strangers are clearly perceived to be from another cultural group, and especially if the strangers have earned, as a group, a bad reputation for criminality or some other unwelcome behavioural feature. In these large cities, where different racial and cultural groups occupy ghettoes in which they live separate and parallel lives, there is now heightened vigilance and suspicion on all sides. The ghettoes arise spontaneously when any small group invades and tries to settle in an existing but different cultural group's territory, because they provide the comfort and protection that the newcomers naturally need. Unfortunately, an undesirable side-effect of this self-inflicted separation is that it heightens the suspicions of both groups. Indeed, the ghettos resemble the ancient tribes in the jungles of long ago, but with the added disadvantages of being more tightly crowded together and of very recent acquisition. It is therefore hardly surprising if, from time to time, outbreaks of minor or serious inter-group violence occur.

Many modern so-called 'multicultural societies' paint a very different picture from 'monocultural' ones. Their governments, conscious of the pressing need to weld peoples from very different cultural backgrounds into one harmonious nation, devote a lot of state-organised educational effort to fostering a national identity. In the USA for example, American history, the symbolic exhibition everywhere of the national flag, the swearing of the oath of allegiance, the promotion of the constitution and the myth of the 'American Dream', are all heavily emphasised in the schools and in the media, and by the politicians (with their constant speech-ending of 'God Bless America'), in an effort to make its citizens feel American first and foremost. When I see frequently on TV the tireless efforts of American politicians and their President to convince us (and themselves!) that America is the greatest nation on earth, I can't help thinking of one of Shakespeare's marvellous psychological insights when he makes Hamlet say: 'Methinks she doth protest too much.' Of course, almost everybody thinks that their own nation and culture is the best, just as most children think that their mother is the best one on earth. In older, stable nations of relatively homogeneous racial and cultural structure, these heroic efforts by the state are not usually necessary, because national identity can be taken for granted where it is universally handed on by most families embedded in an already united group. In countries riven for decades with conflict between two large cultural groups, such as in Northern Ireland during 'the troubles', identity symbols were (and still are) fiercely and proudly displayed on the streets by the two groups in order to emphasise their own territory, cultural affiliation and differentness, and sadly, to intimidate the opposing group. The terrorist organisations in Northern Ireland used to wear army battledress, black balaclavas and badges, and each side had their own national flags and colours prominently displayed in their ghettoes, and in their group marches or street demonstrations. The criminal gangs that are now a prominent feature in 'multicultural' Britain also use some of these methods to promote group identity and solidarity, and have their own codes of conduct. Moreover they often use brutal punishments for infringement of their rules of behaviour. Many of these subcultures promote fierce loyalties, and are very resistant to change. Resistance to cultural change is a characteristic of all humans, who have a very strong atavistic need to identify with some small group, to give a feeling of comfort and security.

In England, display of the red cross of Saint George has for the last few years become much more common than it was before, presumably as a message to recent immigrants given British nationality and passports that they are not English, and as a sign of the feeling of threat to the national identity and culture. It is also used by extreme nationalists during protest marches to indicate their hostility to mass immigration. It seems that a considerable part of the native population, having suffered the loss of free speech, and perhaps having been made anxious by the independence movements in Wales and Scotland, which threaten the break-up of Britain, is trying to send a symbolic protest message to the governments that have allowed and encouraged mass immigration. It looks as if many of the English (and Scottish and Welsh) native populations are now rejecting the badge of being British as a title with no real modern, cultural significance. People of many different racial origins who have recently migrated to Britain have been given British nationality and passports, and yet these migrants are felt by the indigenous population to be interloping foreigners with whom they have little in common. The resentment felt by the natives is also fuelled by the fact that they were not consulted about the drastic consequential change to their culture caused by their so-called 'democratic' governments, who took the unwelcome decision to welcome the immigrants over their heads. It is hardly surprising, if this be a correct reading of the feelings of the natives, that the ignored electorate now seeks a badge of identity that emphasises their separateness and differentness from the groups of newcomers. The current Cameron Government has tried recently (2012) to use the London Olympic Games and the traditional British Union Jack to restore a sense of national identity, apparently with some success, but I doubt whether this exceptional effort will have a lasting effect. Indeed, more recent (September 2013) surveys have shown that indigenous English, Welsh and Scottish people are now turning to their individual countries for their feeling of identity and are rejecting their British identity as no longer having any real meaning. Many of the Scots are determined to achieve full independence, and have already achieved the British Government's acceptance of their referendum on that goal, even if they are currently unsuccessful.

It is not surprising that relatively young nations with 'multi-cultural societies', aware of their internal cultural conflicts and different languages, religions and racial groups, pay so much attention to the problem of creating and maintaining a sense of national identity. Nor is it surprising that Britain, along with its Western and Northern European neighbours, is now undergoing serious social problems as a result of the recent and continuing mass immigration of foreigners with markedly different cultures. It is clearly thought by the liberal intelligentsia, who have had a stranglehold on the morality of the Western world (at least in the broadcast media), that these are only transitional problems on the way to their deliberate social objective, and that efforts should be made to assist the assimilation of the invaders. However, the prior example of the USA does not seem to hold out much hope of success. It looks as if the traditional American ruling class of European origin (the Wasps) have lost their cultural and political hegemony, due to the rising, and apparently unstoppable, tide of immigrants from non-European and Muslim countries, and especially from Mexico with Spanish as their first language. What will happen soon in states with an increasing majority of Spanish-speaking citizens? There are already messages on the internet from such citizens (and some academics) announcing that California will secede from America 'without a shot being fired' and will soon re-join Mexico. Another example of this phenomenon, as recent as 1995, was that of French-speaking Quebec, which was very close to separating from Canada, ridiculous though that outcome would have seemed to an outsider. The Basque and the Catalan people of North Eastern Spain and South Western France have for a long time aspired to become independent states, perhaps inside the European Union. These two movements are keen to hold referendums, and may do so against the wishes of their national governments. Naturally both the French and Spanish governments are against full autonomy for these two independence movements.

It is difficult to predict whether actual dismemberment of large multicultural countries will occur in the next few decades. Certainly large federations and empires have difficulty in maintaining their cohesion, as democracy spreads and allows people the freedom to decide for themselves on the basis of strong, more local identities. These political conflicts are based on the desire, on the one hand, of ordinary people to run their own affairs in local regions with historical and cultural identities, and, on the other hand, on the desire of powerful, rich political elites to hold onto their power over large territories and populations. Undoubtedly the example of the 2014 Scottish Independence Referendum will act as a spur to other independence movements, both in Britain and further afield, no matter the result. Personally I welcome such movements, because 'small is beautiful', and democracy flourishes more easily at the local level. Federations of small independent states may turn out to be the new growth area in democratic politics, as in the Swiss system of direct democracy. Democratic countries that have culturally diverse populations that have not assimilated into a single harmonious nation state, may well start to disintegrate into smaller cultural groups that will demand referendums on independence within a federation.

Culture then, is the essential glue that holds members of a community together, and is clearly of the highest importance to human social life, because it *engenders trust* amongst a population. It creates the major feeling of identity that encourages cooperative behaviour, and allows people to go about their daily activities without social anxiety. In other words, if one has been successfully educated (or indoctrinated) into the prevalent culture one can communicate and interact with other members with a sense of familiarity, trust and comfort. Cultural signs enable people to recognise immediately whether a stranger is a member of the same group or not, and to make reasonably accurate assumptions about the other person's likely behaviour and values. The differences between cultural signs may be obvious or very subtle. Quick assessments may be of great importance in a chance encounter with a stranger, especially for the weaker, less 'savvy' or more vulnerable of the two persons.

Culture therefore has a vital social function in fostering co-operative behaviour and trust within the cultural group, but has a severe disadvantage in modern 'multicultural' existence, where it is always in danger of initiating and maintaining conflicts between people of different cultural groups living in close proximity to each other. What is thought to be 'good' behaviour in one culture may be 'bad' behaviour in another, thus easily leading to misinterpretation, misunderstanding and potential conflict. But, in the worst case, even mutual understanding, a favoured nostrum in liberal quarters, does not inevitably lead to acceptance and harmony. The trendy liberal idea of 'moral relativism', the philosophical movement that promotes the notion that one should respect other people's cultures, is obviously flawed if one is concerned with human well-being. It presumes that there are no moral absolutes, such as some of those enshrined in the biblical Ten Commandments. We may understand why chopping off a criminal's hands is thought to be an appropriate punishment for stealing, in the minds of some Muslims who embrace strict Sharia law, but our understanding of their beliefs does not ensure that we will respect the practice, nor the culture that is based on such a view of morality. We have surely moved on from a medieval set of values based on the interests of tyrants and men, to a point where the interests and values of every human being must be the objective of all our modern societies.

It is obvious that the culture and family subculture in which one has developed from infancy moulds one's beliefs, values, behaviour, moral code, character and social perceptions to a high degree, and although later educational experiences may produce modifications, most of us will still feel most comfortable with people from our own culture. This is because we can 'read' other people's minds without effort, and interpret more or less accurately what they will next say and do, and because everything in our social neighbourhood is familiar and comforting. Conversely, foreigners from very different cultures, with strange appearances, clothing, behaviour, religions, accents or languages, present one at first encounter with a new situation that may turn out to be interesting and mutually fruitful, or disturbing and painful, or of no particular interest. The circumstances of such encounters and the personalities of the involved people usually determine the outcome. To take one obvious example, that of an English native meeting a Muslim woman shrouded in a black burka, so that only her eyes can be seen, the gulf of mutual non-comprehension could hardly be wider. I once sat in a hospital waiting room looking at such a garbed person, wondering whether it was a woman or a man. How can a British person, or any normal human develop a feeling of trust, when faced with such an alien cultural symbol of difference? Her clothing seems to some of us to be bizarre in the extreme, and a symbol of alienation, male dominance, and an insult to our culture. In September 2010 the French Senate overwhelmingly approved a ban on covering the face in public places.[5] In Britain a similar ban was not approved by Parliament, although a majority of the public were in favour of a ban.

Most people strongly hold to the beliefs, habits and customs of their own culture, the elements of which they learned during childhood, and which are reinforced during each day of an adult's social activities within the cultural group. The

---

5   www.telegraph.co.uk (14.09.2010): News Archive: French Senate
     approves 'Burka ban'.

strength of these cultural norms can hardly be exaggerated and, as a result, people usually believe their own culture to be superior, and those of other groups to be inferior and maybe totally unacceptable. Clashes between cultural groups therefore seem to be inevitable, because compromise is very difficult to achieve between parties with strongly entrenched views. These conflicts have been one of the main themes of history, and the last two World Wars, with their hatred, ferocity, wasteful physical destruction and barbarity, are within the living memory of some of us. The human psyche evolved to deal with the problems of tribal survival, and now seems to be driving us to self-destruction in the very different circumstances of modern life. Our evolved brains and cultures have produced the two differing modes of social interaction that are now the mainspring of cultural conflicts in an increasingly crowded world – namely co-operation with the 'in-group' and aggression towards the 'out-group'.

Perhaps inevitably, in a society where the majority of people previously had a common culture, as in Britain and in Western European countries before about 1950, the sudden injection of a mass of immigrants from diverse cultures is likely to give rise to serious conflicts. These conflicts may be severe and protracted, because each group holds dearly to its own beliefs and values, and is certain that the other group is wrong. Conflicts will become heightened when the host country's laws are contravened, such as the example of forced marriage, which has been practiced in Leicester by groups from Pakistan and Bangladesh. Many Muslims think that the state's laws should not intrude into family life, and some of them are campaigning for this view to be incorporated into British culture, even if it means special exemption from British laws for them. This may be a bizarre notion to us, but it could be argued that such developments are the inevitable consequence of a 'multicultural society'. Whatever the outcome of such a proposition for different laws or rules, one side or the other is likely to be displeased or outraged. Many native Britons are displeased at the introduction of halal butchering to please the Muslims, an example of the appeasement policies of the various British governments, especially since we may well be eating halal meat that has not been properly labelled. In this way our own culture is being insidiously undermined.

It might be thought that in a recently evolving 'multicultural society' such as modern Britain, which has adopted many special measures to help integrate its minority racial immigrants, there would rapidly develop a 'fused' culture, and that, as a result, the immigrants would gradually lose their original cultural affiliations. This notion has led to efforts to give the children born here an integrated school education, following similar efforts in Northern Ireland. Unfortunately this measure can at best be seen to be only temporarily successful, owing to the very enduring quality of people's cultural memories, partly no doubt a result of the schools' well-intentioned reminders of their cultural roots, but also due to the strong influence of family, community and religious belief.

As an example of this phenomenon of enduring cultural affiliation we need only remember the cases of 'British' Pakistani men Omar Saeed Sheikh and Richard Reid. The former person was described by the Pakistani authorities as the mastermind behind the kidnapping and brutal beheading in Karachi of the American journalist Daniel Pearl in January 2002. Richard Reid was the arrested 'shoe-bomber', who was convicted of having tried to destroy, by means of explosives hidden in his shoe, a trans-Atlantic airliner bound for Miami from Britain on 22.12.2001. Both men were born and educated in Britain, (and Reid had an English mother), but this had not prevented them from identifying with enemies of this country and joining Al-Qaeda, a terrorist organisation devoted to our destruction. At best, it seems likely that many of the descendants of the original immigrants will be confused as to their cultural identity and, at worst, some will strongly affiliate with their parents' original identity and completely reject a British identity.

It seems that cultural conflict, to at least some degree, is an inevitable consequence of mixing groups of people together who insist on maintaining their own cultures, as many people do. It also seems clear from many historical events that cultural affiliation is very enduring, and resists efforts to merge it with a host culture – the American Dream of the 'melting pot', now discarded in the harsh light of reality. The dream seemed at first, and for many decades, to be succeeding, probably because most of the immigrants originally settling in the USA were of European cultural stock, but latterly there have been many signs that the programme has run into serious social problems, (including the 9/11/2011 airliner attacks by al-Qaeda terrorists on the Twin Towers in New York, which killed almost 3,000 people), now that the more recent immigrants are coming from Arabia, Asia, Africa and Mexico. In fact America is heading for the same 'multicultural' conflict-ridden fate of modern Europe.

Cultural conflicts have been the main narrative thread throughout recorded history, from the period of the classical Egyptian Pharaohs fighting the Nubians and the Hittites, to the modern era of the two horrendous World Wars in the 20th Century, and the Balkan war in 1998-9. Even now, when serious efforts are being made to eliminate warfare as a solution to international disputes, and to persuade all countries to obey international law, we have horrendous and protracted major conflicts in Israel/Palestine, Syria, Iraq and Ukraine, and other smaller ones in Libya, Sudan and Congo. We also have the modern development of terrorist organisations that are motivated by hatred of other cultures, and which can strike at any time, in any place, and in many different ways. Even when we manage to succeed in combating their worst intentions, we suffer the enormous costs of maintaining expensive anti-terrorist intelligence and police services, hundreds of thousands of surveillance cameras and the disruption at border controls. In other words we have to lose many of our cherished freedoms in exchange for maintaining a feeling of security. Freedom and security constitute a zero sum game – the more security the less freedom, and vice versa.

Unfortunately, although most people in multicultural societies are peaceful and benevolent, there are usually minorities amongst them who are extremists, and who are prepared to plan and execute atrocities against people from other cultures. The extremists are, by definition, those who take the most extreme interpretation of their cultural customs and religious teachings, and are often determined to sacrifice their own lives to achieve martyrdom. All cultures seem to produce extremists, but cultures that believe strongly in their own superiority, and which are ruled by authoritarian regimes, are often dedicated to domination of the world, and therefore produce more, and more dangerous, extremists. The extremists are often people who have not developed normal human feelings of compassion and empathy. Some may have a genetic disorder, but many others have suffered abuse and neglect during childhood, or have been brought up in a culture based on aggression and hatred. The vast majority are men, who in general have inherited aggressive traits which once had survival value, but now are harmful in our modern societies unless modified and channelled into useful activities during childhood. What is even more worrying is the fact that some young people seem to be quite normal and benevolent and yet in their teenage years can be drawn into an extremist organisation, and be turned into terrorists. Presumably this phenomenon is based on psychological traits common to young people: the tendency to be rebellious, to seek excitement and even danger, and to be easily influenced by charismatic leaders, and to lack experience and scepticism. They are, in other words, enthusiastic and energetic, but easily brainwashed by demagogues. We must, I think, pay more attention to *understanding teenagers* and their developing value-systems during this period of their development, and harness their enthusiasm for positive and exciting causes, such as overseas projects to help poorer people in foreign countries. Parents and teachers should make sure that they are in touch with children's feelings as the latter pass through puberty, and especially if they are dealing with a child that is withdrawn and bad at communicating, or is rebellious. This is an area of psychology worthy of more research, and my guesses may well be wrong: we need more scientific data on this modern problem.

As far as culture in general is concerned, we need to turn our attention to the factors that promote or diminish hostility and conflict between cultural groups, if we are to proceed in the near future with some hope of dealing better with this pressing and dangerous facet of human nature. It should be helpful therefore to examine in some detail some of the factors that seem important in the structure and content of culture, and to discover to what degree these individual factors influence the clashes between the members of different cultures.

We tend to underestimate the importance of culture, especially when we are brought up in a mainly homogeneous society, in which we take for granted that we are all very similar in our basic behaviours, attitudes, values and moral codes. Many people, especially those who are liberal-minded, emphasise the obvious similarities of all human behaviour, and ignore the subtle but important differences that can cause so much misunderstanding and misery.

What is certain is that culture is never going to go away, and neither is cultural conflict, for the foreseeable future.

§

CHAPTER TWO

RELIGION

OUR INVESTIGATION SO FAR has found that people hold dearly to the beliefs, behavioural habits and customs of their own culture, and, as a consequence, usually consider those of other groups to be strange, unacceptable or inferior. This is particularly the case where religious beliefs and practices are concerned, and one of the worrying changes that has been forced on the British social scene in the last few decades is that of the impact of invading alien religions.

Before the recent mass immigration began in 1948, Britain was a nation with a nominally Christian religion, with the predominant churches being of several Protestant and Roman Catholic denominations, with smaller numbers of other religions such as Judaism. We have a long national history of struggle, often vicious and bloody, between the two main faiths, but over the last three centuries or so the former conflicts have been slowly resolved on the mainland, in the cause of ecumenism. In Northern Ireland, the struggle has continued up to the present, and cannot be said to have been finally resolved. More importantly for the present discussion, is the fact that religious belief and practice was in steady decline in Britain, so that the nation was considered to be largely secular in its beliefs, practices and attitudes. The established Church of England was, and still is, losing devout adherents. Despite this major concern within the Church of diminishing numbers of believers, it has recently been preoccupied with several less important issues, such as the ordination of women bishops, and homosexual ('gay') marriage. These issues have been hotly debated, and are clearly of great importance to the disputants, based as they are on biblical interpretation and fundamental beliefs.

The Roman Catholic Church has recently suffered a major loss of credibility, as a result of the appalling scandals in the Irish Republic and other countries, concerning the widespread sexual abuse of children in the care of the priesthood, and the almost unbelievable cover-ups by the senior clergy. Although prediction is notoriously fallible it does look likely that religious conviction, and regular church attendance, will continue to decline in Britain, at least amongst the natives. Indeed, Rowan Williams, the former Archbishop of Canterbury has, in April 2014, written that: 'Britain is now a post-Christian country'. But he and I may be proved to be wrong, because there is the possibility of a revival amongst the native Britons, because many of them feel the need to combat the influence of Islam, and to shore up their British culture against the invading cultures. As a Chinese philosopher is alleged to have said: 'Prediction is difficult – especially about the future.'

It seemed too many people in the 1960's, including myself, that we were, along with all the other Western developed nations, becoming more rational, tolerant and civilised, and less inclined to accept the authority of the Bible, the churches and their hierarchies. Of course, a major contribution to this change of attitude is the gradual advancement of science, with its extension of experimentally validated knowledge, and its stunning technological achievements. Our parents and grandparents, although more religious than the present generations, were gradually losing their faith in the face of the above changes. Nevertheless, we still think of ourselves as the inheritors of a culture based on the Judeo-Christian religions, and holding most of their moral values. We also think of the influence that the Protestant work ethic of Northern Europe spread amongst many of the European nations, and which made a substantial contribution to the scientific and technological advances that have revolutionised our living standards. Science seems to have better answers to questions about the universe and its creation, and to be discovering the natural laws that determine how matter works, and how the human body and mind develop and operate. Darwin's 'dangerous idea' has revolutionised our knowledge of the creation of living things, including ourselves, and few intelligent people in the Western countries now believe in a supernatural, creator-God. Unfortunately, in abolishing God we are surely making the mistake of demolishing the Christian moral code, and thereby attenuating the world-wide organisation that welcomes all humans into the Church 'flock', without inventing a comparable substitute. In its place we now worship consumerism and capitalism, with its emphasis on individualism, ruthless competition and 'the devil take the hindmost'.

Suddenly this important aspect of our culture, namely the decline of the influence of religion and the secularisation of society, gradually arrived at during the last ten centuries or so, has been shattered by the influx of some five (some say eight) million people and counting, many of foreign racial groups with different and alien religions which dominate their cultures. This religious invasion might have been expected to result in immediate and serious clashes with the remaining indigenous religions, but the actual result has been very different. Although protesters were active in the early days of the invasion, those protesters were, in the main, workers and trades unionists concerned at the possibility of losing their jobs to newcomers undercutting their wages. The Christian Churches at first welcomed the immigrants, presumably because they saw them as religious believers, albeit of different faiths, but at least not atheists. We had the paradoxical experience of seeing the nation's Christian churches being shut down or converted to housing as their congregations declined, and at the same time watching the many mosques rapidly sprouting up in all our cities. We were soon getting used to watching groups of Muslims praying in the streets as well as at the mosques. Clearly these immigrants are very devout people, with strong beliefs in a medieval religion which they intend to continue to practice.

Their culture is obviously very important to them, and most of them make no attempt to hide their beliefs and customs. In other words, they are sending clear signals that they have no intention of assimilating into our culture. Their preachers (Imams) soon gave serious provocation by *openly promoting religious hatred* and soliciting murder of infidels (non-believers). The Islamisation of Britain was, and still is, the ultimate agenda of the extremists and fundamentalist Islamists in our midst. They were, and are, radicalising their youths, organising terrorist activities, accumulating weapons, and sending youths to terrorist training camps in Pakistan and elsewhere. This is not to say that all Muslim immigrants are extremists, but to some extent and not surprisingly, the Muslim communities sympathise with them and protect them. After all, they consider us to be 'infidels', and the Islamists are dedicated to taking over the Western democracies on their way to dominating the world. Unfortunately our politicians have totally misunderstood this dire threat to our culture and way of life and, in the name of tolerance, equality and 'multiculturalism' have encouraged the 'enemy within'. In the process they have naively assisted in the demolition of our own culture.

It is not easy to understand what makes religious belief in general such a frequent underlying factor in horrendous bloody conflicts, especially as many of the world religions profess the importance of peaceful behaviour. It is clear that not all adherents of any of these world religions are antagonistic to members of other religious groups, and some religions preach peace to all mankind, but at the same time many religions have extremist followers, who think it is their duty to spread their gospel, and to attack 'non-believers'. Indeed extremist Muslims are not only determined to take over the whole world; they are easily threatened by any perceived insults to their prophet Muhammad, and think that violence and murder are legitimate forms of response to insults, disagreements or different religious beliefs. This cultural attitude, somewhat surprisingly, is not only held by some first generation immigrants, but even more vehemently by some young men who have been born and educated in the state schools here, the so-called 'home-grown' terrorists, who are willing to become suicide bombers and martyrs.

Religions have a strong hold on their adherents, incorporating a fundamental belief in their unique version of a god or gods, and a world view with a moral code which is strictly taught (but not always strictly practised). They also have a set of rituals, including prayers and worship of the 'creator', 'prophets' and 'saints', days of observance of various significant historic religious events, and rites of passage involved with important social events such as birth, marriage and death. They often have a revered book or books (scripture) which are studied in childhood and consulted throughout life. Children are indoctrinated into the religious mysteries, and are expected to conform to a code of conduct, under the expectation of great rewards in heaven or paradise, and of everlasting torment in the 'afterlife' for committed sins. Thus emphasis is given to the belief in a spiritual life dominated by unearthly and controlling being(s), which cannot be rationally examined and therefore is, by definition, beyond any criticism. Demands for evidence are brushed aside. Indeed, many religions are based on revelation or personal experience, either that of the individual adherent, or of an historical prophet. Of course, this dependence on an ancient, written authority is a powerful tool for the priestly caste, who act as tyrants backed by their unchallengeable authority. One might characterise all religious scripture as 'the tyranny of the dead'. And of course, power (and wealth) is held by the priests, because they alone can interpret any part of the scripture. In other words, most religions are in effect *power organisations,* with autocratic hierarchies that derive their power from an unchallengeable creed that lays down the detailed way that its adherents must live. Religions tap into the universal hard-wired psychological trait which tends to make humans believe in a supernatural creator-God or gods.

A saying attributed to the Jesuits claimed: 'Give me a child for the first seven years, and you may do what you like with him afterwards'. Strong religious beliefs are inculcated from infancy in most religions, and are used to guide the adherent throughout life. The practice of a particular religion, and the shared beliefs, also serve an important social function in the prevailing cultural group, binding people strongly together into a community. This factor is more important than any other in the acculturation of religious community members, owing to its formal structure, its educational and social organisation, and its high standing amongst community members. The shared religious belief, inculcated from infancy, gives community members a feeling of great social comfort, a sense of belonging to a caring and helpful group, and gives them moral self-worth. Because the adherent has been indoctrinated during the period in life in which one is most susceptible to learning a fundamental world-view and moral code, these religious beliefs are very resistant to later contradictory and rational belief-systems. The efficient teaching practices and moral codes of all religions nevertheless have many praiseworthy and positive outcomes, which seem essential to the building of a harmonious and stable community, based on the strong cultural bonds which often survive for life. Atheist critics of religion usually emphasise their disbelief in a supernatural creator, but often overlook or underestimate the positive cultural aspects of religions, and their actual strong and worldwide organisations doing pastoral work amongst poor and deprived people. Most religions will also try, at least in theory, to proselytise people, regardless of their racial origins, and thus help to reduce racial conflicts if they are successful, but, more often than not, promote serious conflicts. Many wars have been fought between different religious communities.

There is a strong and unfortunate tendency for members of any one religious group to feel morally superior to other religious groups and non-believers, and to want to demonstrate their differentness by their own practices and badges of affiliation. They usually believe that single faith schools give their children a better education based on their own faith, and thus hope to ensure that the next generation lives according to the parents' beliefs. Religions usually have a firm and detailed script for the day to day guidance of the faithful, with the promise of an undeniably wonderful life after death for the obedient, and of a certain, horrendous, and everlasting punishment for the disobedient or sinful. The threats of punishment for sinful behaviour are used to produce guilt, which can be a crippling psychological problem for the naïve victims. Religions are also long-lasting organisations for the control of large numbers of people who can be exploited for the enrichment of the earthly leaders. They give much comfort for most people who have a craving for certainty in the face of the many unknowns in life, including death and the 'afterlife', and provide a welcoming social group which constitutes the 'flock' under the pastoral supervision of the local priest. It seems that religious adherents have a strong need to belong to a community-wide and world-wide organisation that has an answer to all questions and problems, has organised and regular social bonding events, and that provides certain and reliable daily psychological comfort. Not surprisingly, many studies have shown that most adults tend to adopt the religion of their parents. One very unfortunate consequence of the use of religious power is the sexual abuse of children, which has been recently discovered to have been widespread amongst the Roman Catholic priesthood, and facilitated by the also widespread protection of abusers by the higher echelons of that church. I have no doubt that similar abuses have been common in other churches and other care-organisations, because paedophilia is itself widespread and is usually organised in 'rings', with powerful people in top management protecting abusers lower down in the hierarchies.

For human societies, as history shows, there is undoubtedly another severe disadvantage in religious belief, and that is the tendency for religious bigotry and fundamentalism. Many religions claim to have the only true God, and to view all other religions as inferior and false. Some may vigorously attempt to recruit followers and to convert people from other faiths. It is only too easy for an extreme adherent to one religion to think that it is his duty to convert 'non-believers', or to eliminate them and their 'false' faith. Of course extremists of any kind are always potentially dangerous, and are not unique to any particular religion, or indeed to religion in general. However, a member of a cultural group with strong religious convictions may be easily persuaded by demagogues or extremist preachers to undertake violent actions against other religious believers or groups, with a feeling of moral justification. Indeed some tyrannical political movements, thought to be atheist, such as Russian and Chinese Communism, German Nazism and the regime governing North Korea, have, or have had, many of the characteristics of fundamentalist religion, including God-like leaders who have to be worshipped. The leaders of many religions take advantage of the religious organisation to enrich themselves, and to gain and maintain power. In order to do this they may need an ever-increasing population of followers, hence the encouragement of parenthood, the prohibition of contraception, and proselytism. The extremist young man needs a moral cause to justify his abominable actions to himself and to others, and religion may well be his choice, and he will be attracted to demagogic preachers. Unfortunately for the Western democracies in general, and Britain in particular, the move towards secularism has been accompanied by a 'liberal', excessive tolerance of alien religions to the point of idiocy, and has invited Islamism to fill the moral gap created by the loss of our native religion. The British political and intellectual elite have encouraged Islamic extremists to create a dangerous Muslim state within the nation. If you think that this last sentence has no foundation in fact, and is the raving of a disturbed and paranoid mind, then read the well-researched and frightening book by Melanie Phillips: *Londonistan: How Britain Created A Terror State Within.*[6]

The hope of us all must surely be that extremism can be gradually attenuated and eliminated. To that end we must embrace in our culture the psychological habits of scepticism, rational thought, obedience to the rule of law, and the ability to manage our affairs without worshipping leaders. But the Islamist threat to Britain is now so far advanced that it will be very difficult to reverse, because the Muslims have become embedded in all our state power-organisations, and are still being encouraged by our establishment elite. Not only are we being threatened by extremist terrorists, but even the majority of 'moderate' Muslims believe that it is their duty to spread their faith and thus create a Muslim empire across the world.

The interesting feature of religious belief from a psychological point of view is that it seems to be a *universal* human characteristic. All the cultures in the historical record, and all the surviving hunter-gatherer tribes that have been studied, show a belief in a supernatural God or gods, albeit with different names, powers and moral codes. We should therefore ask: 'What caused our evolution to devise this tendency to need a religious belief, and what survival function did it serve?' When our ancestors lived in hunter-gatherer tribes of about 150 people, they were at war with their neighbours for much of the time, in order to defend themselves and their territory, to strike their neighbours pre-emptively, and to take female slaves. The tribes were led by the strongest and fiercest male, just as were the pack-leaders of their animal ancestors. This 'alpha

---

6   Phillips, Melanie (2008).

male' leader would be the source of their success and a repository of knowledge and skills essential for the tribe's survival. In all ancient cultures that have been studied there has been ancestor worship, and, as in ancient Egypt, the dead ancestor would be worshiped as a God. It seems to have been a natural and logical thought that the ancestor/god would be looking after the tribe in his after-life, just as he did in life, and his actions would be a natural explanation for the vicissitudes of life on earth, be they bad or good. As in Egypt, the life-giving sun with its daily travel through the 'heavens', and nightly disappearance into the earth or ocean, would often be thought to be the reification of the ancestor-God. All the rituals would have been slowly accumulated in an effort to please the god and to stave off his wrath. In ancient Egypt and in Meso-America, worldly leaders had extraordinary power and became Gods on earth, as well as in the after-life. This enabled them to use a huge proportion of the community's labour force to build gigantic temples and pyramids for their burial tombs, and to take with them precious objects into the after-life. So powerful were their Gods thought to be, that often human sacrifices were the routine way of appeasing them, and, hopefully, thus influencing the weather and other events. Aztec priests routinely sacrificed thousands of captive people at one religious ceremony.

It seems therefore that the universal human tendency to develop a religious belief system, involving the worship of a 'God' or gods is a hard-wired brain element which evolved in our ancestors as a form of ancestor worship. This would have had a survival function, in that the tribe would have a unifying culture based on the oral history of the myths and legends of their ancestor's exploits, skills and bravery. Just as children learn from their parents and other adults the basics of their culture and their knowledge, the tribe would have the benefit of a code of conduct and customs that would fit them to survive in a competitive world, without having to 'reinvent the wheel.' The attributes of the 'God,' such as omniscience, omnipotence and the ability to reward and punish behaviour, would tend to keep the curious and rebellious members from straying too far from the tribal norms. The tribal leader, who would often be the son of the previous dead leader, would dominate the tribe by exhibiting the necessary survival skills that he would have developed by learning from his father and following the 'religious' code.

Later, when agriculture was invented, the increased food productivity enabled larger groups of people to live together in a settled and more comfortable way of life in cities, and with more leisure time. In most if not all cases, as the civilising process got under way with its specialised divisions of labour, and cities became much larger, the rituals, myths and ceremonies were organised and taken over completely by an emerging, professional, priestly class. When writing was invented the literate priests compiled the holy books, and interpreted them to the illiterate workers. Often a tension would soon arise between the community leader or king and the priests or high priest, as to who should exercise power. If compromise prevailed, the two leaders usually agreed to share power between their individual domains, and often cooperated over mutually advantageous wars against external enemies.

It seems clear, whatever the psychological causes operating within faith groups may be, that history shows that different religious groups living alongside each other seem to generate mutual hostility and severe conflicts. This hostility may continue over many centuries, and religious groups often live in ghettoes adjacent to each other, living parallel lives with few social contacts between them. The appearance of peaceful co-existence may however be shattered by outbreaks of bloody violence, triggered by small incidents, a rumour perhaps or a murder. Of course, all wars have not been religiously motivated but, even in politically-motivated wars, the opponents are often both supported by their individual religious organisations, and we see the bizarre phenomenon of 'God' being on the side of the opposing belligerents!

Secular states in Western democracies have very recently begun to think that wars should be a last resort as a solution in any sort of dispute. However, the idea of conquering other peoples and their territory has not been finally eliminated from the human psyche, even in representative democracies, most of which still have so-called 'defence' forces. As recently as early 2014, we saw the Russian military takeover of Crimea, and tensions between the military forces of North and South Korea. Humanity has clearly not yet discarded the old habits of war and conquest, even when religion is not the underlying cause. Nevertheless, in both of these recent examples, the tyrants that control the aggressive forces are God-like leaders of communities that worship them, in cultures that imitate the beliefs and actions of 'secular religions' (if that is not an oxymoron).

Religious extremists are still able to appeal to the medieval mind-set of warfare against non-believers, for the obvious reason that priesthoods can still exercise their power over the minds of congregations of people who are not yet fully civilised – from a Western point of view. Indeed, sometimes most early education is religious, as in the Muslim madrasas. The faithful may not be stupid, but they have not been educated to the level where they can think sceptically, and they cannot entertain the possibility that their spiritual leaders are perverting their religion for their own gain and aggrandisement. Not only that, but until their education is based on a scientific world-view, with its reliance on evidence rather than authority, they do not have the ability to see that they can achieve a high socio-economic status by their own efforts, rather than by pillaging and exploiting other peoples.

In Britain before World War II, the two major religions—the established Church of England and Roman Catholicism—had reached a peaceful mutual tolerance after many centuries of conflict.

By about 1950, after suffering the agonies of World War II and its aftermath of rationing and consumer deprivation, the population had become more united, used as it was to sharing emotional experiences, scarce goods, air raids, and the fighting against a vicious European neighbour. Despite the fears and casualties, which it might be thought would reinforce religious conviction, the population continued the pre-war slide into religious non-observance, although many still considered themselves to be Christians. The mass migration of alien religionists to Britain started in 1972, when Idi Amin deported the people of Indian ancestry from Uganda, and some 30,000 who held British passports arrived here. This influx was followed by uncontrolled mass immigration from the Indian subcontinent, from Africa, and later from Eastern Europe and other parts of the world. Most of the Asians are Muslims, as are some of the Eastern Europeans.

The effect of this unrequested and unwanted change in Britain can hardly be exaggerated. It is as if we have had an invasion of peoples with the attitudes, beliefs, and habitual ways of looking at the world similar to that of the religious Europeans and Arabs of the Middle Ages. The earliest post-war immigrants came on the MV *Empire Windrush* from Jamaica in 1948, to work for London Transport, British Rail and the NHS. Their religions included Rastafarianism, which brought with it the habit of heavy cannabis smoking. In addition the black immigrants from this former British colony introduced the use of more harmful drugs, knives and machetes as aids to drug-peddling, other criminal activities and street mugging. Why anyone would want to import into Britain people from a culture as criminal and violent as that of Jamaica is difficult to understand. But then my first thought was of the social consequences, whereas the business executives and the politicians were probably thinking of the quick political fix of cheap labour, willing to take on poorly paid jobs. I doubt whether they gave any thought to the possibility of the unintended consequences that this seemingly benign innovation would bring about to Britain's culture.

An outstanding early incident, which highlights the cultural shock to relatively peaceful London, was that of the hacking to death of a policeman, PC Keith Blakelock, by a large mob of black youths on the Broadwater Farm Estate in Tottenham, London, on 06.10.1985 during a 'race riot'. The mobsters were apparently trying to decapitate him, and his *post mortem* revealed forty stab wounds. The riot followed the death of a Jamaican woman from heart failure, during a police search of her home. The rioters used machetes, knives, shotguns and petrol bombs, and seriously injured another police officer by dropping a concrete slab on him. Further riots were quickly snuffed out by the Criminal Justice System handing down severe penalties to those convicted of taking part in the riots. Meanwhile British natives wondered how such a monstrous crime could have happened in their hitherto peaceful country. So far, some twenty-nine years later, no one has been definitively convicted for this brutal murder, committed by immigrants who apparently boasted openly of their actions and intentions.

We have since then had conflicts between some newer groups from the Asian subcontinent, and calls for single-faith schools suitable for each religion. The Muslims in particular have built many mosques and madrassas in our large towns, presumably funded from Saudi Arabia, and are clamouring for Sharia law to be recognised. They have congregated in ghettoes, some of which, despite police denials, are practically 'no-go areas' to ordinary natives and the police, creating neighbourhoods that look like scenes from the Indian sub-continent, with females wearing burkas and hijabs – outlandish garb by English standards, and which look like signals of rejection of our culture. There is no doubt that many Muslims are not just settling here as refugees from persecution (or more likely for economic advancement) – **they are actively colonising our country. Nor is this a wholly underground movement;**

their religious leaders openly promote the Islamisation of Britain and Europe. For a very detailed account of this process and its monumental consequences the reader is strongly advised again to consult the aforementioned book by Melanie Phillips.6

The effects on Britain and our European neighbours of the continuing invasions and colonisation by alien religious groups have been, and will be, profound. The phenomenon in Britain amounts to the most radical social upheaval that our culture has undergone since the invasion of the Normans in 1066. It is difficult to imagine a more threatening and destabilising impact on our native culture. The astonishing fact is that our politicians seem to be unable, or unwilling, to take effective action to stop the invasions, indeed they have been, and are still, encouraging it. Whilst they originally started it, and conducted a propaganda campaign to persuade the native electorate to accept it, and its imagined benefits, they are now realising at last that mass immigration has presented us with many serious social problems. This predictable state of affairs should have been obvious to anyone with a nodding acquaintance of the many historical and current bloody conflicts between religious groups around the world. We shall later examine the motivations and actions of the politicians and the establishment elite, in order to understand why they have landed us in such a serious social crisis.

At this point we can understand that religion has had, and does have, even in modern times, a great part to play in most cultures. In some of these cultures an intolerant religion dominates the other cultures in every aspect, including the certain belief in their own God or prophet, Islam being a prime example in Arabia and many other countries. Some cultures, such as those in Western Europe, that are based on a religion which has recently become attenuated and peaceful, with many adherents now non-practicing, non-churchgoing, and not believing in a supernatural God, but nevertheless firmly basing their moral code on that religious heritage, are very vulnerable. Unfortunately, the tolerant culture is likely to be easily overturned by the intolerant one, unless the former is made very aware of the virus in its midst, even at an early stage when the proportion of colonisers is low, but rapidly increasing.

Tolerance, like many psychological characteristics, can be a wonderful aid to social cohesion within a culture, but it becomes a weakness when overdone in the circumstance of threats from without and within.

§

CHAPTER THREE

TERRITORY

ONE OF THE FEATURES of an ancient culture is that the members tend to inhabit a particular territory which they claim as their own, because they and their ancestors have lived there as a group for some long time without dispute, or have won long ago in battle and therefore believe that they have established a right to the territory. Like many species of animals, humans have a territorial 'instinct' in the sense that most of us require personal space and secure territory, and are prepared to resist other people's incursions into what we think is our own area. Again, this instinct may be 'hard-wired' into our brains because of its early evolutionary importance to members of a small tribal group in competition with others for scarce resources, just as with many animals. At a more trivial level, much conflict within a community between neighbours is focussed on boundary disputes, hence the legal aphorism: 'Good fences make good neighbours'. Even a few inches of ground can be hotly disputed, and the dispute can last for years and involve fierce arguments, and sometimes actual violence or even murder. Many wars between countries have been fought over disputed territory, and this feature underlies the present Palestinian-Israeli conflict, the Crimea and Ukraine war, and the continuing Kashmir dispute between India and Pakistan. Even within families, private territory can be strongly defended, such as a child's bedroom, father's study, a place at table, or an easy chair.

Gang fights are often sparked off by territorial disputes, and frequently result in murder. On housing estates different social subgroups (gangs or 'tribes') fiercely defend their own patch (or 'turf'), and invade that of their rivals to carry out acts of violence, destruction and vandalism, designed to intimidate or revenge. So protracted and serious can fighting between religious communities become that walls may have to be built to keep the two factions apart, as in Northern Ireland and Israel/Palestine. If peaceable people who are identified as belonging to one group (gang, religion or race), are housed in the claimed territory of the other group, they may well be harassed, attacked and hounded out. The result of these territorial conflicts is that each group comes to live in a separate ghetto, partly self-imposed and partly imposed by their hostile opponents, where each feels safe, as has recently happened between the Shia and Sunni tribes in Iraq. This harassment may happen to people who, although identified with one of two competing groups, do not have any strong affiliation to either group, but may be expected to join one group or the other: 'You're either one of us or one of them'. This forcible demand to take sides is exemplified in the Northern Ireland joke punch line: 'Yes, you may be an atheist, but are you a Protestant atheist or a Catholic atheist?'

In Northern Ireland, any stranger can recognise at once, on many housing estates, which group territory he is in, because the street pavements are painted with one national colour or the other, flags fly from windows, and walls are painted with slogans and emblems of affiliation. This seems to be the human equivalent of the common animal behaviour of territorial 'scent-marking'. Territory is clearly a prized cultural possession because it gives a feeling of security, and where inter-group hostility abounds it can be expected to be strongly defended. Although most of the above description seems to be that of 'primitive' people, or at least of people behaving in a primitive fashion, we should recognise that these atavistic urges lie just below the surface of us all, however civilised we may think we are. Most of us protect our homes, gardens and even parking spaces, and thus show that this territorial instinct is a universal human characteristic, which is unlikely to be easily diluted or suppressed. Indeed the words 'Fatherland' and

'Motherland' enshrine the importance of the cultural territory to many nations. Because of the modern crime epidemic in Britain we now have active 'Neighbourhood Watch' groups, to provide the defensive 'eyes and ears' in our city and rural neighbourhoods, to deter burglars and other criminals, and to help the police by providing the intelligence which is essential to their protective task.

Wars are often undertaken to acquire new territory under the pretext of uniting culturally related groups on the one hand, and to resist such invasions and to defend the threatened territory on the other hand. In a peaceful society the psychological characteristic of territoriality may not be much in evidence, but that is because there is no perceived threat when neighbours recognise each other's space, and therefore there is no need for any defensive posturing. Nevertheless, this universal human trait is merely lying dormant, and can quickly be resurrected by any real or imagined threat to one's territory. We have only to remember Winston Churchill's speech and rallying call in 1940 when Britain was under immediate threat of invasion ('We shall fight them on the beaches....we shall fight them in the hills... we shall never surrender'), to realise how easy it is to arouse our defensive territorial passions.

Not surprisingly therefore, when new cultural, racial or religious groups are seen to be invading one's home territory, most of us will be automatically concerned at least, and dismayed or angry at worst. Of course, some may feel more threatened by this turn of events than others, depending on other factors. By and large those most adversely affected by the influx of 'foreigners', (or 'aliens' as my compatriots are called by the authorities in Cyprus), will be most disturbed, and proximity acts as a constant reminder that one's territory has been invaded. The area of housing that the immigrants come to occupy will naturally be seen as territory which rightly belongs to the natives. Because many immigrants are initially poor, they have been seen by the British natives to be obtaining benefits and assistance from the Local Authorities and yet the natives close by will often be poor themselves but denied such help. Consequently the immigrants are perceived by the natives to be receiving privileged treatment, including immediate housing, cash payments, jobs and supportive help. Thus defensive territorial anger is reinforced by feelings of economic envy, resentment at the perceived unfairness of the Local Authorities – and hatred. Some groups in the larger host society, such as business people, politicians and the 'race relations industry', may well be benefiting from the influx, but they do not usually live near the poor immigrants. They do, however, arrogantly feel it to be their right to 'educate' the underprivileged suffering natives and to lecture the immigrants about their duty to 'integrate'.

It would be very surprising indeed if this scenario did not inflame the instinctive feelings of hostility towards invading cultural groups which have been developed in all humans by the process of evolution. Those people who live cosily far away from the threat, in a little patch of England still almost unchanged throughout their lifetime, are in no position to criticise or lecture those at the sharp end of the problems, which they themselves have created. The territories, shops and homes now inhabited in many of our large cities by recent immigrants, were not so long ago peopled by native Britons and their families, who are now sorely provoked by having been displaced by foreign people, whom they see as unwelcome invaders who are benefitting from their own government's policies of positive discrimination.

Where have the original inhabitants of Brixton, Ealing, Bradford, Rotherham or large parts of Birmingham gone? Did they go willingly? Were they asked whether they wanted to move in order to provide a territory for these invaders with their alien cultures? Do they still feel resentment at what has happened to them and their displaced communities through no fault of their own, and without their being consulted? What must they now think when they see on television that hundreds of thousands of immigrants are still arriving? And what must they think of the politicians, who are now panicking because of the mounting social problems and yet are still telling them that we need *more* immigrants, because they are good for our economy, because they do the jobs that no one else wants to do, and because we need them to look after our ageing population? Even some of us who have not been directly affected feel considerable resentment at the displacement from our towns of our compatriots – a perfectly natural and reasonable feeling of cultural empathy.

I well remember a newspaper correspondence in the 1970's: aggrieved immigrants and their sympathisers were complaining that the newcomers were not being given enough help to practice their own culture in some London borough. An elderly English lady replied after many complaining letters had been published, to say that she was born in and had lived in her neighbourhood for some sixty-odd years, and that she was now the only white person left in her street. 'What about my culture?' she asked. I do not recollect that anyone gave a satisfactory reply. Indeed there can be no satisfactory reply. The most likely reply from one of the immigrants would be: 'Go and live somewhere else', although I do not recollect such a reply being published. In fact, that is what some Hispanics in California have said on the internet: 'White men go back home', and 'California will soon return to Mexico without a single shot being fired.'

Many of the immigrants, being humans with the same instincts and needs as ourselves, have now established their own territories, by a relatively peaceful conquest encouraged by our political establishment, and now dwell in self-imposed ghettos where they can live within their own comforting cultures, because they also do not feel happy living in our culture, which is foreign to them. They wear their traditional clothes, soon build many of their own splendid mosques and temples (despite being poor on arrival!), speak their own languages and adhere to their own religions, customs and cultures. Their children may quickly outnumber the native children in the local primary school, and eventually they often take it over entirely. Thus they wittingly or unwittingly emphasise the foreign nature of their origins and culture, and thus maintain the hostility of their displaced native neighbours. Worse still, the Afro-Caribbean blacks in particular have infected our culture with the severe violence, drug peddling and criminal gang organisation from Jamaica; the Muslims have brought their medieval religion with all its warped and outdated morality; and many other groups, including the Eastern Europeans, have brought their criminal gangs.

Of course, some immigrants, especially of the next and subsequent generations who are born and educated here, will substitute many British cultural elements for those of their parents' cultures. However, enough of their culture of origin will remain, such as their religious affiliation and the inescapable racial physical characteristics, to remind their native peers that they are from a different culture, and have displaced natives from their traditional territories, houses, shops and jobs. Even when mixed schooling seems to be reducing cultural differences and mutual hostilities, so that children have friendships across the cultural divide, it is likely that conflicts will tend to resurface once adulthood brings about more awareness of cultural affiliations and their consequences. Even as I type (December 2012), the news from Northern Ireland of a serious outbreak of violence, arson and rioting bears this out. The peace process there had appeared to have solved the decades-long 'troubles', but the decision to stop flying the Union Jack over Belfast City Hall was a typical cultural spark to inflame some of the loyalist community into violent protest. The tensions between the two religious groups are still smouldering in 2014, with the relatives of the 'disappeared' still demanding justice, and accusing Gerry Adams, the Sinn Feign leader, of complicity in past atrocities.

In Britain, we now find ourselves, in the later phases of a sudden, unplanned and serious mass invasion of immigrants from other cultures, in the worst possible situation imaginable – namely with large and expanding pockets of conspicuous foreigners apparently taking over many parts of our cities, and thus generating immediate and sustained mutual hostility. This phenomenon constitutes a catastrophic assault on our culture and our way of life, with a foreign occupation of our long-held territory, and has direct parallels to past historical invasions where such assaults were the result of military invasion and conquest. But in the modern case the invasion and conquest of Britain have been the result of the cupidity of the governing and intellectual elite on the one hand, and the passivity of the population bullied into supine acceptance by a continuous forceful propaganda campaign, on the other hand.

Of course, the present invasion has been facilitated by modern means of easy and fast travel, and is stimulated by the efficient means of communication, which spur poor people to migrate in large numbers to seek immediate economic improvement in their lot. The invasion has been, and still is, organised by gangs of professional foreign criminals, but their task is made easy by the apparent reluctance or inability of our liberal opinion-formers and governing elite to elaborate a rational and effective plan to control the influx. Because of the conflicting views on the subject, the disruptive efforts of the ever-greedy 'human rights' lawyers, the ridiculous rules handed down by the European Union and the lack of political will, the gangsters and their immigrant customers are making the best of our dissension and political incompetence.

One of the Blair New Labour Government's 'initiatives' was, I fear, bound to fail, because they had not recognised the causes of the wrecking of their 'multicultural' project. It appeared from their public announcements that they were going to set up a few initiatives, aimed at attempting to persuade foreign people to 'integrate'. They didn't seem to realise that if people on both sides of a cultural divide don't wish to integrate, as I suspect is the case for the majority, and which has been clearly stated to be the case by some immigrants and some natives, then governmental efforts will come to naught. The great example of the American Dream, (the famous 'melting pot'), in which all the different races and cultures would become American, is now recognised as being largely a failure, despite constant and ubiquitous efforts to emphasise the hoped-for cultural assimilation – hence the large and ever-present displays of the American flag, the hands-over-the-heart during the playing of the national anthem, and the politicians' signing-off prayer: 'God bless America.' One might be forgiven for thinking that if God has answered that prayer, then the Americans must be extremely thankful that he hasn't cursed them.

In Britain, a lot of people, their dissenting views stifled in the past, have apparently voted with their feet. Those people who have the economic means have moved out of the big towns into a rural periphery free of foreigners, where they can bring up their children in their own culture. A very popular and long-running TV programme is called: 'Escape to the Country', and a more recent programme is called: 'Escape to the Continent'. What, might one ask, are people escaping *from*? The programme-escapees are mostly well-off, middle-class, youngish and middle-aged professionals and business people, who are looking for a rural village community in which to bring up their children, and to live a quiet and peaceful life. Of course, this is not a totally recent phenomenon, and many people have, for decades, migrated to large cities whilst young, despite the risks of crime, to take advantage of meeting more people of their own age, to attend universities, to access the increased opportunities for career advancement, and to enjoy the vibrant cultural attractions. Later, when married, if lucky enough to have made enough money to be able to settle down somewhere more peaceful and relaxed, couples have often moved out of the city into the country, more suited to the needs of their small children.

Nevertheless, it seems to me that this social move is now immensely popular and there may well be new motivations operating to increase the demand, hence the unending popularity of the TV programmes. I think that the new main motivation may be to transplant themselves and their children into a small remaining ghetto of their previous native and peaceful culture. Concerns about their children's schooling of course loom large, and the typical English village school is still usually peopled by native English teachers and pupils, in stark contrast to the black, Asian and Eastern European makeup of the typical, large, town schools, with their myriad of first languages. If asked, the adults would not say that they were trying to get away from the immigrants that have taken over so many of our large cities, because the English do not like to appear to be unfriendly or xenophobic, and know that the prevailing 'politically correct' wisdom is that we are all the same and should welcome 'multiculturalism'. My view is reinforced by the fact that immigrants mainly live in their self-imposed ghettoes where they obviously feel most comfortable in their own culture, just as we do. It is also reinforced by the fact that since segregation of 'blacks' and 'whites' in America has been abolished by law, there is evidence that people of African descent are even more physically isolated from the white Caucasians than before, presumably because some people in the two racial groups have voluntarily moved to get away from each other. A motivational factor may have been the tendency for young families to move to neighbourhoods close to schools with pupils of the same racial group and social class.

Unfortunately the personal solution adopted by affluent natives in Britain, of moving out of the large cities into the countryside, is now becoming less successful, because the problems of the big cities are also creeping out into the countryside. The latter phenomenon is being accelerated by the deliberate actions and initiatives of the Government and its 'race relations industry', whose stated intention is to continue with their efforts to get foreign immigrant people to spread out and 'integrate' throughout the length and breadth of the British Isles. The objective is that every town and village should have its immigrants in sizeable numbers, in order to achieve the utopian dream of 'multiculturalism'. Other British people, especially those retiring from employment who have realised the capital locked up in their houses, have opted to migrate to a part of some European country where there is not only better weather, but also a British ex-patriot community. Many have migrated to France, Cyprus, Florida or Australia for similar reasons. In many cases, the hope is that they can still live within their own sort of cultural community, albeit transplanted into what they hope will be a relatively peaceful host country, preferably with a basically British or European culture. In other words, these British migrants are also trying to find a small community of compatriots where they can practice their own subculture within a European culture, now that they feel like foreigners in what is left of New Labour's artificial 'multicultural' Britain.

In 2013, a BBC correspondent, Mark Easton, who had the news that native Britons were now in a minority in London, announced excitedly on TV that: 'London is no longer a capital city – it is an international city!' His excitement appeared to me to reveal that the BBC had achieved one of its social objectives of assisting the colonisation of Britain. For many years I have not had the slightest desire to go to London with all its cultural attractions, despite having studied there in the 1950s, because my last visit in about 1965 left me with the feeling that it was fast becoming a foreign territory, to say nothing of the criminal capital of Europe.

The position in Britain today, with more and more territory being invaded by people from other cultures, and the transformation of the large cities into foreign-occupied lands, has arisen in a haphazard fashion with no proper planning, preparation or control, but with a more-or-less hidden, social-engineering project by the establishment elite, combined with the desire of many businessmen for cheap labour. No one knows where this process will lead but the omens do not look hopeful. There are now various racial, religious and culturally diverse 'tribes' living in different areas, and the Government's aim of 'integration' looks like a lost cause, despite their panic 'initiatives' to force people to do what they plainly do not wish to do.

All people, of whatever colour, race, religion or culture tend to want to live together with their own kind for mutual comfort and support. That does not mean that they inevitably hate foreigners – in fact quite the opposite. I am sure that we would be much more likely to get on with each other, and respect each other's cultures, if, in the main, we lived in geographically separate national territories, thus eliminating any cultural threats. The idea that the more closely diverse sorts of people live together and intermingle, and the more familiar they become with each other's cultures, the better they will like each other is, I'm afraid, another utopian dream. Close contact and better information about other people and cultures might well cause antipathy to increase, or indifference to remain as it was. In Britain this antipathy to foreign cultures in general, and to Jamaican, Muslim and Eastern European cultures in particular, is plain for all to see, but the politicians, with their inevitable short-term view and over-arching self-interest, are just hoping that all will be for the best in the worst of all possible worlds. Look at the facts: where in the world are the most troubled areas with violent clashes between the inhabitants, and where are the areas with practically no violence and low crime rates? At the moment (mid 2014) we have wars between different cultural groups in Syria and Iraq - the most horrendous, brutal and destructive civil wars in living memory; Russians and Ukrainians on the brink of civil war; Sri Lanka has not long finished a brutal civil war; Sudan, Yemen, Libya, Egypt, Nigeria to name some of the countries with warring tribes of Muslims; the USA with its post-slavery 'troubles' between blacks and whites, and its cultural frictions between those of European descent and the newer various cultural groups – Muslims and Hispanics; and closer to home, the long-running saga of the Northern Ireland 'troubles'. On the other hand Japan, Iceland, Canada, New Zealand, Australia, all with relatively homogeneous cultures, are managing fairly easily to avoid fierce disputes, violence and high crime rates and to provide their citizens with the peaceful and harmonious culture that most of us long for.

You may say: 'That's obvious – if most of the people in a country have the same history, racial origins and culture of course they will get on easily together under the rule of law, and disputes will be mainly personal, easily settled, and of little concern to the majority. The small number of immigrants from other cultures will probably be there because they either wish to integrate with a preference for the host culture, or wish to live quietly in a small group practicing some of their own culture, whilst enjoying the freedom and peace of the host culture. In other words, they are happy to be left alone, and are no threat to their hosts. In addition, the hosts may find them and their culture interesting and friendly'. Well, if that's obvious, why are we or, more accurately, why are our political masters and liberal intelligentsia, hell-bent on infecting our culture with as many groups of vastly different cultures as they can find? This is a serious question, needing a serious answer, not the endless repetition of the multicultural mantras of the politicians.

Certainly in Britain and in Europe, to say nothing of Israel/Palestine, Africa and America, there is much unhappiness, and there are many serious social problems and a lot of hidden and sometimes overt mutual hostility, coupled with a strong tendency for different cultural groups to live separate and parallel lives. Even amongst people of similar racial origins, but of different religions or sects, such as in Northern Ireland, Syria or Iraq, there is much evidence of cultural and territorial conflict.

I do not think anyone can be happy with the results of the several British Governments' haphazard, poorly understood and momentous social experiment over the last few decades, nor is there much evidence that they have actually reached the stage when they are willing to admit their grievous errors, and to abandon their project. The current Cameron Government looks as if it is trying to get some control of the immigration flow, largely as a reaction to the rise of the UK Independence Party (UKIP), but it is greatly hampered by the rules and laws of the European Union on the one hand, and the cynical tactics of our avaricious 'human rights' lawyers on the other hand. The recent protracted criminal cases of Abu Qatada and Abu Hamza illustrate the difficulties that the Government has had to cope with, when trying to deport even self-admitted and illegal, immigrant, terrorist organisers to their countries of origin. Whilst they have attempted to do what most of the natives consider to be right and proper, to say nothing of being greatly overdue, they are criticised by Ed Milliband's Shadow Home Secretary, Yvette Cooper, for the delays, without her admitting that he and she were members of the 'New Labour' Government that let these vicious Muslim extremists into the country in the first place.

All of this modern history gives the strong impression of total political and intellectual confusion, whilst the monumental social problems continue to worsen as the country continues to be colonised by alien cultures. Under the rules and laws of the undemocratic European Union, our Government is powerless to control the continuation of mass immigration, and our native territory is defenceless. No one knows how and when this story will end. Up to now (August 2014) this misconceived social experiment has led to much unhappiness in both native and invading groups, to the 'Balkanisation' of our homeland, to an unprecedented crime epidemic, to sporadic attacks on individuals, and to severe racial riots in several of Britain's large cities – phenomena unheard of and unimaginable before the start of the mass immigration. I do not think that any rational and well-meaning person can be happy with the result so far of this unplanned and unwanted social-engineering experiment. Even many of the more moderate immigrants, who have greatly benefited from the economic improvement that they have achieved in their search for a better life in Britain, are not apparently happy with their position in our society. They may well be feeling that they have jumped out of the frying pan of poverty into the fire of cultural chaos. Recently Lennie Hendry, a successful black actor, said on TV that there were not enough black actors and film directors! So he is still not happy, even though Britain has given him the chance of being successful in his chosen profession, and he is making more demands on our culture and territory.

I think it must be said therefore that the current intellectual and moral confusion amongst the political intelligentsia in the Western democracies has allowed the situation to get completely out of control. Unfortunately it is the poor, politically helpless and underprivileged working class people of Britain and other Western European countries who have suffered the most from the adverse consequences of this monumental social catastrophe.

I shall now move on to consider another factor involved with culture which is seldom mentioned, but which illustrates how cultural differences can operate to divide human groups, although nothing to do with race or religion.

§

CHAPTER FOUR

SOCIAL CLASS

SOCIAL CLASS IS AN ASPECT OF CULTURE that has received, as far as I know, little consideration with respect to the current problems surrounding mass immigration and cultural colonisation in Britain. It seems to me to be important to these phenomena in three ways that are complementary.

The first way in which social class impinges on immigration is that the social class of immigrants affects the perceptions of both the immigrants and the natives, and the expectations that each group has of the other one. Social class identifies different sets or groups of people according to their economic and educational circumstances, and is, in effect, a name for *subcultures* within societies such as ours and other Western countries. Whichever social class or subculture one belongs to, the fact is that people feel most comfortable with members of the same class and somewhat awkward with members of another class, especially if the socio-economic gap is wide. This is not surprising after our previous examination and conclusions on the importance of culture. If the person we are talking to speaks in the same way (in the same language), behaves in the same subtle ways, looks as if she is in the same economic group as shown by signs of wealth or poverty in her appearance, lives in the same or a similar neighbourhood, appears to share the same important values and to have had a similar education, we are easily able to anticipate for most of the interchange what she is going to say about most subjects. This is because she has had an upbringing in our common national culture and, what is more, in a common subculture, and she has therefore had a similar set of educational and social experiences from birth. After all, the child's upbringing, delivered by her family, her neighbourhood peer-group and her educational system, is the means by which the child learnt the most important lessons of how to deal with the world in general, and her personal, social world in particular. Her mind and world-outlook have been programmed from birth to adulthood often in a fairly systematic fashion, directed by her parents and reinforced by her siblings, friends and the state or privately organised educational system in which she was educated.

The gulf of misunderstanding and antipathy that separates people of different social classes illustrates the importance of culture in uniting them in one subcultural group, whilst dividing them into separate groups leading parallel lives. Sociologists named these sets as 'in-groups' and 'out-groups'. Even two people from the same national or racial cultural group may be totally alien to each other if from widely different social and educational backgrounds. A chronically unemployed woman, born into a 'problem family' and perhaps burdened with many social problems, will have no point of contact with a compatriot from the upper social class, such as a member of the House of Lords, the aristocracy or even ordinary, middle-class professionals. Each would be unable to communicate meaningfully with the other except when engaged in the most simple transactions, and each would be unable to understand the needs, the available opportunities or the life-style of her compatriot. Their day-to-day language, their accents, their economic circumstances, their lifestyles and their social backgrounds would be vastly different. They might as well be inhabitants from different planets. As likely as not, neither would wish to have any continuing social intercourse with the other – in other words, the very idea of 'integrating' would not even cross their minds. Some people from both classes are full of hatred for the other class, which they hold responsible for most social evils. The members of each class usually wish to shun the company of the other one, and to continue living in their own familiar social group and subculture, in their own territory or neighbourhood. Thus, even two people of similar racial origins, embracing the same British culture, are easily divided by their two different sets of subcultural characteristics. Indeed, they are quite unlikely ever to come into contact with each other in any meaningful way. So here, we see, if you accept the likely outcome of my imagined thought experiment, that racism and religion are not the only causes of all social and psychological barriers between people. In fact, although I have deliberately drawn an extreme picture to illustrate my point, this social-class factor to a lesser degree operates in most of our lives. We usually live amongst people of similar socio-economic and educational class, choose our friends, our mates, our marriage partners and our children's friends from amongst people like ourselves. Furthermore, we feel most comfortable, to a greater or lesser degree, with people very like ourselves. Thus we see that social discrimination is universal and, therefore, clearly very important, especially when the relationships are fundamental and lasting, such as in mate, friend and neighbourhood selection.

Subculture, as exhibited in the social class system, is just as important in our daily lives as the background culture that unites us all in our joint national identity. We also recognise easily other subcultural regional identities, such as Scottish, Welsh, Yorkshire, Geordie or Cornish. These regional identities, based on subcultures, are part of the interesting 'tapestry of life', and the subject of many jokes that caricature the behaviours of the regional inhabitants, but seldom give offence. The social class system, for which the British are supposed to be the most prone if not the originators, is nevertheless part of most modern cultures, and a version operates even in America, although they seem often to deceive themselves that it does not. It is a powerful social force, as illustrated by the fact that it might well be easier for two doctors, lawyers, miners or lorry drivers from different countries to get on at first meeting, than for either of them to do the same with a compatriot of a 'lower' or 'higher' social class from their own country, because of their similar professional, vocational, educational and subcultural backgrounds. In India, even today, there still exists a rigid caste system, with the people of the lowest caste being seen to be of less value than animals.

In developed countries, we still usually unconsciously or consciously immediately assess the mental state and social class affiliation of a new acquaintance, particularly if he has a vested interest in presenting himself as a trustworthy person, for instance as a salesman. The stranger may even be a confidence trickster or a maverick of some sort, or may, on the contrary, turn out to become a new life-long friend. Occasionally we may be proved wrong in our initial assumptions, but we are not very often wrong, because humans are, on the whole, very good at intuitively assessing facial expressions, verbal and non-verbal communication, and other nuances of social interaction. We are also affected by regional and class accents, which are cultural components giving some indication of people's origins, education and occupations, just as do body language and dress. Of course, we may sometimes be mistaken, and become the victims of our own prejudices, especially at first contact. Nevertheless, unconscious judgements are naturally made all the time and will be modified as more information is processed during a social contact.

If we interact with an obvious stranger, and particularly if he is clearly from another race or culture, we are likely to be guarded in our initial assessments. This is because we are aware that some of the usual clues available to us in our own culture are now likely to have different meanings. Not only are gestures, body language and dress likely to be different or, worse, to have different meanings, but also some facial signs of emotional states are also likely to be different – although most of these are found universally across all cultures. In particular, it is difficult to understand someone's subtle meanings when one of the participants in a conversation is speaking in an unfamiliar way. There is plenty of opportunity for misunderstanding. We may well be able to guess at a foreigner's socioeconomic class, but we are not as sure as we would normally be in our own culture. Foreign accents make it difficult to understand subtleties of meaning as easily as a familiar accent, especially for the hearing-impaired person. That this is so, is supported by the fact that recently many companies have relocated their call centres back to the UK from India, in order to please their customers, and they even advertise the fact. Unfortunately they have then adopted automatic telephone helplines in order to reduce costs, although customers think automatic telephone helplines are annoying devices, and prefer to be talking to another human rather than a machine.

The second aspect of social class in relation to immigration is the wide difference in the consequences of immigration for the people of both the immigrants and the natives, from different social classes. The middle or upper-class immigrant, often wealthy and skilled in using his wealth to gain advantages for himself, his family and friends, has been welcomed by the native establishment and has easily made new friends amongst the host members of the same social class. Such people are used to moving in international circles of 'movers and shakers'. Some immigrants, often fleeing authoritarian regimes in their own countries or even persecution, may contain members who are professionals or wealthy businessmen. These people are particularly welcomed by the ruling and political class in Britain, ostensibly because they make an immediate contribution to the economy, but possibly, also, because they are perceived as belonging to the same social class, and therefore bring with them professional skills. Undoubtedly politicians and other officials will feel at ease when dealing with people whom they perceive to be highly educated, wealthy and of previous influence in their own countries. We have indeed marvelled at the ease with which wealthy Asian immigrants have, almost immediately on arrival, integrated into the higher echelons of British political and commercial life, especially in the days of the Blair Government, which became notorious for the 'cash for honours' scandal. This was of course a straightforward cynical financial transaction, redolent of prostitution. Regrettably the Conservative and Liberal parties followed suit, apparently to recruit influential immigrants, possibly also by offering honours for cash 'loans' or gifts to party funds. I do not remember any evidence of this, but it looked suspiciously like a repeat of the Blair arrangement. This phenomenon is another source of native resentment, and the spectacle of recently arrived wealthy immigrants being offered honours denied to worthy and long-established natives, only serves to fuel the current cynicism and suspicion of politicians.

By contrast, the poor unskilled immigrant, whether legal or more likely illegal, has nothing but cheap labour to offer and everything to gain by migrating to a wealthier country, especially one like Britain with open borders and a sophisticated welfare system available to all comers. Moreover, he is not recognised as a fellow member of the native working class; he is seen as an unwelcome rival and scrounger who is unfairly and successfully competing for valuable resources in short supply. In addition he and his compatriots are invading the working-class areas in large numbers, taking over native territories, housing, shops and jobs, and thus offering the greatest provocation to people who have no need of further problems, who are powerless to rectify their new calamitous situation, and are not listened to by the politicians when they try to protest. It is little wonder if they resort to conflict and violence, especially when the message from the 'posh boys' above is that 'immigration is good for us'. This message clearly depends on the question: 'Good for whom?' or, as Cicero said: 'Cui bono? – 'Who benefits?'

The poorest immigrants are the ones most likely to be found amongst the illegal entrants, and these are the ones most likely to meet with native hostility. The natives are likely to assume that all poor immigrants are illegal, and the resentment that is engendered by this assumption is magnified when our own underprivileged poor people become the unlucky and unwelcoming hosts in their communities, and then have to watch the Local Authorities giving the newcomers special help which is unavailable to themselves. Indeed, the people who suffer from the problems engendered by mass immigration are almost uniquely the poor working-class natives, whilst those who have the power to control these events are members of the upper and middle classes in the establishment, who are completely insulated from the adverse consequences of their policies, and moreover are clearly benefiting from the invasion.

The poor immigrants tend to be housed in rundown and neglected areas of our large cities, and these areas already have more than their share of social problems. Little wonder therefore if the problems multiply, and seem to become insoluble. Not only that, but our own underprivileged people are amongst the most poorly educated, and are the least equipped to begin to understand why their fragile subculture is under assault. Nor are they easily able to be able to cope with the extra strains that their new predicament has heaped upon them. Unemployment is often already a major problem in such areas before the immigrants arrive, and if the newcomers suffer this social evil also, or take the few jobs available because they will work for lower wages, we have the explosive mixture of two mutually hostile groups of young, unemployed or underemployed men with little to do except to make mischief. Mutual hostility, violence, sporadic vandalism, drug misuse, crime and gang warfare, are both inevitable and resistant, to attempts by the authorities to control.

Even if the native residents in a deprived area are wrong about the supposed preferential treatment meted out by the authorities to the immigrants, every little sign of the latter's economic advancement may well give rise to rumours which magnify the resentment and hostility of the natives. The young immigrants, particularly of the next aspirant generation, are soon likely to perceive that they are poor and deprived in relation to the native people from other districts, and may begin to feel resentment at their own lowly social and economic status in our culture. This lowly status will be attributed by them not to their social class, but to racial discrimination, and this view is fostered by our own 'race relations industry'. Some of them may have high aspirations for economic advancement, for that was the main reason for them or their parents to migrate to Britain in the first place. By comparison, the neighbouring young native men, whose families have probably lived in these deprived circumstances for generations, are likely to have very low aspirations, and, in any case, will not attribute their position in the lower ranks of the working-class to racial discrimination. They will however, interpret (correctly) the fact that the favoured immigrants are receiving all the benefits that the welfare state heaps upon them as preferential treatment ('positive discrimination' beloved by the liberals). For example, 'homeless' immigrants arriving with their families usually get social housing given to them over the heads of natives whose names have been on the local councils' social housing lists for years, and what could be more provocative of native hostility than that?

These two groups of young men are extremely likely to come into serious and prolonged conflict. Young, poor, ill-educated and unemployed, working-class men often spend much of their time on the streets in gangs, looking for one sort of excitement or other. In their families they are likely to hear talk of resentment and hostility aimed at their neighbours, and this will give them the moral sanction for verbal abuse, occasional violent attacks, vandalism of shops, and for outbreaks of periodic rioting for which they may well have been preparing for some time. When a riot is sparked off, the event seems to come as a complete surprise for those community leaders and the authorities, whose members are of a previous generation and of a different social class. They are not likely to have had much intimate day-to-day contact with local youth culture, nor with the gangs involved, and certainly not much influence with either group. The intensity of the ensuing violence and vandalism may also come as a severe shock, which is just an indication of the communication gulf between the youths and the authorities. Not unnaturally, as deprived young men tend to harbour anti-authoritarian feelings, the police trying to re-establish order will get mauled by both sides. Although riots appear to be caused by some incident, such as a murder, or death at the hands of the police, the arson and looting that form a frequent part of the mayhem may well have been long in the planning. People who feel underprivileged, and know well that members of the middle-class are much better off, may think that they have a moral right to take any advantage of social unrest to grab consumer goods for themselves. In a way, this is a modern form of old-fashioned class war. Of course, some of the rioters will be professional criminals, who will always seize the opportunities provided by social breakdown to further their activities, and they may well plan and instigate the mayhem. Indeed, since much crime has been introduced by immigrants into Britain and this soon results in obvious increased wealth amongst the criminals, it is hardly surprising that the poor, native, young men copy these easy methods of making a good living.

It is therefore to be expected that these events will be repeated time and again across the country, and indeed in other European countries and America. All the ingredients for civil commotion are present in many of our large cities, simmering away quietly, until some trivial or more serious incident causes the brew to boil over. Sometimes it may be an isolated attack on a person or shop. Sometimes it may be deliberately started by demagogues, or be the result of a provocative parade or march. Here we should note the similarities with Northern Ireland, where the conflict is usually labelled as religious or sectarian rather than racial or cultural. If the underlying cause is resentment and hatred of any origin, whether based on social class, religion, or race, the ground is already prepared for the spark to ignite the fire. The modern social communication networks in this digital age contribute to the efficient planning and execution of mass riots that have occurred simultaneously across the country, thus taking the police by surprise. And, of course, the professional criminals are working hard at their nefarious activities, and are only too happy to foster social unrest, because it stretches the resources of the police and provides better opportunities for criminal enterprise.

The third and most important aspect involving social class is the cultural and economic gap between the decision-makers – the politicians and their advisors – and those underprivileged people who suffer the consequences of their decisions. It is hardly surprising that the enthusiastic promotion of the 'multicultural society' has been adopted over the last few decades by a social class that suffers none of the serious adverse consequences, and indeed *benefits* from mass immigration. One can hardly help noticing that in England most of the native people who loudly proclaim their support for continuing immigration are members of the middle and upper classes who form the establishment, and that they are completely insulated from all the social problems. It might be thought that the members of this elite and older group would be neutral, indifferent or even hostile to mass immigration, on the basis of a general resistance to change. In any event their comfortable lives are usually untouched by the neighbourhood tensions, the competition for jobs and housing, the violence and the riots. This contrast of personal experience across the social class divide is therefore an interesting aspect for further study, and the actions of the establishment will be tackled in Chapter Eleven.

Another feature of contacts between people of different cultures is the way that both groups react to each other depending on their relative numbers. This feature is of much greater importance to the outcomes of such contacts than might at first be thought and has been given little attention so far. Scientists automatically pay great attention to measurement and numbers when studying any subject, in order to get a precise picture of the problem; politicians and lawyers however, tend to think in mutually opposing categories that seldom bear much relationship to reality. I shall therefore explore this aspect of numbers in the next chapter.

§

CHAPTER FIVE

THE NUMBERS GAME

IT IS OFTEN POINTED OUT by the immigration enthusiasts that all Britons are immigrants and the descendants of immigrants, and that immigration has always occurred throughout our history. Immigrants have brought skills and new ideas that have greatly benefited our economy and culture. In addition, it is said that we have always welcomed strangers to our shores, and that we should continue with this liberal and tolerant tradition, especially in relation to those fleeing from persecution. These facts seem to them, therefore, to support a plausible argument for allowing the flow of newcomers to continue without concern and without limit, and for welcoming all immigrants, legal or illegal.

We should examine these ideas in some detail to see whether its superficial and liberal appeal can be maintained under critical scrutiny. The British nation has, according to the historians and geneticists, arisen largely from an original settlement of people after the last ice age followed by invasions of the Anglo-Saxons, the Vikings, the Romans and the Normans. However, the process of amalgamation occurred many hundreds of years ago as a result of invasions, bloody conflicts and forcible conquests, and clearly was not a happy or welcome business for the conquered, mutilated, raped, killed and displaced natives. It resulted in the suppression or loss of many of the features of the pre-existing cultures, as usually happens in such circumstances. This part of British history is not therefore one that most people would think it desirable to imitate today. Perhaps more importantly for our present investigation, the long period since this forcible and painful amalgamation was completed means that the resulting nation has had plenty of time to forge a strong sense of group identity, and a well-established common culture. To say therefore that we are all immigrants, as if we, the British indigenous people, arrived yesterday to insert ourselves into our island culture is plainly ridiculous, and has no relevance to today's circumstances. Maybe some of the 'liberal' intellectuals who utter such nonsense feel that they are immigrants, but most of us certainly do not, nor do all of my friends and acquaintances. Personally I consider myself to be one of the British aboriginals, or indigenous natives, whose known ancestors have occupied the British Isles relatively unmolested for well over three hundred years according to existing records, and maybe for thousands of years. Therefore I think that we have a reasonable – even indisputable – claim to be the modern indigenous or native occupiers and owners of the British Isles. We have already, in Chapter 3, established that territorial ownership is an important factor of cultural identity.

Immigration into Britain has continued throughout our more recent history in the shape of the Huguenots (17th and 18th Centuries), the Irish (sporadically), the Jews (1930's), and other smaller groups and individuals from time to time. Whether these people were all welcomed or not is a matter for historical scholarship, but I suspect that the views of the natives differed according to their individual experiences, and perhaps the main response was one of relative indifference. The British are not usually easily roused to anger and are generally friendly and civilised unless greatly provoked. 'Tolerance' however may be a euphemism for low level disapproval not severe enough to cause people to protest or to take action. It is generally thought that the English in particular are a phlegmatic nation which lives largely by Oscar Wilde's saying: 'I don't care what people do, as long as they don't frighten the horses'.

Two aspects of the more recent historical inflows are of importance in the present context: these latter-day immigrants were mainly Western Europeans, and their numbers were relatively small, in sharp contrast, on both counts, to the contemporary situation. It is therefore unlikely that any threat to our culture was perceived by a substantial part of the native population. The important point here is that *small* numbers of European immigrants with very similar cultures were apparently absorbed without much social instability, and were probably welcomed for the most part, often because they brought with them wealth, cheap labour, and/or skills. We ourselves are of European ancestry and therefore have a strong cultural affinity with most European nations (despite our having been involved in many wars with several of them up until very recent times!). We are at one and the same time aware of both our cultural differences, which are minor, and of our cultural similarities, which are major. Importantly in this context, we are of similar racial origins, and we have a basic culture rooted in the Judeo-Christian religion and the earlier Greek and Roman civilisations. In addition, we share a long-standing scientific and rational outlook, live under similar legal systems and representative democratic political governments. Nevertheless we should not ignore the fact that even in Great Britain, united since 1707, and where a tradition of tolerance and mutual respect has evolved slowly between the Welsh, Scots and English over more than three hundred years, there is now a move towards splitting into the three independent nations again. This is yet another example of the enduring importance to people of their own culture, history and racial origins, and for the need for these to be acknowledged and respected by their neighbours. It appears that one of the basic psychological difficulties that we all have with group affiliation and identity is that our atavistic instincts evolved when we lived in small family and tribal groups, and therefore we find it difficult to identify with large groups, which inevitably present us with social encounters with people exhibiting many diverse, strange and unfamiliar cultural differences.

For example, despite the modern tendency to see ourselves with a secondary European identity as well as a primary British identity, this has not been achieved without a lot of difficulty, and the catastrophic wars between nations in Europe are not very far behind us. So, despite the European Union project, and the efforts by some to amalgamate gradually the different European states into one overarching community, there are difficulties at every turn when national interests are being strongly defended. It is a universal, human, psychological trait to be more aware of our differences than of our similarities – another survival feature rooted in our evolutionary tribal past, but perhaps of less utility in our modern closely linked large societies.

In considering immigration into Britain from an historical perspective to throw light on present problems, I believe that *the matter of relative numbers is a crucial factor.* It may at first sight seem to be paradoxical that in almost all cultures the stranger is made welcome, given food and shelter and greeted with friendly curiosity, and yet, in these same cultures, wars and conflicts with neighbours are common from early historical times up to the present day. Relative numbers are the obvious factor determining the response of a settled community to an encounter with strangers (people outside the immediate family, tribe or community). This factor is itself based on the perceived threat. A single stranger, or a small number of strangers, especially if distressed and in obvious need of assistance, brings out the helpful, friendly response even if the strangers are seen to have different racial or cultural features. The strangers are the ones with the greater anxiety because they are helpless, clearly in inferior numbers and therefore the weaker party and, initially, not sure of their reception. Small numbers therefore present no cultural threat, even when the strangers are intending to settle in the host territory, and all the pressure is on the members of a small group to take up the native culture so far as they comfortably can. 'When in Rome, do as the Romans do' runs the old proverb – and good advice it would seem to be, because it makes the strangers acceptable to the hosts. If this be done with enthusiasm it is likely that the hosts will be charmed, because a compliment is being paid to their culture, and they are likely to respond by being as helpful as possible in teaching the ways of their society. If, on the other hand, the strangers make an overt show of holding on to their own cultural customs, with little attempt to learn the new language or take up the local customs, they run the risk of giving offence to the host natives by what seems to them to be a rejection of their culture. If, as with many of the Muslim immigrants in Britain, they openly despise the host culture, then serious mutual hostility is likely to spill over into violence.

If the invaded tribe, village, city or nation is confronted with a considerable group of strangers or foreigners, whose numbers immediately pose the possibility of, at best, a heavy demand on host resources, and, at worst, the threat of attack or other unpleasant behaviour, then the welcome is likely to be muted or absent, and likely to be replaced by a natural, defensive hostility and violence. The threat is perceived to be particularly strong if the strangers are present in very large numbers, say of near equality or even superiority, and if they are armed or behave in a warlike fashion. The defensive response will grow in strength if the number of invaders continues to increase, despite vigorous efforts to stem the tide. The perceived threat, then, is to a large degree coloured by the relative numerical force or proportion of the two parties.

In most modern situations however, we are usually well informed as to the newcomers' intentions in advance, and we believe that most modern people accept the rule of law, that is, the law of the host land. We also like to think that we may be approaching the happy time when we can reach universal agreement that war is to be avoided at all costs, and that warlike confrontations might be a thing of the past. Unfortunately, we clearly have not yet arrived at that ideal point, and many conflicts and even wars continue as I type. Indeed, it seems likely that conflicts over territory, resources and cultural threats are going to continue for decades or maybe hundreds of years to come, and may even increase in number as the growing world population, combined with rising expectations of economic equality, continues to stimulate the mass migrations that are such a prominent feature of contemporary life. As global warming begins to reduce the amount of territory suitable for human settlement, as it assuredly will, the struggle for territorial rights and resources will intensify between the haves and the have-nots. At the moment, the perceived threats that are most common, and the ones with which we are concerned in this essay investigating the mass migrations into Western developed countries, are undoubtedly cultural, namely: religious, economic and territorial. I have already established that some of these aspects of the present problems are of serious import, if only because the human emotional responses to these threats are deep-seated, dangerous and are hard-wired into our brains.

Even in countries where mass immigration is not a current problem, conflicts between different cultural groups continue to dominate political and social affairs. In Northern Ireland, Sri Lanka, the former Yugoslavia, South Africa, Indonesia, Iraq, Egypt, Libya, Turkey, Congo, Israel/Palestine, Malaysia, Sudan, Syria and Ukraine, to mention some that have figured prominently in recent years because of civil struggles or wars, we see that it is difficult for diverse cultural and racial groups to live in harmony, especially when both parties feel numerically strong enough and well organised enough to think they might dominate the other or, at least, do what they like despite the national legal system. As I type, the appalling civil war in Syria continues unabated and has already displaced and killed many hundreds of thousands of people. The dissidents (or 'freedom fighters') fighting the Assad regime consist of many different tribal and religious groups, and whilst fighting a common enemy have had difficulty in forming a united opposition or government-in-waiting. Hostilities have broken out once again recently between Israel and the surrounding Palestinians, and it looks as if many will die on both sides in future hostilities despite the current semi-permanent interlude in this long-running war, and despite the efforts of the United Nations to broker a permanent solution. Both sides in all these conflicts feel that the other side is to blame, and both are determined to win the battle for territory. No doubt each side also feels strong enough to win because of comparable numbers of fighters, and/ or superior weapons.

A small cultural group assimilated within a much larger and different one can often live a parallel life without drawing any, or much, hostility towards itself, because it poses no or little threat to the host group. One reason for this is that the members of a small group will realise that they have little chance of successful settlement if they do not keep a low profile, and they do not therefore act in a provocative fashion. They will certainly be aware of the disproportion in numbers, and will, therefore, not be tempted to think that they could usurp power from the host community. Some of their members may even make successful efforts to integrate into the host culture, and others at least will tend to treat it with considerable respect. This pattern was typical of the Chinese in London many years ago, and is being repeated in Cyprus currently by the British community there. That does not mean that there are no individuals in both communities who feel resentment or hostility but, by and large, resentful people are in a minority, and the efforts on both sides by many others to understand and respect each other's way of life, succeed in maintaining relative harmony. The single immigrant, or the member of a small group of immigrants, is most unlikely to risk rejection or hostility by the host group, therefore there is a strong tendency to want to make an effort to assimilate into the host culture. Indeed the immigrant in this position of numerical inferiority is most likely to appreciate his good fortune in being able to live in a culture that he admires, or which gives him freedoms not available in his culture of origin. He may well have chosen to migrate because he prefers the host culture to the one that he has left, or he is the recipient of economic benefits that outweigh any disadvantages that he is experiencing in the host culture.

In a given, small neighbourhood in a modern, host nation, hitherto of relatively homogeneous racial and cultural composition, the intrusion of a single person or family from a different cultural background will usually arouse curiosity and a range of feelings from warm welcome to indifference or, possibly, mild hostility. If similar individuals or families begin to follow, the natives are likely to become gradually concerned that the composition of their neighbourhood is changing in a way that is not welcome. At this point the newcomers are likely to be living in close proximity to each other and socialising largely within their own cultural group for mutual support and comfort. When the relative numbers begin to approach something like one to ten, some outright expressions of native hostility may well occur. Of course this imagined scenario will be more likely in a leafy suburb or village, where neighbours are friends and acquaintances, rather than in a large, anonymous city where people live in ignorance and indifference of their neighbours. In our modern conurbations almost everybody tends to feel a stranger for most of the time, unless they live in a ghetto of compatriots. Unfortunately, due to the fact that almost everybody seems to be a foreigner, and that there are many closely-packed crowd situations, these large cities provide perfect conditions for criminals such as pick-pockets, muggers and credit-card thieves. This picture contrasts markedly with that of the village or small town, where most people feel much safer, because many are friends and neighbours watching out for each other, and strangers are soon spotted, and monitored if behaving suspiciously.

By the time that the increasing proportion of immigrants in a neighbourhood or small city looks like approaching parity with the natives, some sort of civil strife is a distinct possibility, but by no means inevitable. The latter outcome is very likely in areas with a deprived working-class population, and very unlikely in an area with a middle-class population, the inhabitants of which are economically well-off and more sophisticated. In these middle-class neighbourhoods, immigrants tend to be in small numbers, and to be well-off professionals or business people like their host neighbours. However, because the native middle-class sophisticates do not usually exhibit overt hostility and aggression to immigrants, does not necessarily mean that they are less concerned, and are in favour of these unplanned changes in their locality. It will be clear to the natives at some point, if the invasion continues, that they have lost a considerable amount of their territory, and that their culture is now fighting a losing battle. It is then too late for a simple solution, and prolonged mutual misery and resentment is often the outcome, unless the losing party (the natives) can make an exit to another locality where they can again enjoy their own culture with their compatriots. This option is often taken by middle-class citizens with money to spare, but is not usually available to poor and working-class people.

The serious social problems are likely to begin when the immigrant group is more of a threat by reason of *comparable numbers*, of assumed illegal entry, of rapidly rising numbers, of easily-identified, alien racial and cultural features, and particularly if the invading group members have the *cultural arrogance* that assumes that they have every right to do as they please, whatever the natives may think. This cultural arrogance is a direct result of the numbers of the immigrants being large enough to give them a feeling of safety and separateness, which is magnified when they have established their own territory or ghettoes. If, as is the case with the recent Muslim immigrants in Britain, their own religious culture also gives them a strong feeling of moral and cultural superiority, then they tend to reject the host culture, and even feel that they have the right to inflict their culture on the hosts. In addition, the behaviour of the host politicians in appearing to bestow privileges and favours on the incomers only serves to inflame native hostility, and to encourage the immigrants to make more demands. The latter phenomenon might seem to be an unlikely factor, but that is just what has happened in Britain for several decades. One has only to observe in Britain today the hundreds of prominent mosques and the city neighbourhoods with the appearance of some Asian country, to realise that great and unwise provocation is being heaped upon the native population. Indeed, it is most surprising (at least to me) that the British population has not rebelled more often with sustained and open hostility and even violence, in an effort to defend their clearly threatened culture. Part of the reason for this apparent tolerance is that British citizens have been bullied into submission by the forceful and relentless propaganda campaign against 'racism'; by the repression of free speech; and the fact that the working-classes have become totally demoralised and fragmented as a result of the loss of their previous solidarity, which was destroyed during the catastrophic de-industrialisation under Margaret Thatcher (1979-1990).

When any country has had, for many decades or centuries, more than one cultural, religious or ethnic group within its territory, with the numbers of the groups being of comparable size, it is almost certain that there will be considerable resentment and hostility beneath the surface, despite superficial appearances of mutual tolerance for long periods of time. This pattern is usually the result of some historical conquest or mass migration, or where the country has been artificially 'constructed' by well-intentioned administrators acting for regional or global political organisations. Sometimes one group may slowly become more numerous and powerful, often by means of a differential birth rate. Even after hundreds of years of uneasy, parallel living together, civil war or violent episodes may break out. Demands for separate nationhood and territory may result in eventual break-up of the country, as in the former USSR, and sometimes after attempts at 'ethnic cleansing' and war, as in the former Yugoslavia. Sri Lanka, Congo and the Sudan have recently been involved in long-running civil wars on these lines, and it looks much the same (2014) in Iraq, Syria, and Israel/Palestine despite considerable efforts by Western democracies to intervene and to stabilise the situations. The differential birth rate, with the less well educated and poorer population sometimes having large numbers of children compared with their neighbouring group, is a threat of very serious import for the latter group, as in Israel/Palestine. It is almost a certainty that the more fertile group will in the end swamp the other group by sheer weight of numbers, particularly when the available territory is very limited.

In general, it is clear that the size or proportion of an immigrant population relative to that of the host country will be likely to produce an outcome which may vary from easy acceptance and assimilation of small numbers at one end, to outright mutual hostility and severe conflict towards large numbers at the other end of the numerical scale. It would therefore seem wise and prudent for a host country to control immigration carefully in terms of numbers, speed of increase, and the type of immigrants that would be likely to want to assimilate and be able to do so quickly. Unfortunately, since World War II, in Britain, the Western and Northern European democracies and in America, no such effective control has been operating. It is difficult to understand why our political establishments have been so guilty of this serious dereliction of duty, which has landed us all in such social turmoil, when it should have been obvious from historical and current examples around the globe that 'multiculturalism' produces serious social problems.

Whilst we are dealing with numerical factors we should also look closely at the problem of the increasing size of the British and world populations. It seems to me obvious that the biggest and most urgent problem that the world currently faces, is how to control its population size at a level which is sustainable in the long term. It is unfortunately a fact that the world's politicians do not even seem to recognize, let alone address, this imminent and serious problem. It is practically never that one hears a politician mention this factor whenever confronting a national problem, and yet it is difficult to find a current social problem that is not affected by population size, both in individual countries and the world as a whole. The problems of pollution, global warming, wars, disease epidemics, traffic congestion, housing, flooding, droughts, wildfires, tornadoes, overburdened social, education and health services, and the scramble for natural resources such as drinking water, food, energy and living space – must all be totally insoluble if the global population continues to increase at its present alarming rate. And yet the world's politicians are obsessed with the old familiar parochial matters. **If we humans do not begin to develop effective population control policies soon, then the immediate and medium-term future must surely be one of incessant conflicts as nations and cultures continue to fight for the diminishing available territory and resources.**

In Britain the population has grown from about 50 million in 1951 to 54 million in 2012, despite a *native* Total Fertility Rate (TFR) of 1.92 children per woman over her lifetime (which is below the replacement rate of 2.095), and despite the hundreds of thousands of natives who have left the country to settle elsewhere during that time. The TFR for the Pakistani and Bangladeshi population in Britain was 4.90 in 2012. The Office for National Statistics in 2011 projected, on the basis of an annual growth rate of 0.6%, that the UK population will be just over 73 million by 2035. The projected population density for 2015 at 264/sq km is one of the highest in the world, and it is projected to be 300/sq km by 2035.[7]

These figures should long ago have sounded alarm bells in high places, as the politicians struggle all the time to solve the housing needs, the pollution, the traffic congestion, the need for more health, education and welfare services, water resources and so on. Did they never study simple arithmetic at school? Have they no knowledge of the devastating effects of exponential population growth? Do they not realise that the problems they try to deal with every day will never be solved, and are getting worse, because the national and world populations are steadily and rapidly rising well beyond what the available national and global resources can support? Rising expectations of higher living standards *alone,* mean that the demands are increasing beyond what the world can provide at the current population level. And, to make matters worse, the available territory for living space and food production is diminishing, as rising sea levels remove the fertile delta lands, and other agricultural lands are slowly being made infertile by reason of over-use. We have been able to postpone for the time being the catastrophes of famine and disease predicted by Robert Malthus[8] in 1798, by the introduction of technological improvements in food production despite the rising world population, but this 'technical fix' has engendered a dangerous complacency. People need not only food, which requires fertile agricultural space, they also need satisfactory living space, and that cannot be manufactured. The expansion of human settlement areas, along with the scramble for natural resources, is already the main threat to wild life with many hundreds of species already destroyed. In the meantime, the

---

7   Office of National Statistics (2012): Population Estimates.

8   Malthus, Thomas (1798).

exponential growth of the world population will soon result in a crisis of biblical proportions, as increasing demands continue to outstrip diminishing supplies.

The problem of world population control is, like that of global warming, not going to be solved unless nations can agree on a joint plan and execute it, and the chances of that happening in the near future look bleak indeed. Some nation needs to set an example, and heavily overpopulated Britain is one such that would greatly benefit from an early start. If the British Government were to be looking for a subject for one of its quangos or think-tanks, why not select population control? We might then see the beginnings of a policy to reduce the population of Britain to a reasonable figure in the ball-park area of say twenty-five or thirty million. Even if we wished to start today with a policy of population control with an inadequate target of stabilisation at current numbers, we would probably be discussing the necessity and the means for decades, before any real measures were agreed and initiated. Unfortunately, there are powerful interests, such as big-business, who will do everything in their power to obstruct such a policy because they thrive on increasing consumer numbers. China had such a policy (the 'one baby policy'), which has been so controversial that it has had to abandon it under public pressure. In a Western democracy any attempt to remove the 'right' of any couple to procreate as much as they wish would surely be defeated. However, there are more subtle and hopefully acceptable ways in which people might be able to change their aspirations and behaviour. The fact that the introduction of education of girls and women has resulted in several countries showing a decline in the birth-rate, is one such hopeful sign, which could easily be exploited in Third-World countries (as if such a measure needs any extra justification!). Rising living standards also seem to reduce the average number of children in families. These two factors could certainly be incorporated in an early start to a world-population-reduction policy, along with the availability of free contraception.

In Britain, the Cameron Government has introduced reforms of the welfare system, including limiting the child benefits to people earning less than £60,000 per year. However, the child benefits for lower earners will still be considerable at £20.50 per week for the first child and £13.55 per week for all other children. **Thus many parents are still being rewarded for each and every child, which is irresponsible in the extreme from the point of view of both national and world overpopulation.**

The dictates of many religions are also seen to be an obstacle to the reduction of populations, because their objective of increasing the numbers of their adherents relies not only on evangelistic efforts to multiply the number of converts, but also on the fecundity of their adherents – the more children brought up in the faith, the wider the movement spreads, and, one might add, the greater the wealth and power of their leaders and usually, the poverty of their flock. However, the trend in the Western representative democracies, before the recent mass immigrations, was towards religious decline and atheism. Even Roman Catholics in Britain were largely ignoring the admonitions of their church against contraception and birth control. In contrast, the Muslim communities across Britain and Western Europe are having many more children than the native white populations, as described above, and that fact should be a cause for great anxiety about cultural domination as well as overpopulation.

It would be better and more rational to stop child benefits altogether. However controversial such measures may prove to be, they should be an essential part of any population-control policy. It is irresponsible to encourage any part of the population to have more children when the country is already heavily overpopulated. Of course, critics will say that people have the 'right' to have as many children as they wish; the state should not interfere with family life; and that such a policy is discriminative against the Muslims. I say that 'rights' should always be granted by the consensus wish of the population in a democracy, and should never be established by the whim of individuals or minority groups alone. Nor are they God-given, nor written in stone, and therefore they should be changed by the majority will of the people when they are responding to their perceived and changed circumstances. As far as the state's interference in family life is concerned, that is what it did when it set up the child benefit in the past, and I don't remember that there was any opposition on that ground at the time or since. Our Government has a first duty to protect the people from whatever threatens their wellbeing, and increasing overpopulation is a very dangerous threat indeed, with all its inevitable and predictable consequences. The discrimination aspect is one that follows from many actions of government and is therefore unavoidable. Governments discriminate by taking money from the richer section of the population and giving it to the poorer section; the legal system discriminates against law-breakers, including motorists who disobey the speed limits, or who use their mobile phones whilst driving.

Of course many politicians will say that this recommendation of population control is pie in the sky but, if that is their only response, it will be another indication, I fear, that they are reluctant to deal with long-term problems, however important they may be for the welfare of the public. Not only that, but they are addicted to power, and, in the modern world as of old, that means that many of them, especially the dictators, want to control as big a territory and as big a population as they can, knowing that these actions inflate their wealth, their power and their influence across the globe. The President of the Russian Federation, Vladimir Putin, has set up a youth organisation in Russia which is reminiscent of the Hitler Youth, to imbue young Russians with the 'duty' to have more children in order to reverse the falling birth rate in his country, which steadily declined for a decade after the break-up of the Soviet Union. Large populations mean the possibility of more economic power and bigger armies, and authoritarian politicians, like religious leaders, often wish to expand their subservient populations. Once again, self-interest appears to be the prime motive. However, one can see why Mr Putin acts as he does, because Russia has the same problem as Europe, namely a native birth rate which is inadequate for replacement, and a Muslim birth rate that is more than adequate, and destined to increase that section of his population to a point which will ensure that it reaches a majority if things do not change. So Putin's actions may well be commended rather than condemned from the point of view of the native Russians, if not from the point of view of the world population.

Returning to the situation in Britain, one might more real-istically hope that all well-meaning politicians would by now be in favour of controlling the numbers of further immigrants, and would help to formulate a long-term plan, and then properly resource the agencies that are supposed to control immigration. The numbers that have already settled in Britain have already overstrained all the public services and, more importantly, have resulted in social problems that we never had before. In November 2012, a Government report revealed once again that the Border Agency still had a large backlog of failed asylum seekers remaining in the country, and that the Agency had even been lying about the figures to the Government! Words fail me. Who will rid us of these troublesome incompetents?

There is bound to come a point when the natives' perception of the increasing proportion of foreigners reaches a level at which their instinctive, protective feelings for their threatened culture are seriously aroused, and something like civil war becomes a possibility. The arrogant assumption, which some liberal British people are inclined to rely on to avert this scenario, that we are a tolerant nation and all will be well, is likely to receive a severe correction. We are just as human and have just the same instincts as everybody else. Our presumed tolerance may well be the result of past fortunate circumstances, such as living on an island, with the comforting feeling of having had the English Channel as our impregnable moat, separating us from all but the most determined and well-armed invaders. Another factor may be a sense of racial superiority that lingers on from the days of Empire. I've no doubt that some of those, who keep repeating their mantras about Britain's tradition of giving 'asylum' to all those crossing our moat in recent years, are also suffering from an attack of feelings of moral superiority over our European neighbours who were less welcoming to the 'refugees'. There's nothing that cheers up a liberal so much as being able to feel morally superior by 'doing good' to some 'inferior' person or group, especially if others who are more realistic are not so inclined at the time or occasion, and can be criticised for being hard-hearted.

One of the items mentioned above concerning numbers should be looked at further. This is the differential birth rate, which is operating in favour of the younger immigrants. Britain's native population had a TFR in 2012 of 1.92 that is too low to replace the previous generations, and thus this factor, in combination with an increasing life-span, means that the proportion of old people to young natives is rising dramatically. The immigrants are mainly young people with different attitudes towards desirable family size, and therefore they are producing, and almost certainly will go on producing, a greater proportion of children compared with the native population. Those from Pakistan and Bangladesh already had in 2012 a TFR of 4.90, and the two demographic factors together will result in a rapid increase in the proportion of immigrants in the next few generations, even if no more immigrants were to settle in Britain. This phenomenon is also evident in the whole Muslim section of the immigrant population, and Britain and other Western European countries afflicted by the same problem are witnessing a modern Muslim colonisation, which is to a large extent deliberately fostered by their religious leaders. It is amazing that such a profound and imminent cultural threat to our long-developed civilisation should have been allowed to materialise without serious efforts to ward it off. The threat is obvious, and has been obvious from the beginning of mass immigration. **We are reaching the point of catastrophe in Britain and Europe from the point of view of the maintenance of our racial makeup and our civilisation, and radical action alone will suffice to halt the obliteration of our culture.**

The importance of these demographic factors, for serious cultural conflict at best, and complete cultural usurpation at worst, hardly needs pointing out. The same phenomenon has been operating for some time in Northern Ireland and in America, especially in California. In both communities the differential birth rate has resulted, or very soon will, in the numerical balance of two cultures being reversed. It is this, I believe, that has brought the IRA murderers in Northern Ireland to 'exchange the gun for the ballot box', because they have realised that they will soon be able to take the advantage which democracy gives to the majority in the voting population. They will soon be in democratic control, and who knows what they will do with the advantage, particularly as their current leaders are IRA terrorists turned 'politicians'. The most likely first, major objective that the Catholic majority will then easily achieve, is that of unification with the Republic of Ireland, with the certain resumption of Loyalist violence. In fact serious Loyalist violence has broken out already in 2014, in response to the decision of the Belfast City Council to stop flying the Union Jack over the City Hall except on certain designated days. Clearly the Loyalists see this decision as a symbol of the diminution of their traditional hegemony, as a prelude to losing it altogether as the Catholics become the majority in the population. Similar demographic changes are happening in New Mexico, (Latinos formed 47% of the population to 39.8 whites in 2014); in California (where the figures were Latinos 39% and whites 38.8%); and in Texas

(Latinos 38.2%, whites 44.4%).[9] Prominent Hispanic community leaders are already looking forward to re-joining Mexico 'without a single shot being fired' and are advising the whites to 'go home'!

It looks as if Britain, other European countries, and the USA are heading for trouble on a grand scale, for we have identified a number of important factors which underlie racial and cultural conflict, all of which are currently operating in our countries. In particular, the numerical demographic imbalance will inevitably continue to get worse unless governments make a sharp change of policy, and follow that up with determined action. If they do not do this and, in their ignorance or arrogance take no notice of the realities demonstrated throughout recent world history, then Western politicians are in for much continuing bewilderment, when they contemplate every outbreak of civil violence as the numbers and proportions of immigrants continue to rise.

It seems that the political systems in Western Democracies are now failing to cope with some of the greatest threats to the wellbeing of their populations, and indeed of Western civilisation. The democratic politicians even seem to be unaware of these serious threats and concern themselves with relative trivialities, such as racial abuse in football matches, expenses scandals, sexual infidelities amongst their party members, and homosexual 'marriage' rights. They are, in effect, fiddling while Rome is being rapidly destroyed in a firestorm.

The intention of this chapter was to examine several numerical aspects of the immigration phenomenon, and we have seen that relative numbers play a large part in determining the consequences of a rapid injection of different cultural groups into a hitherto relatively homogeneous country. The initial phase of such an injection may seem to be without serious problems, but if

---

9 www.pewresearch.org (16.10.2014). Latino Voters and the 2014 Midterms.

the number of foreigners continues to rise with more arrivals, accompanied by the effect of differential birth rates and native emigration, then serious conflicts will inevitably arise, and soon become more frequent as the perceived threat to the native culture increases. The initial complacency and incompetence of our politicians will be accompanied by bewilderment and confusion as city riots break out again in the major towns. In a radio programme (The Moral Maze, 09 February 2002) one of the pundits expressed astonishment at the concern which was being voiced by native listeners at the number of immigrants in this country, thought by her to be insignificant. I wondered whether she lived in, or had visited recently Ealing, Brixton, Bradford, Rotherham, Oldham, Birmingham or Leicester. We should not forget that people's *perceptions are based on their own experience*, which is likely for most people to be local and limited, and/or strengthened and confined to impressions gained from the media. As I remember Prime Minister Harold Wilson saying in another context: 'National unemployment may be low, but to the unemployed man it is 100%.' To the natives in one of the above cities or localities the number of immigrants must already appear to be more than 50% of the population, regardless of what it may be in a leafy middle class suburb or a rural village. Indeed, we now know that foreigners form the majority of the population of London, which was for hundreds of years our capital city.

What is certain is that with continuation of the present state of affairs, the proportion of immigrants to natives is bound to go on increasing, and all the factors examined above would seem to indicate that so will mutual hostility and serious social problems. Despite this conclusion, held by many natives, the establishment intelligentsia seem to continue in their belief that 'immigration is a good thing for the country' and, indeed, 'essential to cope with our ageing population and skill shortages'. When I hear these mantras uttered it reminds me of a story, which may be true or possibly apocryphal: former American President George W Bush went to China on a charm offensive, to establish better relations with the Communist politicians. GWB said to Chou En Lai, the Chinese President: 'We welcome Chinese immigrants to America.' Chou En Lai replied with a wry smile: 'How many you want? – one million?, ten million?, a hundred million?' I don't know what GWB said to that, but it illustrates the fact that Western politicians tend to think in categories and not in numbers. *Numbers matter;* a small number of carefully-selected immigrants may well be good for a country, *but a huge and increasing number of self-selected ones most certainly is not.*

Indeed this principle applies to almost all comparisons, because in day-to-day speech we simplify by using mutually exclusive categories rather than an arithmetical range – for example: good or bad, guilty or not guilty, alive or dead, large or small, rich or poor, stupid or intelligent – whereas in reality all these and many other qualities, states or characteristics change their value from one extreme to the other along a continuum or spectrum. Scientists measure everything they study in order to look for correlations and patterns in their data, but unfortunately, politicians seem to be completely ignorant of any such numerical indications of possible cause-and-effect relationships. Food is good for us, indeed essential for life, but too much is harmful and even possibly lethal. So to say glibly that something is 'good for us', leaves out the questions of 'how much'?, 'what sort of something'?, 'good for whom'? And that simple principle applies to immigrants and to population. About the only numbers politicians are really interested in are economic and financial ones, and even there they think that the figures of GDP and 'the economy' can go on growing indefinitely in a more-or-less straight line. Remember Gordon Brown's notorious prediction? – 'No more boom and bust.' What an amazing public demonstration of his ignorance of economics, reality and numeracy.

The end result of the continuing unwanted and unplanned, catastrophic social change to which we are being subjected is, I fear, the inevitable escalation of inter-cultural violence, and even eventual civil war – which we may well lose. That is, unless we can convince our politicians that immigration should almost entirely cease – a difficult ask, but one that I will address later on. The good news is that the Cameron Government, despite the inevitable complaints from the liberal intellectuals (and, of course, most of the established immigrants), has begun an attempt to tackle the border-control problems, and appears to have realised that immigration has to be severely curtailed. Unfortunately the promises of our politicians in relation to this topic have been dashed so many times that the electorate has little faith that firm and effective action will be taken soon, especially because our membership of the European Union makes such action illegal. Even as I type, the Inspector of the Border Control Agency has reported that hundreds of thousands of applications for British citizenship are awaiting decisions.

In the next chapter I will examine the tensions which arise in most gradually evolving, long-established organisations, between the conflicting forces for change and stability, and which are operating in our Western democracies while they are being colonised by foreign invaders.

§

CHAPTER SIX

CHANGE VERSUS STABILITY

IN ANY SYSTEM OR ORGANISATION, human or natural, there is usually a tension between the forces of change and stability. Nothing remains permanently and totally stable and change appears to be inevitable, whether on the cosmic or the human scale. In human affairs there is usually some control system that endeavours to achieve a balance in any organisation, such as a commercial management, committee or government. One of the continuing tasks of human controlling agents is to manage the pace and direction of change whilst many competing forces try to influence the process, some operating within a consultative system such as a democracy, and some operating outside the system, such as commercial competitors, criminals or terrorists. Obviously some of these forces are trying to accelerate the pace of change, whilst others are trying to retard it, maintain the status quo, introduce alternative changes, or even return to a previous solution or practice. In Western democracies this conflict of forces is usually represented by two opposing, major, political parties who have most of the power of government, alternating often between one and the other. If, as sometimes happens at elections, the majority winner does not have enough representatives to be able to legislate successfully against the combined total of the other parties, it may form an alliance with one or more of the minority parties. These power struggles occur in some shape or other in Local Government affairs and in any situation where power is being wielded, although any form of tyranny suppresses all opposition ruthlessly.

The need to manage the process of change is basically because a complex functioning system is likely to break down if changes are too fast or too drastic, or perhaps if they are too slow. In other words, the system which was set up or evolved to carry out some function usually has to work efficiently in its present form whilst it is adjusting to the changes, however desirable or necessary these may seem to be for future performance. Natural biological evolution points the way – the continuous or intermittent introduction of frequent small changes is more likely to be beneficial to a complex functioning system than the imposition of infrequent, large changes. In fact evolution usually is to be preferred to revolution. In the genetic sphere this principle is well recognised – gene mutations of large effect produce catastrophic effects, whilst mutations of small effect are the ones that usually provide the necessary phenotypic changes for evolutionary selection to work on. The more complex any functioning system is, the more likely it is that a sudden major change will be catastrophic and destructive. Most people are therefore intuitively conservative as long as life seems to be tolerable, as it does for most of the time in a well-functioning democracy, and are antipathetic to ideas of revolution and its highly probable, unpleasant social consequences. Nevertheless, if all else fails, and the forces of resistance to change become intolerable, revolution may be the only remedy, despite the fact that it usually causes much suffering, and usually one tyrant is replaced by another. It is much easier to destroy a complex functioning system, however bad it may be, than to replace it with a better one. Thus the human struggle for liberty has a long history of both incremental changes and revolutions, but few people would say, even in Western democracies, that the process has yet succeeded. Indeed, it may never come to an end.

In human affairs there are added psychological complications. The young (naturally, because of their enthusiastic and optimistic drive, combined with their lack of experience of change), are generally in favour of change, which automatically reduces the value of knowledge and experience; whilst the elderly (naturally, because they wish to hold onto their power), are in general in favour of stability, which sets a premium on knowledge and experience, based as these are on long-term learning. The older generation have worked hard for many years, and wish to enjoy the fruits of their labour, but they still tend to retain control of affairs and most of the nation's wealth. The younger generation are keen, in turn, to do likewise, but have to take control as soon as they can, and they often do so by embracing new methods, techniques and technological innovation. The wealthy older people have a near monopoly of power and naturally wish to retain it; the poorer and younger citizens naturally wish to wrest the power and wealth from their elders and political masters, and distribute it more fairly. The result of the operation of these psychological factors is to increase the tension in most human organisations between the forces in favour of stability and those in favour of change. Thus there tend to be power struggles in all human affairs, and this needs to be acknowledged if we are to make rational decisions on matters that are important for society. A salutary recent example of the failure to take account of these factors was that of the so-called 'dotcom' revolution in the field of internet commercial start-ups. In 1999-2000 it appeared as if youthful entrepreneurs were sweeping everything before them in their exuberant enthusiasm for technological change. As we all know now, nemesis soon followed hubris, and the financial 'bubble' burst. The mistake was not that of embracing the technological changes, which are still inevitably continuing, but of thinking that a drastic and revolutionary change could immediately overturn, without pain, the functioning, complex system that had evolved from past experience. The old proverb: 'Much haste, less speed' warns against this type of human failing.

One of the problems of mass immigration at the organisational, social and cultural level is that the changes in society have been much too drastic, and too fast, and have no agreed objective –

as a result of the failure of governments to control the process throughout the past six decades. The present Cameron Government has not yet gained control, although it appears to be trying to do so, following the failure of the previous Blair and Brown Governments to plan and execute control from the beginning. There have been no systematic attempts to consult the native population, no well-thought-out policies based on rational analysis, and only reactive *ad hoc* 'initiatives' attempting to deal with the consequential social problems, when they have inevitably arisen. In fact, as previously described, the main tactics of successive governments have been to try to convince us that there is no problem, and that we are really fortunate in finding ourselves to be the undeserving recipients of a 'multicultural society'. This extraordinary state of affairs is due partly to the total confusion of the politicians, as shown by the fact that they sometimes announce 'tough' new measures in attempts to control the social problems, and sometimes continue to try to convince us of the 'benefits' that the immigrants are said to bring.

Even if the population had been convinced by the Government propaganda, and had been in favour of an agreed influx of immigrants, the above considerations of managing the momentous societal changes would indicate that the most sensible strategy would have been to adopt a policy of tight control, and slow, carefully-managed implementation. Such a strategy would have enabled a proper system of data collection, careful selection of immigrants likely to benefit our society, efficient reception and dispersal procedures to be set up, along with effective measures to aid assimilation. It would have also allowed time to train staff to administer the necessary measures, and to allocate the appropriate financial resources without straining the national economy. Such a plan would have gone a long way to minimising the possibility of native hostility and immigrant demands for special treatment.

A slow, controlled implementation of a well-designed programme would have allowed careful monitoring of progress to take place, so that adjustments to the programme could be instituted at an early stage in the light of the experience in Britain and similar countries. No successful attempts to manage the situation in such a rational fashion seem to have been organised, despite the fact that the Blair and Brown Governments were addicted to targets and micro-management, in many other areas of national activity, such as education and health care. It would thus appear that our politicians did not even recognise what was happening, or, if they did, maybe they thought the momentous social changes which everybody else was concerned about were of little interest to the establishment. Perhaps they were preoccupied with other matters, such as maintaining the 'special relationship' with the USA, and with following America's lead in foreign policy. What is more likely, however, is that they knew what was happening, but that a carefully hidden self-interest was their main motivation. Whatever the reasons, it is clear that the social changes in Britain and other European countries over the last sixty years or so have been of unprecedented magnitude, and of disastrous effect, partly because the speed of the changes has destabilised our communities, and overloaded public state and local services. In fact many of the long-established native communities have been destroyed, and many others displaced. Our large conurbations are now peopled largely by immigrants who have displaced the long-established natives, with residual areas of poor and deprived Britons, and a periphery of leafy suburbs housing the remaining wealthy middle-class natives. Many prosperous people have fled to rural villages, and retired people have migrated to other countries with a Western European way of life.

The mere fact that a country has a harmonious and peaceful community, such as existed in Britain before WWII, is a sign that social and cultural changes have been small and slow, allowing adaptation and general approval or at least acceptance. The mass immigration from alien and different cultures that we have suffered over the last sixty-odd years, amounts to a rapid and cataclysmic change, unwanted by most people, and which, predictably, has resulted in serious disharmony, and moral breakdown due to the conflicts between different value systems.

There can be no argument that our politicians, of all parties, but especially those in the 'New Labour' Government who were deviously pursuing their own agenda of gerrymandering the population, have badly let us down and continue to do so. They did not, in the face of unprecedented social problems and conflict between different cultural groups, face up to the obvious social catastrophe that their collective conniving was wreaking upon what was once one of the most civilised countries in the world. It was civilised partly because it had a very long history of slow evolutionary change against a solid background of relative stability (albeit punctuated by civil wars and invasions). Too much change brought about too quickly by the self-interested political establishment, especially under the malign influence of exterior evil forces which are allowed free range without regulation and control, and even encouraged, is an obvious recipe for disaster. A stable culture, which most people desire to live in, is a delicate and fragile institution. It takes hundreds of years to produce, with many vicissitudes and casualties along the way, and yet so little time to destroy – like all valuable and complex human institutions and enterprises.

It seems certain that the present uncontrolled and mainly illegal immigration invasion threatens the overwhelming of our native culture. There are signs, such as the current (2014) mood of disillusion with politics amongst the British electorate, who are turning away from the three traditional parties as 'being all the same', that people are protesting at their impotence to influence the governing elite. Two thirds of the electorate are not usually voting, and the other third are tending to vote in increasing numbers for the United Kingdom Independence Party (UKIP), whose main aim is to leave the European Union (EU), whose rules and laws frustrate our national aims. The three traditional political parties are, in varying degrees, in favour of remaining within the EU, and seem to think that they can negotiate changes to that organisation's rules that will repatriate important powers to our Parliament. Similar trends are occurring in other countries within the EU, whose non-elected establishment is determined to proceed with its main utopian aim to forge an 'ever closer union' – a United States of Europe.

This idealistic idea is being pushed forward at a time when there are several political movements across Europe in which people are demanding more independence, such as those in Scotland, Wales, the Basque country and Catalonia. The main and wholly commendable idea of setting up the EU after WWII was to prevent any future wars amongst the European states and, for this aim, success has so far been achieved, with the single exception of the Balkan war of 1999. No one would argue with the aim of closer cooperation between all the European states to prevent wars, and to accelerate the process of free trade which tends to spread wealth more equally, and to promote cross-border friendships. But unfortunately the political establishment elite of the EU has its own over-arching agenda and is trying to bring about radical and far-reaching changes much too fast, and without a democratic mandate. It is only natural that the governing elite should seek ever greater power and control, because history shows incontrovertibly that *this is what all leaders with power do.*

Britain has a long history of struggling for liberty and democratic government, and I am sure that the present disillusionment with politics is the result of our having experienced monumental social, cultural and detrimental changes to our way of life, as a consequence of the EU's rules regarding open borders and freedom of movement, which our governments have been unwilling or unable to resist or modify. The whole point of democracy is that the 'demos', or people, are in control of their own affairs. Major changes in a democracy should have the approval of at least the majority of the electorate and, as far as the invasion of recent immigrants is concerned, our several governments have not only not had a mandate on the question of mass immigration, but they have tried to suppress all opposition to such change, which has devastated our culture and displaced our peoples from their long-held neighbourhoods and territories. And even now (after the elections of May 2014) the politicians still 'do not get it' and think only of presentational problems: 'We must get our message across'. It seems that they cannot appreciate that perhaps the electorate do not like their message. The politicians' problem of understanding the wishes of their constituents is their own fault: they concentrate on trying to get the voters to accept their own message, rather than listening to the message of the voters. 'There are none so deaf as those who will not hear'. This is the mark of the arrogant liberals, who are convinced that they know best.

This failure of the governing elite to take on board the concerns and wishes of the people is a subject of considerable importance because, if it is not soon corrected, it may result in such dissatisfaction and resentment that civil strife may break out, and people decide to take matters into their own hands. The rule of law is a bulwark of democracy, but it too must have the endorsement and support of the people. It is fortunate indeed that UKIP, as a new and credible political party that has listened to the population and their wishes, has been organised so that a democratic solution is available for those people who feel disenfranchised by the traditional parties. If UKIP had not arisen at this moment of monumental and widespread political disillusionment it is certain that voters would have turned to extremist parties, as has happened in France and Greece. Happily, the next general election in May 2015 will give British voters a chance to send an effective signal to the Government that they wish to leave the EU, which has done so much harm to our culture without any democratic consent. We need drastic but real democratic change in British politics to avert revolution on the one hand and destruction of our culture on the other hand.

One other interesting phenomenon related to the matter of change versus stability is that of opposite movements occurring at the same time. In the present context we are aware of the strong campaigns being conducted throughout Western democracies for more local independence, and, at the same time, there are other campaigns for a larger federation. Thus the European nation states, which have lasted for about three hundred years are being attacked from both sides. This paradoxical phenomenon requires some investigation and explanation, although I think the answer is fairly obvious. There are separate groups of people working in the two opposed movements, motivated as always by their perceived self-interest. The independent movements are gaining popularity with ordinary voters in several European countries, who wish for more control and direct involvement in the local affairs that immediately concern them. This wish is supported by feelings of cultural identity which are so important to most people, who naturally find it difficult to identify with large, multicultural groups, as described in Chapter One. On the other hand, the movement towards a large federal combination of nation states in Europe is promoted by politicians backed by large commercial corporations with a lust for more power and wealth. These people are not concerned with the wishes of ordinary people, and are elitist and self-serving. The mark of this group is the strong tendency to push their federalist agenda by undemocratic means. I need hardly mention the example of the European Union with its aim of 'ever closer union', nor the fact that all over the EU there are burgeoning, new, political parties, picking up the protest votes of the disillusioned electorates. This phenomenon has been growing for some years, and initially the traditional politicians were arrogantly dismissive of the new parties, but are now beginning to panic in the face of the distinct possibility that they may soon lose their long-held power in a 'velvet revolution', which will devolve power down to the people, where it rightfully belongs.

I must return at this point to our investigation of the cultural scene. The next chapter deals with one of the most lamentable and distressing aspects of the current British cultural scene, namely the crime epidemic, and examines its relationship, if any, with immigration and multiculturalism.

§

CHAPTER SEVEN

THE CRIME EPIDEMIC

SINCE ABOUT 1950, soon after the arrival of the first cohort of immigrants from Jamaica (22.06.1948), the crime scene in Britain began to change for the worse, and this trend has continued fairly steadily ever since. Even the Government was forced later to acknowledge that we had a soaring crime rate (28 February 2002), despite their oft-repeated commitment and efforts to reduce it. The Director of the Prison Service expressed his concern (29 February 2002) at the fact that the prison population had then reached a record level, causing heavy strain in prisons trying to cope with the problem of overcrowding. Not only had the rates of old, familiar types of crime greatly increased, but newer and more pernicious forms had appeared. The drug problem was completely out of control, and the criminal gangs that organised it deliberately targeted children, to the horror of all parents who were, and are, helpless to protect their youngsters. Shop-lifting and credit card fraud quickly became major industries and resulted in a heavy financial burden on commerce but, of course, these burdens were inevitably passed onto the ordinary consumer. Vast rackets in the sale of meat unfit for human consumption were discovered by health inspectors. On 18 March 2002 we learnt that electric stun guns were being sold to criminals as a new addition to their armoury of standard handguns.

Street mugging, stabbings, shootings and drug-related crimes in London and many other cities became only too familiar events, most of which were almost unknown six decades ago except in the largest conurbations, and even there they were of very small extent. At the same time we were aware that we were just catching up with the state of affairs in some other countries, such as the

USA, Mexico and Jamaica. In the now far-off days of pre-World War II, Britain prided itself on its police force, with its image of the friendly local bobby, armed only with a bicycle, a whistle, and a truncheon, which he kept out of sight and rarely had to use. This realistic image of the bobby (which I experienced in my youth and well remember) was enshrined in a very popular TV series called 'Dixon of Dock Green'. Britain basked in world-wide respect for its peaceful, friendly, law-abiding democratic culture and its system of 'policing by consent'. Seventy or so years later, it is seen as the crime headquarters of international terrorist Islamists and criminal gangsters.

For those without personal experience of that earlier era, and who are now thinking that this nostalgic picture is being painted by an old buffer in his dotage, imagining his childhood in a mythical 'golden age', I recommend a detailed and witty account of post-war Britain: 'Notes From A Small Island', by Bill Bryson, an American travel writer who lived in Yorkshire for almost two decades.[10] Although his travels around Britain were made in the post-war era, his descriptions of small town and village life give a flavour of British culture, which was lingering on after the large towns had been infiltrated by the immigrants and contaminated by their cultures.

A decade after 1950 it became noticeable in documentary TV programmes based on CCTV and police operational video films about criminals and their activities in our towns, and in daily news items, that a large proportion of the new crime epidemic was being committed by people who were clearly not British natives. This is still the case today, and is corroborated by the fact that our expanded, but still overcrowded, prison system is known to have a disproportionately high number of people of non-British origin. This is also true of the prison scene in the USA, where

---

10   Bryson, Bill (1996).

black citizens form a disproportionately high number of the prison population and have done since American Independence in 1776.

This phenomenon requires an attempt at an explanation. I do not think that more than a modest contribution to the differential crime statistics in Britain can have been due to police 'racial discrimination', even in those far-off and less sensitive days, especially if one confines the investigation to serious crimes. Certainly, few people suggest this currently, now that the police are more aware of the need for great care in dealing with all suspects on a fair basis. Few people that is, except for those in a vocal section of the immigrant communities who seem to be totally biased in their perceptions. 'Police institutional racism' is most unlikely to be a major factor as far as serious crime is concerned, where strong forensic evidence is usually needed for conviction.

If we assume therefore that disproportionately more crime is being committed by the immigrant populations, we need some plausible reasons for that phenomenon. I do not think it likely that people from different racial populations would have a different genetic propensity to commit crime. It seems much more likely that we are looking at another cultural feature, and this idea is supported by the fact that not only did the rate of familiar crime rise, but new criminal activities appeared which related to the patterns of crime in the countries of origin of the immigrants. For example, in Jamaica the use of machetes, knives, mugging, drug-abuse, and of violence in general was much more common than in Britain at that time, and possibly is even now. It soon became a feature of the drugs scene that immigrants from the West Indies were the main source of importation of proscribed drugs, as they travelled to and fro between the Caribbean countries and Britain. Of course, contamination with these cultural features soon caused the spread of similar crime patterns to the native population, particularly because children were being targeted by the drug dealers. Unfortunately it is almost impossible to obtain reliable and comparable statistics on the crime rates of different countries because the rates are obtained in different ways, and comparisons are therefore not valid. It is not even easy to make comparisons between the data compiled in one jurisdiction, such as our own, over different years, because methods change over time, nor is it possible to be sure that all crime is recorded by the police. When a set of data appears to indicate a correlation between a particular type of crime and a particular group of offenders it is also difficult to untangle the possible causes of the connection.

As if these difficulties are not enough to deter one from trying to establish causes and effects in this field of inquiry, there are many people with racial prejudice eager to rubbish any conclusions they would prefer not to be broadcast, however carefully they have been arrived at. Notwithstanding the above caveats, I will try to gain a general picture from various sources which seem to be as reliable as one can find.

In 2002 an official in Jamaica estimated that one in ten Jamaicans flying to Britain was carrying illegal drugs. To encourage the immigration of people from a violent, corrupt and drug-ridden culture into our own culture is to infect it with a more deadly and destructive agent than if we were to import lethal organisms such as those responsible for Aids, Ebola or the bubonic plague. The latter circumstance would trigger a major health plan to contain the epidemic and eliminate the spread of the infective agent. However lethal such an organism were to be, it is likely that we would gain control fairly quickly, as we have done with Aids, and our culture would in the long run remain relatively undisturbed. The infection with the values and behaviours of dangerous and violent cultures has proved to be much more deadly, because such cultural features (or 'memes') are very difficult to control, and therefore very long-lasting as the effects spread within the host culture. In fact it looks as if our culture may well not recover at all, since the costly and continuing efforts at control so far have had little effect in reducing the illegal import and consumption of drugs to a low level, and have failed to stop the associated, serious, gang warfare and other criminal behaviours. Officials, such as the senior Chief Police Constables who recently (October 2013) have admitted that the 'war on drugs' has not succeeded, are now suggesting that the use of hard drugs should not be illegal because the users are victims in need of NHS treatment, and that only the drug peddlers should be prosecuted. Decriminalisation is the default strategy of the law enforcement agencies, and a sure sign of an overwhelmed, defeated and impotent police force. At a stroke of the pen the problem can apparently be 'eliminated'. So far our politicians have only embraced this strategy in relation to cannabis for self-use, but that may not be the end of the idea. In 2014 a TV report claimed that in the Netherlands the authorities were about to close some fifteen prisons because of a lack of criminals! Such a miraculous decline in criminal activity should be treated with scepticism; the most likely explanation is that a decision has been made to decriminalise a whole tranche of criminal activities. How wonderful it is to be able to eliminate a serious and intractable problem with a stroke of the pen!

These criminal activities, which have been imported with the mass and uncontrolled influx of people from alien cultures, unfortunately infect the native host culture with behavioural features that are most unwelcome. Drug misuse is a particularly deadly behaviour because the drugs are addictive and the victims have their own and their families' lives destroyed. The criminal suppliers target children with free supplies initially, knowing that the victims are likely to become addicted, so that they can then be easily exploited. This successful tactic was enshrined in the amusing but accurate song: 'The Old Dope Peddler', by that brilliant satirist Tom Lehrer.

Thus the drug culture takes over many sections of society, but especially the underprivileged and vulnerable poor people, and the addicts then cause further serious social problems, such as stealing to fund their habit. Much secondary crime is therefore committed by the victims, and the whole noxious trade is organised by the professional criminal gangs who use knife and gun violence to defend their territory from rival gangs. There is little doubt that most of this criminal activity was, and is, committed by black youths and native young men on the streets of Britain, but organised by older men in international gangs.

The large sums of money deriving from the drugs trade soon lured white natives into its snare. Street muggings, thefts from children of mobile phones, car theft and burglaries soon followed, and all seemed to be, partly at least, related to the drug scene with a heavy involvement of young men of Caribbean origin. That is not to say that this phenomenon would not have occurred to some extent in this era if no such immigration had occurred, but doubtless it was, in Britain at least, organised by people from a violent, corrupt and drug-ridden overseas culture. Nor should we ignore the fact that the inevitable cultural contamination infected many of our native young men, who were resentful at the displacement of their communities by the immigrants, and began attacks on the blacks, whether criminal or innocent. One such notorious case was that of the murder of Stephen Lawrence in 1993 by several white young men, who were convicted and imprisoned.

A later immigrant cohort of 30,000 people of Indian origin began to arrive in Britain when Idi Amin expelled the Asian community from Uganda in 1972. These immigrants, holding British passports, were mainly business and professional people who quickly integrated into the British middle-class, and made a contribution to the economy, having taken full advantage of the positive discrimination policies of the political parties and the BBC. But they were followed by many more poor Asians from India, Pakistan and Bangladesh. There is no doubt that the

Blair and Brown 'New Labour' Governments welcomed the flood of immigrants, and kept no records of the numbers, whilst keeping up the constant propaganda flow of positive slogans and 'political correctness' in order to suppress opposition. Later on, new cohorts from Northern Africa and Eastern Europe began arriving, making use of the European Union's irresponsible policies of open borders and freedom of movement and labour. These large and uncontrolled later flows of mostly illegal immigrants were of course organised by criminal gangsters, who were probably the first to take advantage of the new rules, which might well have been written by themselves.

Many factors have doubtless been involved in the increase of crime rates since about 1950, but I have drawn attention to what I believe to have been the most important one, and one not often publically acknowledged, even as late as 2014, namely the effect of the drastically changed racial and cultural mix in Britain. It seems obvious to me that the more homogeneous and stable the population, the more everybody feels bound together by virtue of their common genetic origins, history, language, morals, customs and values: in other words, bound together by their common culture, forming a greatly extended 'family'. In such a society people are expected to conform in many ways and usually do so, but most of all in their civic duty, which is taken for granted, to help each other. There is a very strong social pressure throughout such a united society for almost everybody to act in a moral fashion, and not to transgress the unwritten code of conduct, which is accepted by almost everybody, and which is inculcated from birth. Although this description is an idealised one and a generalisation, it was closely applicable to most of Britain before mass immigration began to cause its rapid destruction. The current so-called 'multicultural society' is a conglomeration of many mutually hostile groups with different cultural and moral values, which in many cases includes a strong criminal element.

The sudden influx of many alien, cultural groups has undoubtedly contributed to our serious, current, crime epidemic and I think we need to take a look at the possibility that being an immigrant, especially an illegal one, may in itself tend to push the foreign person into crime. When a poor immigrant from the third world, or from an impoverished European country, arrives in a developed country illegally she seldom does this without help. The whole experience is new, she has many things to learn, and often a difficult, long, and dangerous journey to make. Not unnaturally she is usually helped by international criminal gangs, who extract large sums of money for their services. She will usually arrive in the country of choice with a large debt to be repaid in a short time to the criminals, who can easily threaten harm to her family back at home if she does not pay up. For example, a documentary TV programme in March 2002 illustrated the plight of young, black, African women in Italy, working as prostitutes to earn the £30,000 that each owed to the gangsters who had arranged their illegal immigration.

The illegal immigrant is therefore already a criminal in her new country, arriving with forged documents, and her immediate future is in the hands of criminals. Not surprisingly for someone in her predicament, and having seen the wealth and easy lifestyle of her 'minders', she will easily view crime as the fast track to a brighter future. She will probably be given a nudge in that direction by her criminal friends, or by her compatriots who are already wise in the ways of earning easy money through crime, drug-peddling and prostitution.

The poor male immigrant looking for a brighter economic future, who is unskilled, without proper documents, who doesn't speak the host language and is therefore unlikely to be able to earn large sums quickly to pay off his debt to the gangsters, who has promised to send money home to his family before setting off, and who does not yet share the host country's culture, is also unlikely to have a high moral attitude to crime. He is, in a word, desperate. Crime will therefore be the obvious choice, indeed the only option, for the rapid realisation of his aspirations, and he has no affiliation with the people of the new country, who in any case seem to have money and goods to spare. He is also, typically, a vigorous and determined young male. He enters the country to which he has migrated therefore as a criminal, dependent on a criminal subculture to ensure that he is not detected and deported. He will have an acute awareness of the vast rewards that criminal activity brings for relatively little effort, and with a strong belief that he could reap some of these rewards for himself.

Indeed, and I want to emphasise this, it is a *universal* feature of human social psychology, that people from different cultural backgrounds tend to have weaker moral scruples when dealing with people from other social groups. This is part of the reason why all people are wary of foreigners. When I lived in Cyprus, friends used to say: 'There's one price for the tourists, one for the foreign residents, and another one for the Cypriots'. I hasten to add that the Cypriots are no worse than anyone else in this respect and this is, of course, a generalisation. Every experienced tourist knows that he will be charged higher prices for goods from shops in tourist areas in most countries. He will also know that most tourists are the foreigners who are preyed upon by the natives of any country with a large tourist industry. One could say that the main, if not the only, reason why countries vigorously advertise and encourage tourism is to milk the tourists of their wealth. What I am pointing out is the universal tendency, exaggerated amongst criminals, to be more prone to prey on people to whom they have no affiliation or lasting relationship. The affiliation of criminals is to the gang – hence the proverb: 'There is honour among thieves'. This phenomenon was, and probably still is, a striking feature of the Italian mafia families, both at home and when translocated to America as immigrants. The affiliation of the immigrant is to his own compatriots. And all are likely to be strongly motivated by self-interest and greed, and to see the host natives as economic prey. In Britain this phenomenon has been greatly encouraged by our social welfare system and positive-discrimination policies, which have imbued the immigrants with an expectation that they will be given top and immediate priority for housing and cash benefits. They may not speak good English on arrival here, but they all 'know their rights', and often harass Local Government officials unmercifully until they get what they want. Only lately has the Cameron Government begun to amend the benefit rules in an effort to curb these legal but ridiculous priorities, which have led to so much resentment in the long-established natives, and the Local Authority employees who are daily harassed by the importunate immigrants.

The modern, large, noisy, hectic and cosmopolitan metropolis is peopled by an anonymous crowd amongst which to live, work and enjoy oneself, and it provides a perfect workplace for the ambitious criminal. It has many different subcultures, all of which have little or no concern for each other. It is usually, also, the preferred habitat for the new immigrant, where he can find a community of his compatriots in which he feels relatively safe, and at the same time can easily find a criminal activity that can be practised on the surrounding, wealthy natives, and almost certainly where he can join a criminal gang to teach him his new trade. Crowds are not only a common feature of large cities, they are the preferred workplace of the pickpocket, the mugger, the shoplifter, the car thief, the drug peddler, the bank-card 'surfer', and the terrorist. By contrast a stable, small, and close-knit village community mimics the ancient ancestral tribe, and will always tend to be a safer and more harmonious place for any law-abiding citizen and her family to live in.

If a new, poor-but-honest immigrant passes through the normal immigration procedures and is allowed to stay, he then has the difficult task of integrating into a strange culture with the further disadvantage of having to learn a new language in many cases, and usually of being poorly-equipped educationally and culturally to compete in the labour market. He is usually in the hands of gang-masters who provide him with overcrowded and insanitary accommodation and a poorly paid job. In a short space of time his dream of rapid economic advancement is dashed, the strong temptations around him must be irresistible, and the slide into crime almost a certainty, unless he has been lucky enough to have found a reasonably paid job. He may soon realise, whether he is earning money legally or illegally, and even if he has more money and a better standard of living than he had in his own country, that he is at the bottom of the socio-economic pile in his host country, where consumerism is the new religion. If, at the same time, he experiences unfriendliness or hostility from the natives of the host country, he is understandably not going to identify with the new society, but will become hostile in return. Because of the normal effect that cultural affiliation has on all of us, the new poor immigrant will tend to view members of our culture, and its rules, as being less deserving of his concern, compared with his own self-interest and that of his compatriots and friends.

Not surprisingly therefore, the recently-arrived, unskilled immigrant will tend to feel little concern for the society in which he finds himself, and will have no expectation that he can quickly remedy his economic and social predicament through the normal avenues of opportunity available to the natives (especially in hard economic times). He has in effect traded one underprivileged situation for another one, with the additional disadvantage of having lost his place in his own culture and the comforts that it and his own family provided. All of this disturbing turn of events contributes to an attitude of mind in which engaging in criminality will be the only realistic option for long-term survival, and for the quick economic advancement which was the original objective and expectation which spurred the young man to leave home to better himself. Predation on an alien society, perceived to be hostile and rejecting of the immigrant, will most likely engender no feelings of guilt or remorse, and the many criminal activities which may well be offered to him by his more settled compatriots will be seen as the only available route to riches or, at least, to a comfortable life and some status in a consumerist society. The gangsters who organised his journey, his shelter and false documents, will be threatening him with dire consequences to him and his family back home if he does not pay up for their services, and therefore patience in acquiring ready money is not an option. In contemplating his predicament he will think, probably correctly, that he has nothing to lose and everything to gain by joining his compatriots in their criminal activities. The basic problem underlying all of this social pathology is the deep feeling of alienation which is the likely common experience of impoverished, illegal immigrants in what seems to be, and may well be, a hostile culture far from home.

On the other side of this picture are the poor native Britons, who see their long-held neighbourhoods being invaded and occupied by strange-looking foreigners who are being treated with instant welfare benefits, social housing and jobs – which are the obvious results of a policy of positive discrimination. Naturally they are hostile towards the immigrants being foisted upon their territories and communities by the better-off 'authorities', and some will inevitably be aggressive and violent towards the unwanted foreigners. In addition the underprivileged young natives will rapidly learn from the activities and attitudes of the immigrants, so that their own culture will be contaminated with a criminal mind-set, which enables them also to reap rich rewards.

The rise in organised crime in Britain and in other European countries is mainly driven from above by international gangs who have thrived while mass movements across open national borders have greatly facilitated their evil activities. They could hardly have hoped for better working conditions. The white slave trade of young women into prostitution, the organised smuggling of immigrants, drugs and guns, the organisation of slavery into domestic work for wealthy foreigners, the trafficking of children for sexual abuse, the car-theft, insurance-fraud, drug-peddling and many other major criminal activities across Britain and the European Union are clearly out of the control of the police and immigration authorities of the Union's member states.

We can only wonder whether the politicians, who thought that the European Union would improve the flow of goods and people across the national boundaries when they opened the borders and removed the obstacles to migration of workers, realised what a success these measures would be! It would be much too cynical (I hope) to think that they adopted this scheme in order to benefit themselves, but one should be permitted to ask whether any of them considered the possible (and I say the obvious and certain) unintended consequences. Surely any sophisticated and intelligent person, especially an experienced politician (many of them are lawyers), realises that the first people to take advantage of any new opportunity whatsoever, especially one created by new rules, regulations and laws, are the criminals. But then many lawyers, like criminals, are opportunists first and foremost, and both groups thrive on crime. Indeed the avaricious lawyers need the criminals as much as the criminals need them.

There is plenty of evidence that Britain has now imported not only the 'poor, tired and huddled masses yearning to be free', but many hardened criminals and fundamental religious fanatics, amongst the few deserving immigrants. It seems that the British authorities were frequently warned by other European countries' national security services about the known Muslim extremists who were entering the country, but for hidden reasons ignored the warnings, so, not surprisingly, the terrorists set up their headquarters in London. Acts of serious terrorism have been carried out, such as the London bombings by four Muslim suicide terrorists on 07.07.2005, in which fifty-two people were killed and over seven hundred injured. Three of the bombs were detonated on the London Underground and one on a bus. Many other Muslim terrorist plots have been foiled by the police and security services.

The Islamic fundamentalists have introduced new practices into Britain which are legal under their Sharia law, but criminal under our law, such as forced marriage of female children and female genital mutilation (FGM). Their domination of women is abhorrent to us, even when not illegal. Gangs of Asian men have organised paedophile rings of vulnerable English girls from care homes who have been sexually abused and handed round to many men as sexual slaves. Some wealthy immigrants have enslaved young women immigrants as house-maids and servants. Fundamentalist preachers (Imams) have openly preached hatred against our native population (infidels), and authors have been targeted for murder, such as in the case of Salman Rushdie. The Ayatollah Khomeini issued an order (or Fatwa) to all Muslims to *assassinate* Rushdie for authoring his book, *The Satanic Verses*, and to assassinate any translators or publishers of the book. The author went into hiding for years and was protected by the British security services (at great cost), but a Japanese translator was murdered and two others survived assassination attempts. Book publishers in Britain then practiced self-censorship of subjects that might offend Muslims, as was my personal experience when I tried to find a publisher for my first draft of this book in 2002.

Whether or not all of this analysis be accurate, it can hardly be denied that the crime scene in Britain has worsened markedly over the last few decades and that mass, uncontrolled immigration has made a considerable, if not major, contribution to this catastrophic decline in our standard of living, in our moral outlook, and in our cultural harmony. No one living in Britain before about 1950 could have imagined in their wildest dreams that slavery, female genital mutilation, voodoo murder, forced child marriage, the wearing of burkas, the building of hundreds of mosques in our cities, and multiple new crimes would soon be common features of British life.

As for the native Britons, other factors have certainly contributed to a loss of moral behaviour, such as the rise of commercial values at the expense of Christian ones, the decline of parental supervision and control, the greatly increased affluence enjoyed by some sections of the community with an increase of poverty for others (the income and wealth gap), the influences of television, of advertising, of pornography, and the spread of technical 'must-have' gizmos into the youth culture. The rapid decline of deference to all forms of authority, and particularly to religion, has resulted in a moral vacuum, which has been filled by a culture of rabid individualism which now prevails in many Western democracies. The increasing wealth which capitalism and its technological production methods have spread to many in our 'consumerist' societies, has combined with the individualism, the lack of deference, ubiquitous advertising, and life in large, anonymous cities, to focus many people's motivation and values on personal and selfish fulfilment in a financial sense. Many of us have become richer whilst the gap between rich and poor has markedly increased, at the cost of the social harmony which prevailed in local small groups of like-minded friends and neighbours, and which most of us previously enjoyed. The very rapid and unplanned social changes, such as the breakdown of the traditional family, the changing roles of women, and the rapid break-up of hitherto stable communities as heavy industries disappeared, have also helped to destroy long-stable social patterns. We have now arrived in the 'me, me society', with its constant demands of 'rights', and the common expectation that the 'nanny state' should provide the necessities of a charmed life. In the current social chaos, and our hour of need, our church leaders and politicians are in a state of moral confusion, along with the rest of us, and are apparently preoccupied with trivial concerns of their own, whilst ignoring the monumental and unplanned changes which are the main cause of our severe anxieties. Whilst more respect and help has become available to disabled people, the increasing numbers of elderly and demented citizens are often exploited, neglected and lonely.

All of this makes it easier for evil to triumph, when there no longer appear to be any absolute moral values shared by the majority of citizens. It is not surprising that some of the young, practising Muslims despise a lot of current, Western, native behaviour and values, and turn away to embrace the traditional values of their parents. The TV scenes of young people in a drunken state spilling out of night clubs and pubs in the early hours, and indulging in gratuitous violence are a stain on our culture. This recent innovation has amazed and disgusted our older generation and the Muslim community, and it is difficult to see how we can improve such behaviour. Perhaps returning the licencing hours to the previous state, and increasing alcoholic drink prices would help, but such measures would be unpopular, and therefore politically difficult to introduce. However, there is evidence from many studies that antisocial and violent behaviour is more common in societies where income and wealth is unequally distributed than in more equal ones. Certainly the income gap in Britain and America has greatly widened over the last few decades, during which many indicators of social disharmony and lowered standards of behaviour have also occurred.

Some of the young Muslim men's minds have now become fertile ground in which fundamentalist demagogues can sow the seeds of rebellion and terrorism, because they perceive our armed forces to be attacking their co-religionists abroad. The young Muslim men are second-generation immigrants who have been brought up and educated in Britain and yet have become 'home-grown' terrorists, eager to train in Muslim countries such as Pakistan, and more recently, in Syria, to fight and die for what they believe is a religious war (or jihad). Our Government may wish Muslim and other immigrants to 'integrate' into our culture whilst holding onto minor relics of their own culture, but this seems to be an impossible objective, and to be born of the arrogant assumption that our culture is obviously superior at a time when it is fast disintegrating.

On 26.08.2014 the Press Association revealed that some 1,400 vulnerable children had been sexually exploited in Rotherham, South Yorkshire, over a sixteen-year period between 1997 and 2013, as described in a report by Professor Alexis Jay. She said in her report that: 'There were blatant collective failures by Rotherham's (Labour) Council leadership. Some children reported being doused with petrol, and then threatened with being set alight, threatened with guns, made to witness brutally violent rapes, and threatened that they would be next if they told anyone. They were *raped by multiple perpetrators*, trafficked to other towns in Northern England, abducted, beaten, and intimidated. Girls as young as eleven years were raped by large numbers of men. The problems were underplayed by senior managers who ran the Social Services Children's Safeguarding Team, and were not seen as a priority by the South Yorkshire Police, who *regarded many child victims with contempt*. The failures occurred despite there having been three reports on the problems between 2002 and 2006 which could not have been clearer. The first of these reports was suppressed because senior managers did not believe the data, and the other two were ignored. Front-line social workers and youth workers, reported Professor Jay, did not fail, in that they repeatedly raised serious concerns on the nature and extent of the abuse with their managers.

By far the majority of the perpetrators were described as of Pakistani origin by their mainly-white victims. Councillors seemed to think the problem was a 'one off' and would go away. Several staff described their nervousness about identifying the ethnic origins of the perpetrators for fear of being thought to be 'racist'. Others remembered having had clear directions from their managers not to do so. In the last four years there has been a series of high profile cases of the exploitation of young girls in Rochdale, Derby and Oxford. The young girls were in 'care homes' (!) run by the councils, were very vulnerable, and were apparently easily groomed to accept the perpetrators initially as their friends.

Rotherham Council Leader Roger Stone immediately stepped down from his post on receiving the report, commendably taking responsibility for the failings. The CEO of the Council, Martin Kimber, said that no Council officers would be facing disciplinary action. Rotherham Council, which had commissioned the report, accepted 'almost without exception' the findings, including the failures attributed to senior managers in the child protection services, to elected councillors and senior police officers.

This thorough and horrifying report must at last surely be accepted as *firm evidence* of the dangers that some foreign immigrants pose to our culture. We already know that in Pakistan and other Muslim countries men frequently abuse and rape young girls and that many men have contempt for 'lower caste' females. The abuse that these vulnerable, young, white girls suffered in Rotherham and other British cities is almost beyond belief. Their pain and suffering has blighted their lives for ever. Why our governments have allowed such men to enter the country and settle here is beyond my comprehension. Only six Asian men in one such gang have been convicted and sentenced, out of hundreds of perpetrators.

Apart from the dreadful abuse of young girls supposedly 'in care', the other noteworthy and fundamental feature of this horrible series of events is that of *the effect of the PC campaign against so-called 'racism'*. The cause of the suppression of the evidence, and the failure to act, were *the direct result of public servants being frightened* to state the obvious fact that the perpetrators were Pakistanis and therefore, in fact, beyond the law. I call this phenomenon

'PC-Induced Institutional Paralysis'. If ever there were a case for acknowledging *the serious harm* that has been done to our culture by the 'anti-racist' campaign this surely is it. But I doubt whether that lesson will have been learned, and public servants, naturally, will still be fearful of losing their jobs by pointing out the crimes and the noxious behaviour of any immigrants. Small wonder: the Metropolitan Police were labelled with the pejorative phrase 'Institutional Racism' by the Macpherson Report into the killing of Stephen Lawrence, and the police are currently being investigated yet again regarding the possibility that their 'stop and search' powers are being used in a 'racist' fashion.

As soon as the Jay Report was published we had the usual BBC response, with Yasmin Alibhai-Brown having to tell us how terrible this abuse was, and how we need to acknowledge openly that certain Muslim men behaved extremely badly. Well done Yasmin. I just hope she can fully realise what happens when the BBC propaganda machine suppresses free speech with its 'racist' slur, and which has now been seen at last to have such *a pernicious effect on public servants, who are terrified of losing their jobs if they speak out.* That other regular BBC liberal, Polly Toynbee, appeared on 11.09.2014 in the Daily Politics Show, to explain that the real problem in Rotherham was that the Council was run by a block of men who didn't want any bad publicity. She played down the fact that the hundreds of evil perpetrators were mainly Pakistanis, and doesn't yet seem to acknowledge that the PC-Induced Paralysis in the Council which allowed the abuse to continue was a direct consequence of the 'anti-racist' campaign that she and all the other BBC propagandists used to suppress opposition to their 'multicultural' enterprise. She also seemed to be upset at the abuse she received on the social media. Her sensitivity surprised me a little because, surely, a hardened media hack like her should realise that there are some nasty people out there, and that not everybody agrees with her opinions. If there are two things that characterise the liberal intellectuals it is that they always think that they are right, and they don't tolerate any opposing opinions. Other Muslim commentators gave us the usual platitudes, including the most common one, that these evil men were just a 'small minority'. We never get the figures, so we are none the wiser as to the size of this or any other quoted minority. My fear is that, as with most catastrophes or bad news, we shall all be shocked for a day or two and then other news will push this item out of our minds, and help us to forget the problem. The Muslim community will soon be in denial, until the next scandal hits the TV screens. It is a profound and common human trait to respond immediately with shock to terrible events that are happening to other people, and to forget, within a few days or weeks, all about them, as we get on with our daily preoccupations. More importantly, we quickly get used to almost any changes that occur slowly, and few people now remember the harmonious society that was Britain a few decades ago. How many people in Britain now remember the London bombings, or the Haiti earthquake, and wonder how the scarred victims are getting on? This phenomenon is also aided by the fact that, within a period of about fifty years, many people will have died and their memories will have been lost. This, of course, is one reason why history often repeats itself as the generations change.

In these now-dire straits our society is beset by many extremely serious problems which begin to look insoluble in the short-term, as well as out of control. *We are sleep-walking into social purgatory.* Along with all the modern problems of rapid technological change, we have unprecedented social and cultural instability. Before 1950 we had a basically law-abiding, peaceful and harmonious society based on a common culture. We have allowed that enviable situation to be suddenly replaced by a so-called 'multicultural society' of our own making, (or more accurately the making of the Blair/ Brown political establishment), consisting of different and sometimes hostile cultural groups, originating recently from many parts of the world, living separate and parallel lives. Worse still, those groups contain many career criminals who are acting like predators on our native citizens, and the Muslim religious extremists are deliberately destroying our culture and replacing it with theirs, encouraged by our governments' confused and naïve attempts to integrate them into a culture and society that many of them despise.

Practically all people in the Muslim community hold fast to their own religion and culture, and perhaps a majority support, even if they do not join, the terrorist movements. Those non-Muslim, impoverished immigrants, who have a weaker affiliation with their culture of origin and a lax moral code, are more likely to fall into criminal ways of improving their wealth and thus of entering our own materialistic society, but adding to our problems by intensifying the crime epidemic. Of course, some in both groups may work hard and try to lead a law–abiding life, but they are still likely to live in a ghetto for support and comfort, and to lead parallel lives. They may not be active criminals or religious extremists themselves, but they may not share our cultural values either, and therefore be supporting or hiding their compatriots with whom they still have a strong, cultural affiliation. As the old proverb reminds us: 'Blood is thicker than water.'

We in Britain are not alone in experiencing a crime epidemic, and all Western democracies are, to a larger or lesser extent, in the same difficulties. Many of them suffer from the same causes, including the social instability which is a fundamental causative factor. The mixing together of many cultural groups in the West, which began in the USA in the 1840's, continued in several huge waves of immigration from Europe to a peak in 1907 and to restriction in 1921. It was partly fired by the liberal idea of 'the melting pot'. In many ways, at first, this experiment in social engineering was a partial success in offering Europe's 'huddled masses' both an asylum from persecution, and an escape from poverty. It should be noted, however, that these immigrants were from European countries, and therefore had a basic culture that was democratic, rooted deeply in the cultures of ancient Greece and Rome, and in the Judeo-Christian religions. Despite this common cultural background it became evident many decades later, despite much effort to weld together these diverse peoples, along with the aboriginal Americans, the negro slaves and the descendants of the original European founding fathers, into an American nation, that there were signs of much inter-communal tension, along with a high crime rate. This social instability has been markedly worsened and accelerated by the more recent waves of immigrants of people from non-European countries, many of them illegal, and from alien cultural and religious groups, such as Muslims and Hispanics.

Significantly the murder rate per annum in the multicultural USA is fairly high for the developed world (4.7/100,000 inhabitants) whilst the rates in monocultural Iceland (0.3/100,000) and Japan (0.3/100,000) are the lowest rates.[11] The rate in Britain before about 1950 was towards the bottom along with Iceland, but it has now risen up the scale to (1.0/100,000). The murder rate is a good indicator, I am sure, of the social health of any society, and is one of the best indicators of the crime rate, although there are some difficulties, as always, with comparisons of crime statistics across different countries. In Britain in the last decade, we have seen many very worrying crime trends, which, as with so many other features of cultural life, follow American patterns. School children now commonly mug each other to steal mobile phones, carry knives and use them on each other, and even murder other smaller children. Some have murdered adults, including their school-teachers. Shopkeepers, innocent passers-by (including children) and police officers are not infrequently shot by gangsters. The violence now being committed by young children is one of the

---

11   www.unodoc.org (2012). The UN Global Study on Homicide.

most worrying signs of a sick society. In addition, we have a large
population of 'single mothers' trying alone to do the difficult task
of bringing up several children, often fathered by different men,
and living on benefits – 'married to the state'. Every year we have
mothers and fathers murdering their children, (a new phenomenon),
and many others seriously abusing their infants. In the latter case
it is noteworthy that the abusing parents are often of different
racial origins, and frequently, are addicted to alcohol and drugs.
Apparently, two women are murdered each week by their abusive
partners. Although our society still has a majority of people who
are kind, caring, friendly and hardworking, there are too many
serious problems, of which the crime epidemic is one, for us to be
complacent about the changes that have occurred since the mass
invasion of immigrants.

Another worrying but inevitable change from the previous
open and relaxed society which was Britain up to about 1950, is
the vast increase in security measures, visible everywhere. Alarm
systems, and over six-million CCTV cameras and security lights
festoon the buildings in the towns, and, to a lesser extent, those
in the countryside. Security guards operate in all large shops,
armed police are frequently called out to shooting incidents
and parade openly showing their automatic rifles in airports
and other public places. Britain was world-famous for being
practically the only large country in the world before World
War II that had an unarmed police force. Now the police have
armed response units on constant standby to deal with shooting
incidents, and sometimes their unarmed colleagues get shot and
murdered during their ordinary duties. Inevitably the armed
police sometimes make mistakes, and as a result innocent citizens
occasionally get killed. The criminals in modern Britain are both
intelligent and very resourceful compared with their pre-war
counterparts. Every few months it seems, they move on to new
targets and the next criminal fashion, before the police have caught

up and instituted effective counter-measures. Recent common criminal enterprises have been the theft of lead from church roofs; theft of copper cables on the railways and from signals on motorways; the deliberate causing of motor accidents to commit fraudulent insurance claims; metal theft of various other types, such as drain covers; and, of course, rapidly expanding cyber-crime. In addition, 'old-fashioned' crimes, such as motor theft, are now organised on an industrial level, including exporting expensive stolen vehicles. A TV programme in 2014 claimed that a car is stolen every two seconds in Britain, and when high value cars are stolen they are exported within hours to continental countries like Cyprus, where there is a high demand for them. Slavery of females for sex or to work as house-maids, in 2014, is a scandalous crime for the country that made such efforts to abolish the slave-trade of Africans after Wilberforce's bill in 1804. This modern curse has hardly been recognised up to October 2014, and many police forces are unaware of the practice in their areas. Most of these professional criminals are not local amateurs – they are organised gangsters with multinational enterprises. The cost to the British economy of all this criminal activity, and the very expensive security and police measures required to cope with it, must now be a phenomenal drain on the British economy compared with the pre-WWII level. I have no figures for this modern expense, but it must be in the billions of pounds each year. It is certainly not included in any government calculations of the 'contributions of immigrants to our economy'.

As in America, our prisons are now overcrowded, and foreign criminals make up a disproportionate number of the inmates. The prison population is the highest ever, and more prisons are being built, despite many Government 'initiatives' to shorten sentences and to use community-based punishments in an effort to keep people out of prison. Many violent criminals, such as murderers, have been discharged back into the community after serving short sentences, and without adequate assessment of the threat that they pose. Inevitably, some of these paroled murderers kill another innocent person. The Criminal Justice System is largely ridiculed by a population crying out to be relieved of the petty and serious crime that blights so many lives, because it is seen to be ineffectual in punishing criminals and in supporting a law-and-order society. There is much talk of helping the victims but not much is done. Most people, I'm sure, think that recidivist criminals should be getting much more severe penalties. If criminals keep repeating the same offences one can only draw the inference that the penalties are ineffectual.

The prevailing feeling amongst many ordinary citizens, aware now of the many criminals in our midst, and surrounded as they are, in the large cities in Britain today, by people of obvious diverse origins, is bound to be one of heightened wariness and vigilance. This feeling may be mitigated in the course of time, and after many casual day to day meetings. Even then this gradual breaking down of initial suspicions and caution in one's dealings with people from different cultures still leaves people vulnerable to occasional adverse experience, or even rumours and disturbing news-media information. This feeling of suspicion towards strangers, foreigners or immigrants from different cultures may be labelled as 'prejudice' by the 'politically correct' brigade, but the implication that prejudiced people are evil or less than decent is often mistaken. The feelings of wariness or suspicion are *universal in all people* faced with very different strangers, especially when the latter have earned a disreputable reputation through their behaviour. The feeling is a proper defensive reaction to a perceived threat and is, as described previously, hard-wired into all human brains. To expect, for example, a frail, elderly, native woman not to feel threatened if she meets a group of young, noisy and boisterous black males in an area where such males are known to have been responsible for street muggings, would be ludicrous in the extreme. 'Prejudiced' that feeling may be, but to expect such natural defensive responses to disappear just because someone of liberal tendencies thinks it 'unfair', and therefore tries to legislate against it, is to depart from sanity and to live in cloud-cuckoo land.

The answer to this sort of 'prejudiced' attitude, which I share with many of my compatriots, is to restore the stable homogeneous communities which are known to provide all citizens with a peaceful and comfortable life. Immigration should be firmly controlled and criminals should be vigorously pursued so that citizens do not feel threatened by anybody in the streets, whether natives or foreigners. However, such a popular and sensible course of action has not always been adopted. The conclusions and recommendations of the Macpherson inquiry in 1998 encouraged a new climate of confusion in the Metropolitan Police Force. The assumption that police officers were unfairly 'stopping and searching' black youths, and the consequent abandonment of this policy, led to the inevitable and predictable result that drug-peddling, mugging, the carrying of knives and guns, and violent street crime increased. Naturally, no police officer was going to risk a charge of 'racism' when his ambitious and 'politically correct' superiors had made it clear that they were determined to 'rid the Met' of 'institutional racism', of which the Macpherson inquiry accused the Metropolitan Police. This necessary exposure of bad practice in our policing appears to have had the unintended consequence of swinging attitudes from one extreme to the other, so that the frontline officers began to fear being called 'racists' when confronted with black suspects.

Public servants have the unenviable task of convincing two opposed groups in our disunited nation of their unbiased practice, and their actions are therefore often criticised by one side or the other. Many natives think that the pendulum of public policy has swung far too far, to the detriment of their own people. There is even the suspicion that the legal system also discriminates in favour of immigrants. The Government and the public services should make no concessions to immigrants, and insist that everybody is equal before the law, as was usually the case in the past. Unless the Criminal Justice system is seen by our citizens to be completely 'colour blind', and to treat all of us equally, it will lose its crucial support of the population.

People who come to live in our country should be told in unequivocal terms that they must *learn to live in our culture as it is*, not expect that they will be able to alter anything and everything that does not suit them. They would already think in that way if they were to come as visitors or as potential settlers in a preferred culture. If, on the other hand, they intend to come as colonists or predatory criminals they should not be admitted, or, if they have been admitted inadvertently, they should be deported immediately after being discovered.

The fact that the authorities do not adopt a sensible and forceful policy towards the immigrants, but, instead, continue with 'positive discrimination' and lax application of our laws, has produced a disillusioned and demoralised native population, many of whom have emigrated. The remainder have lost interest in the political system that has let them down, as is indicated by the gradual decline in voting at elections. The public now feel that they have no influence on political decisions because the politicians are 'all the same', whilst the politicians wonder why they have lost touch with the electorate. Some of the natives are also losing faith in the police, although the police are not to blame for the Government's policies, and if these trends continue, and the public begins to imitate the immigrants' non-cooperation with the police, then we shall be near the point of no return.

In the meantime, if immigrants want to have a better reputation within the native population, then they should try to earn it. If they do not want to be considered as a criminal threat to ordinary citizens then they should behave like the law-abiding majority. They have often enjoyed special privileges since they arrived and been given every opportunity to fit in, and if they have not done so, then there is something seriously wrong with them, and the onus is on their communities to put things right, and not to keep whingeing and complaining at the native population and its culture. Of course, not every immigrant is a criminal, but it is a civic duty for all citizens to cooperate with the police when they are trying to maintain law and order, and it is not helpful for the reputation of foreigners if they do not help the police to catch criminals within their communities. Producing a wall of silence out of compatriot solidarity, or complaining when the police intrude into 'their territory', is only going to arouse severe hostility amongst the natives who believe in policing by consent, and impartial implementation of the law.

One last point about immigrant crime and its cultural origins: the West Indian and African immigrants come from cultures that have serious crime and other social problems, such as violence, drug abuse and family breakdown. It is to be expected that these features would be carried with the immigrants into the host countries. A feature of particular importance in these groups is the strong tendency for the fathers to be absent from the families, so that the children are brought up by their mothers and other close female relations. The boys are thus often denied the experience of suitable, black, male, role models at the early stages of their development, and at later stages may experience unsuitable role models in the criminal street culture. The tendency for primary schools to be staffed mainly by females does nothing to ameliorate this problem, which may be a strong factor in the genesis of much violence and crime among young, black men in our cities. This has, I think, been at last recognised, and attempts to rectify the situation are being made, by recruiting black, male, role models into primary and secondary schools with many black pupils.

There is little doubt that mass immigration has played a major part in the rising and very serious crime wave in the large cities of Britain and Europe, for the reasons described above, and this process is continuing. This analysis is not intended to give the impression that we never had any crime before this modern social experiment began, nor that no criminals in Britain are natives. The crime wave at the petty level is now out of control, and many native youngsters plague their communities with 'antisocial behaviour', which can vary from the trivial to the serious and persistent, making vulnerable people's lives a misery. Serious crimes, organised by gangs of foreigners, preoccupy the overstretched police and security services, to say nothing of the huge expense to the economy of all the state and commercial security measures now necessary for our protection. However, these costs are certainly not taken into account by the politicians who say that immigrants benefit our economy.

At the most serious level, we now have 'home-grown' terrorism of a magnitude which is a totally new and previously unimaginable feature on the British mainland before mass immigration began. A senior officer in the security forces said, on 02 September 2006 in a TV programme, that his force is currently keeping surveillance on several thousand potential terrorists in Britain. In later weeks (September 2006) the security forces arrested some twenty or so Muslim young men who were suspected of plotting imminently to blow up several airliners crossing the Atlantic Ocean to America. In July 2005, four Muslim suicide bombers, born in Britain, blew themselves up in London on a bus and several underground trains, causing fifty-two civilian deaths and more than seven hundred injured, innocent travellers.

We were also told that there was a 'pipe-line' between Britain and Syria, along which many Muslim young men were being ferried, to join training camps in order to go on to Iraq to fight against British and American troops. It is not my intention to discuss here the pros and cons of our previous intervention in Iraq, but to illustrate the fact that British society is now showing *severe fault-lines* along the cultural divides. The British public does not need to be told that these phenomena are extremely serious for our society, nor that there is little likelihood of getting control of the problems caused directly by the failure of our Governments to take effective action to limit and control immigration. Sadly, most of the present young generation of natives will have little or no idea of how peaceful and harmonious British society was before World War II, because all their direct experience is of the current scene. **They do not know what they have lost and are now losing, and they do not seem to know what is going to happen to their children and grandchildren, who will live in a Muslim society if no radical preventative action is taken in the West. And they do not seem to realise that this Muslim society will take them into a new Dark Age, ruled by an authoritarian group of male religious extremists similar to the Taliban in Afghanistan.**

It is indisputable that the unplanned mass immigration, of hundreds of thousands of young men in particular, from foreign cultures into our hitherto peaceful islands, has been the major factor in causing the crime rate to soar. How the intelligent lawyer-politicians did not foresee what the result would be, is something I find difficult to understand. Consider before this chapter ends, just one indicative example amongst many: young men are usually sexually active, as most people know, so what would be likely to happen when all those young men descend *en masse* on another community? Yes – you've guessed it. The criminals would be well ahead of everybody else, already organising the trafficking of young women into prostitution, which they would fully expect to be a booming trade, and from which they would expect to reap huge rewards. In this sorry situation we should, however reluctantly, be grateful for their enterprise, because if they had not filled a gap in the market we should be faced with an even worse problem than we now have – an increase in abductions and rape of our native young women. Despite their enterprise, paedophile rings have already been operating within England, grooming and then sexually abusing young vulnerable teenage girls from social care homes. Six Asian men were convicted and sent to prison in 2012 for running a ring which organised the sexual abuse of such girls. The hideous Rotherham scandal of 2014 has been described above, and almost certainly will not be the last. Of course, the British tax-payer has to pay for the substantial imprisonment costs of these and many other foreign criminals (more benefit to our economy?). I can only conclude that either the foreign criminals are much smarter than our politicians or that many of our politicians do not care what happens to our culture and our population, because they are looking after their own narrow interests. Why otherwise would they still be trying to persuade us that immigration is good for us and good for our economy? And does anybody believe them?

In August 2014 we learned that about five hundred 'British Muslim' young men have gone to fight in Syria and Iraq in support of the jihadist Islamic State (IS) which has committed barbarous acts on Yasidi civilians and invaded Iraq. They have already beheaded two American journalists and threaten to do the same to a British hostage. Our security services are now preoccupied with trying to identify these British terrorists, so that they can deal with them appropriately when they try to re-enter Britain. This very difficult task will cost us a great deal of money because the threat of their staging more brutal acts here is high. More 'benefits' of immigration? What a lucky country we now are, with so many 'benefits' being heaped upon our unworthy heads! The liberals who believe such rubbish are, of course, still in denial. Luckily, most natives are now beginning to desert the unrealistic Liberal Democrats, although it is very late in the day.

It has not been my intention in this chapter to tackle all the causes of the crime epidemic in Britain today because many different causes have been, and must still be, operating today. One cause, which is now being recognised to be operating across all countries, is that of the rising economic inequalities between rich and poor people within countries and between countries.[12] During the last twenty-five years the income-inequality gap in Britain has widened under the influence of a free market ideology. In 2000-2013 the CEO's of the top 25% FTSE 100 companies had a median pay rise of 86%, compared with their average workers' rise of 2%. In 2009, the top bosses' pay was 145 times their average workers' pay, and that related to about 290 times the pay of their lowest paid workers.[13]

I have instead tried to analyse the factors which plausibly have been contributing to the sudden, precipitous and unexplained rise in crime rates that began about sixty years ago, and that have been mirrored throughout the Western democracies. It seems obvious to me, and to many of my compatriots, that the modern mass migrations, that have been the main sociological change coinciding with this period, would be the prime candidate for investigation and analysis of the causes. The suddenness of the social instability, the clash of very different cultures, and the illegal entry of many of the immigrants, surely point to these phenomena as major causative factors in the crime epidemic. It is therefore surprising that there is little mention of these possible causes by the authorities most concerned with tackling this serious problem. The police don't mention them as possible causes; the lawyers don't mention them; the politicians and even most of the chattering classes make little mention of them. This apparent blindness to the probable causes of one of the most serious, internal, social problems of the modern scene is somewhat perplexing. The only explanation of this almost universal silence seems to be that everybody is

---

12   Wilkinson, Richard & Pickett, Kate (2010).

13   www.highpaycentre.org. (28.10.2014): Income inequality in the UK: Explaining the data: The growing pay gap.

frightened to speak out for fear of offending the immigrants and their supporters, and of being accused of 'racism'. The fear may be well-founded. When small street protests against immigration have been organised by political extremists such as the British National Party and the English Defence League, counter-protests have been mounted by left-wing extremists and emotions have run high on both sides. Violence has usually broken out and, as usual, the police endeavouring to keep the antagonists apart are the targets for both sides. Thus the recognition of the underlying causes of the crime epidemic, and other social problems, is left to the native extremists.

My fear is that the underlying hostility, between those in favour of immigration and those against it, is very powerful and dangerous, for the simple reason that discussion of the subject has been discouraged from the beginning of the first signs of opposition to the 'multicultural' policy. Free speech and expression have been systematically suppressed, and therefore the unheard objections of the public have been turned into resentment and cynicism about politics and politicians. At the same time the politicians have inevitably lost touch with public opinion, and they are thus confused and perplexed when the apparent calm of daily life is suddenly broken by the storms of inter-racial violence, or 'race rioting'. I shall therefore discuss later the subject of free speech and its antagonistic philosophical idea of political correctness.

The next chapter however will be devoted to analysing another aspect of culture, fondly espoused by the liberal intelligentsia, namely cultural diversity.

§

CHAPTER EIGHT

CULTURAL DIVERSITY

THE HUMAN MIND SEEMS TO THRIVE on diversity. We seek new experiences, whether dangerous, tranquilising, social, sexual, environmental, geographical or cultural, as long as we are in control. Of course, people differ in this appetite as in many others, but, particularly when we are young, anything new or different seems exciting. As we get older we develop nostalgia for the experiences of our youth and tend to find change less attractive and more confusing or disturbing. But for most people, variety, to some degree or other, is more stimulating and enjoyable than monotony and sameness. Boredom soon sets in if our environment does not provide at least some opportunity for variety, for an element of surprise or even danger. Young men in particular often seek out dangerous experiences, and sometimes go to extremes in their quest for the 'ultimate adrenaline rush'. This latter, human, hard-wired trait has been an important evolutionary survival trait and has been, at least partly, responsible for mankind's recent rapid exploration and domination of the world's habitats, and the exploitation of the world's resources. It continues to stimulate our young men in particular to want to explore outer space, despite the serious dangers and the early casualties. Unfortunately, it has also been partly responsible for the continuing, seeming addiction to warfare and for male violence in general.

However, and this is a recurring theme throughout this book, discussion of any hotly debated topic often takes the form of 'mutually exclusive categories', whereas most of us favour a position between the extremes of a continuum. For each individual person in relation to any proposition, subject, experience or human need, there is a position on a hypothetical numerical scale which indicates that most people hold a position somewhere in the middle between the two extremes. Take clothes fashion as a trivial but familiar example: few of us would slavishly follow the whims of the arty designers, whose somewhat extreme productions are exhibited annually on the catwalks, even if we had the money to do so, nor would many of us be happy with a Maoist workers' uniform worn by all. We feel more comfortable wearing clothes somewhere in the current fashion mainstream, but with minor modifications that are a sign of our individuality or subgroup identification. And so it is with the experience of cultural diversity in all its forms.

'Variety's the very spice of life, that gives it all its flavour', as William Cowper said. Recognition of this universal, human, psychological need, coupled with increasing affluence and therefore more choice, underlies many modern movements to increase variety or diversity, thus enriching human experience. The industrial revolution and the mass production methods that followed have, for the developed world at least, abolished for most of us the fear of being deprived of basic necessities. This recent improvement in our living standards has led on to the possibility of satisfying another need – that for stimulating experiences, whether for new television programmes, bungee jumping, white-water rafting or holidays abroad. People in the Western democracies now live in a consumerist society and are spoilt for choice.

We are now aware, however, that mankind's burgeoning consumerist communities, and ever-expanding populations spreading across all the land masses, are destroying the habitats essential to the survival of wild life. We have caused the recent extinction of hundreds, or even thousands, of species already, and are threatening the extinction of many more. One major, current preoccupation is therefore that of preserving biodiversity. We are all aware that the activities of the expanding human population are causing the world to become a more uniform place as we modify the natural environment to suit our basic needs for food and shelter, and for the natural resources we consume. The increasing uniformity of the urban environments in which most of us now live makes our daily experiences less interesting, so that people now like to travel to far off places to experience 'the last wilderness' as a relief from urban monotony. We also like to travel on holiday to experience different cultures and, perhaps, to throw off the behavioural constraints that limit peoples' behaviour in their home neighbourhood.

It is not surprising, therefore, that we wish to preserve the rich, cultural diversity displayed by different social, racial and religious groups around the world. A world in which everyone looked the same, behaved in the same ways, spoke the same language, and exhibited the same subtle habits and customs that go to make up human cultures, would be, for most people, a very boring and uninteresting place. Some nations have been subjected to an authoritarian Communist political system, as in North Korea currently, with its familiar picture of masses of people wearing identical uniforms marching like automatons. But in the USSR this 'egalitarian' system collapsed suddenly, and in China it looks as if it is on the way to collapsing more slowly, as contact with the Western democracies, the trade in manufactured goods, and the digital information highway, awake an awareness of the possibility of a more varied and better life.

It seems reasonable, therefore, to assume that few people would welcome the loss of cultural diversity. But just as with biodiversity, there seems to be a marked trend towards the loss of cultural diversity, propelled in this case by the inexorable advance of our clever technology and modern trans-global communication. The world has become a smaller place, or to use a modern cliché, we all live in a global village now. Many of the estimated twenty thousand ancient languages have been lost, and many of the remaining estimated six thousand are gravely threatened with early extinction. Modern methods of communication facilitate the universal and rapid uptake of ideas, values, fashions and technologies, and generate worldwide ambitions to possess the latest industrial products. McDonalds, Coca Cola and Hilton Hotels stride across the world. A package holiday provides the traveller with all the familiar daily requirements, and at the same time insulates her from the local culture. Not only that, tourism can ruin the local culture, because the local economy comes to rely on supplying the needs of the incoming 'invaders', including providing them with a contrived version of the local culture as a form of entertainment. The contact between two different cultures never leaves both uncontaminated, and thus cultural diversity in tourist destinations, like biodiversity, is threatened with a slow death.

However, despite these formidable forces for the global spread of uniformity, humans are very resistant to losing their own cultures and identities, and many groups are now making a conscious effort to preserve their languages, religions, and customs. There is now a discernible and growing movement in many countries towards a desire for the preservation of local cultures and languages, along with a desire for a new form of nationalism. The September 2014 referendum on the independence of Scotland from the UK was a prime example of this movement. People seem to be saying that they want to revive their ancient national identities, and to have more power to arrange their local affairs. The Scottish referendum has shown, without a doubt, that the people of Scotland were very excited to be taking part in this political question, and most of them demonstrated their deep pride in their own distinctive culture. Paradoxically, at the same time, politicians are trying to increase their power and, to that end, want to build bigger and bigger federations, such as the European Union. Their motivation is quite clear: they are not interested in the wishes of their people, and they want more power, personal aggrandisement and wealth for themselves. All the signs that I can see indicate that this paradoxical situation is just a modern form of the age-long struggle for liberty and freedom, and my guess (and hope) is that the people will win in the end, as they surely will.

The question we need to address is: how do we facilitate the preservation of human cultural diversity in a world where the forces of technology are extremely powerful (aided of course by advertising, trans-global commercial corporations and instant communication), and seem to dominate and destroy our cultures without any expressed democratic control, whether we like all the consequences or not?

Politicians in the developed countries of European origin seem to have adopted a policy of allowing and encouraging mass immigration based on the utopian, liberal idea that all the incoming migrants will quickly adopt the culture of the host nations, and somehow retain their own cultures as well. This bizarre idea has few or no historical examples to give us any realistic expectation of its success for large groups, although some individuals may make a good attempt. Certainly, in Britain today there is plenty of evidence that the immigrant communities themselves are far from happy with the efforts of our government to get them 'to integrate' and to 'become British'. The evidence of immigrant people's behaviour and demands indicate quite clearly that many of them have no desire to integrate, and some despise and reject British culture, including a lot of the younger Muslim generation who were born here. In North America and in most of Europe much the same pattern seems to be repeated.

Let us therefore look at the possibilities for cultural integration. There seem to be four (and possibly five) common patterns of cultural co-existence in the modern world, arising from the different historical developments of various peoples and their cultures:

In the first type, people harmoniously share a common culture, language, religion and ethnic origin, and occupy a territory with a geographical boundary recognised by their neighbours, whether hostile or friendly. Usually such peoples have occupied their territory for at least several hundred years without significant intrusions from without, often due mainly to their geographical isolation. The populations of Iceland and Japan exemplify this pattern to this day. Usually the society is peaceful, everyone is comfortable with their neighbours, minor disputes are easily settled and crime rates are low. This is to be expected, because a common culture ensures that people share the same basic values and behaviour. In particular, children are taught to feel part of the culture and to take care of their neighbours and compatriots. Of course, this is a vast generalisation, but in general, disputes and differences of opinion do not usually result in violence or rioting in the streets, in these countries. Visitors from other cultures, working, studying or holidaying, constitute a small proportion of the population and are no threat to the host culture. They usually choose to spend a limited period of time in the host culture for a variety of reasons, but mainly out of curiosity and to learn from the hosts. Only a very small proportion of the visitors decide to settle in such cultures, and the settlers form only a small proportion of the host population.

The second pattern was typified by Britain up to about 1950, where a basically stable, native population, formed initially by ancient historical migration into a relatively isolated and unoccupied territory, was then followed by much later injections of hostile peoples from other cultures, in this case by the Vikings, Romans, and Normans over several thousand years. These more modern invading and violent cultural groups were fiercely resisted by the aboriginal natives, but the latter were defeated and colonised. Over many hundreds of years most of the culture in the south of Britain was mixed with that of the recent invaders, some of whom stayed and settled. In the mountainous areas in the north and west of Britain, the invaders were less successful, and the aboriginal natives managed to retain much of their own culture down to modern times. The British pattern of cultural development is therefore one of a series of very painful invasions and wars, settling down over the last four hundred years or so into a common peaceful culture, with smaller subcultures existing within the majority culture, but the minorities holding on doggedly to some of their own customs and language. In fact, the modern period is demonstrating the revival of national desires for more independence in both Scotland and Wales, possibly partly motivated to try to avoid the fate of England and its mass modern alien colonisation.

The third pattern is illustrated by the recent change in Britain. In the period of the last sixty years, Britain in general, and England in particular, has experienced large, but for most of the time relatively peaceful, invasions of immigrants from very different cultures. However, the relative peace has been achieved largely by virtue of the strained tolerance of the host nation, and the *ad hoc* efforts of the Government to do everything possible to pander to the demands of the invaders. Despite these somewhat heroic efforts to placate the demands of the immigrants in the hope that they will integrate, and to policies of positive discrimination, there have been serious sporadic outbreaks of conflict between them and the natives, including acts of rioting and terrorism. Many of the immigrant groups tend to live parallel lives in ghettoes although some groups are more integrated, mainly in public situations such as workplaces. The hitherto peaceful culture of Britain, once renowned the world over, is now in a state of Balkanisation with consequential serious outbreaks of conflict between different cultural groups. If, as seems likely, the invasions and the disproportional birth rates continue, so that the size of the immigrant population increases in relation to that of the natives, then the social fabric, so painfully arrived at over hundreds of years, will be irretrievably torn to shreds. This third pattern is shared to some extent with most of the Western European democratic countries.

The fourth pattern is similar to the third one, but where several or many cultural groups have lived side by side for a comparatively long time (more than one hundred years or so), with much tension and mutual hostility, such as in the USA. For much of the time these tensions are hidden below the surface, but periodically riots tend to break out. Different cultural and racial groups tend to live in ghettoes, despite the efforts of the politicians over many tens, or even hundreds, of years to get people to integrate. To this end laws are passed to prevent discrimination in public services, such as schools and workplaces. Sometimes, as in East Timor a few years ago and again recently, the long-established surface harmony is suddenly replaced by ferocious civil disturbance in which mutual atrocities are unleashed. Usually the different cultural groups live separate and parallel private lives during the quiet times, meeting mainly in public places, such as schools, workplaces and sports facilities. This pattern is most typical of large countries with a wide geographical spread, where peoples from different cultural backgrounds can find an area which suits their own particular needs, whether for living amongst their own kind in a mini-state, or in a ghetto in a large town or a cosmopolitan metropolis. A more recent example (2014) is the outbreak of violence in Ukraine, almost certainly planned and executed by Russian forces for strategic military purposes, and the empire-building motives of a tyrannical political regime. It is only too easy for such forces to exploit the underlying tensions between different cultural groups for their own purposes.

The fifth pattern is perhaps more a utopian dream than a demonstrated practical reality, and has been mentioned above as the social engineering objective of the last New Labour Government in Britain. Here it is believed that everybody should live together regardless of their cultural and ethnic origins, mixing freely without discrimination in their private lives as well as their public ones. This belief may be based on a Christian biblical idea: 'The wolf also shall dwell with the lamb, and the leopard shall lie down with the kid.' The multicultural harmony will, it is believed, be based on mutual respect, and recognition that all peoples are happy with their diverse origins and private customs but are united in a common culture at the same time. The problems with this pattern are that it is based on a theoretical contradiction (everybody has two cultures); that there is a total lack of historical precedent that it can be made to work for a period of hundreds of years; and that there is plenty of evidence that attempts at constructing such artificial communities have usually failed. In addition, it is clear that most people vote with their feet when they have the opportunity, and prefer to live with people of their own culture and genetic origin. Even if this utopian idea could be made to work, the eventual outcome would probably be the loss of most distinguishing cultural characteristics, including racial admixture, and the loss of the cultural diversity which we all seem to think should be preserved.

Why should we all agree that biodiversity is best retained by protecting as many of the individual species of flora and fauna in their natural habitats as possible, but that in order to protect the many different 'species' of human culture we should mix them all up together to encourage 'assimilation' and 'miscegenation'? The conjunction of these two different ideas seems to be somewhat paradoxical. The slightly different American idea of the 'melting pot', in which different peoples would be melded into one cultural group is now discredited as a practical failure. The alternative proposal of trying to live together in one over-arching culture, and at the same time, retaining all our different cultures doesn't sound a very successful idea either – the modern American idea of the 'salad bowl'. These ideas sound as if they were dreamt up by a committee of 'liberal intellectuals' who have ignored all the historical and modern evidence before their eyes, and have focussed instead on their utopian dreams. In fact, several of these patterns seem to be developing in Britain's 'multicultural society', and no one seems very happy with the result of this confused and unplanned experiment.

So which of the four main patterns should we be aiming to achieve, assuming that we have a choice, and the political will to take charge of our own destiny? The first pattern might well be the choice of most people, and yet this must appear to be another utopian dream to those millions across the globe who suffer horrendous violence from their neighbours for years just because they are perceived as belonging to a different culture or racial group. It is, however, not just a dream but is still a reality in the monocultural countries already mentioned, and was close to the pattern in Britain before about 1960, when the recent immigration invasions began. If this pattern were to be seen more clearly to be what it is, namely the main one that has demonstrably succeeded, then more people would aspire to it, and gradually the political will might be developed to make it a universal aspiration. Of course the successful 'monocultural' countries have been the fortunate ones who have not (yet!) been invaded by foreign cultural groups after the aboriginals settled, mainly because they were geographically isolated islands. The formidable difficulty for other countries which might wish to copy their 'monoculture' is that of trying to reduce the current multicultural mix. I shall therefore have to try to deal with that problem later.

England and Britain now typify the second pattern, and show how quickly centuries of internal harmony can be shattered by the uncontrolled influx of new groups with totally different cultures. Surely no one in her right mind would have chosen to bring about this change if she had any inkling of what the unintended consequences would be? Would any of the natives who were living in post-WWII Britain have wanted a large invasion of Muslims if they had any idea of the problems they would bring to their peaceful and happy country? The question surely answers itself. Many of the present older natives would choose at once to return to the former harmonious state if they believed that were possible. One only has to read the emails which are circulating daily between English people to realise what a large amount of support would be given for a return to the Britain of 1950. Nevertheless, if the political will were to be aroused, this objective might not be impossible to achieve, even though there would be much difficulty. Certainly, as the present immigrants amount to some 10% of the British population and rising, there is no time to lose. If we don't manage this option in a slow, steady but determined political manner, we must surely risk civil commotion or worse, as the British natives are at last becoming roused to action. The 2014 local and European election results, with the UKIP advance in both, have surely sent a loud message to the three traditional parties that the indigenous population want no more uncontrolled immigration. If UKIP had not arrived on the British political scene, many native people would be voting for more extreme parties, as has happened in France where the *Front National* party of Marine Le Pen has routed the traditional parties. It is clear from the results across the EU that many Europeans have rejected the policies of open borders and freedom of movement, which have resulted in the mass immigration invasions. If Europe is not careful the rise of right and left wing extremist parties will gain substantial support, and civil commotion of a very serious degree will shatter the utopian dream.

Unfortunately, our upper and middle social classes are voting with their feet and moving, when possible, to quieter, peripheral parts of Britain or to sunnier European countries where they can live in their own British cultural ghettoes, at least for most of the rest of their lives in retirement. The poorer people, who are stuck in the large towns in underprivileged areas cheek by jowl with poor immigrants, will from time to time attack individual immigrants and their families, and organise riots whenever possible to express their resentment, and to take advantage of the civil commotion to grab consumer goods from burning shops. They will be reliant on extremist political parties for support, and to express their contempt for the mainstream parties and the establishment that have caused their neighbourhoods to be invaded and colonised.

The fourth pattern, typified by the USA, is currently showing signs of impending instability. The Hispanic and other groups now form a majority in California, and some political groups are already looking forward to breaking away from the USA, either to declare independence or to reunite with Mexico. If they achieve this aim, it may stimulate the Afro-Americans in the Southern states to follow their lead, and also demand independence. Maybe the remaining white people of European ancestry will opt for other independent states or for joining Canada. For such countries as the USA, the only long-term solution may well be breakup into smaller units or states, each with a much more homogeneous cultural population. The Balkanisation of the USA seems to be a possibility. Indeed, we have already seen this pattern emerge in the break-up of the former Yugoslavia, albeit after horrendous violence in the war of 1998-9. It would clearly have been better if the process of splitting had been brought about in a civilised political manner rather than through the process of war. It may sound far-fetched to think that the USA may in the not-too-distant future become the 'Disunited States of America', but even in Britain the individual countries are moving towards independence. And in Europe too, where the liberal and socialist utopian movement for greater federalism is currently (after the EU elections in May 2014) in danger due to the severe economic strains, and the cultural threats of continuing mass migrations, there is no certainty that successful integration will be achieved. The dangers of civil strife will increase if colonisation by Muslims, Africans and other groups is not halted, and no effective measures are taken to stabilise and maintain Western European culture.

The fifth pattern does not exist anywhere in the world as far as I know. Even if it did exist, and it achieved total harmony, with no tensions or conflicts between people of different cultural origins, the eventual result would surely be a loss of many of the distinguishing characteristics, and the cultural diversity which gives us much of the spice of life. Although the imagined potential harmony of this utopian pattern might seem to make this aspiration a desirable one on that count alone, it seems illogical to strive constantly for the preservation of biodiversity but to exclude mankind's cultural diversity from the scheme. Why should we want to preserve the giant panda, the killer whale, the red kite, and every species of beetle, insect and wild flower, and yet want to pursue the aim of eliminating our own genetic and cultural differences? I am sure that for most people of all origins the answer is that we do not wish to pursue such an aim.

If we therefore wish to live on this planet in relative harmony and freedom from serious strife, it seems that we should preserve the pattern of general cultural and racial homogeneity in those few countries where it still exists, and we should move as steadily as possible, through a civilised political process, to bring about a similar pattern in those countries where the presence of relatively recent immigrants has caused the original harmony to become seriously disrupted. This latter exercise will probably only be possible without serious civil commotion when the immigrant groups represent a proportion of the population of about 10% or below. Where even this objective is not possible without civil war, then the breakup of the country into smaller units may be the only practical solution, as happened to the USSR in recent years, and may soon start to happen to the USA. It is interesting to note the same trend in Britain, where Scotland is moving towards independence, with Wales not far behind. In Britain however, the process is occurring in a slow, civilised and democratic manner, due mainly to the genetic and cultural groups being almost indistinguishable from each other. The European Union is moving in the opposite direction in an experiment to amalgamate nation states, both big and small, into a co-operative federation which can compete economically with larger and more powerful countries and other groups. This experiment, as we now know, has run into very serious difficulties despite the fact that most of the Western European countries have a fairly similar democratic culture based on the Judeo-Christian religions. National cultural differences are nevertheless important to the various populations and their feelings of identity, and these cultural features tend to obstruct the efforts of elitist politicians to unite the European continent. People naturally can identify easily with small groups, but find it much more difficult to subsume their main identity within a very large group. Indeed, 'bottom-up' plebeian campaigns are now tending to want to break up larger political groupings despite the 'top-down' efforts of the politicians to form ever larger conglomerations. This somewhat paradoxical situation is, as explained in Chapter Six, a result of the opposed efforts of two self-interested activist groups: the cultural groups wish to have more local control over their own lives, whilst the politicians want to gain more control over ever larger economic entities in which to feel globally important, and in which to enrich themselves. Overarching federal governments should not be allowed to interfere with any activities that local authorities can manage quite easily and more successfully, because Local Authorities are in touch with the wishes of local people. In other words, federal governments should be strictly controlled by Local Authorities, instead of the current reverse system.

If all countries in the world could achieve and retain relative, internal, cultural homogeneity, we should all be able to live in peace and harmony whilst retaining the external cultural diversity that seems to be a desirable, stimulating experience. In order to appreciate the range of flora and fauna developed over millions of years by Darwinian evolution we now expect to have to travel to where the animals and plants live in order to see them in their natural habitat. We do not mix them all up together in our own neighbourhoods (except in zoos and botanical gardens, which are now changing from their traditional entertainment functions into one of saving threatened species in breeding programmes) in order to experience their manifold wonders. When the introduction of foreign species into other environments has been attempted in the past, intentionally or inadvertently, it has often caused severe problems for the creatures and for us. Even the introduction of alien plants to Britain, such as Japanese knotweed, has sadly caused the loss of native species and widespread nuisance at best. Australia is also a prime example of the problems that the introduction of alien species, such as the rabbit and the sugar-cane toad can do to the native animal species.

Such biological mixing experiments, sometimes designed and sometimes the result of accidents, are radical and irresponsible, with often unexpected and irreversible consequences, and are all too easy to introduce in a shrunken world where travel from one side to the other takes only a day. The introduction of rabbits into Australia is perhaps the most well-known and notorious example of the damage that is done when man interferes with ecosystems without proper scientific consideration. But some will say that such considerations do not apply to humans – we do not wipe out other groups by invading their long-held territory because we are all of the same species, and do not now compete in a fight for survival. Rather, we recognise our common humanity and co-operate in the common endeavour of achieving happiness and prosperity for all.

At the level of physical survival we may now be approaching this ideal, although history tells us of many episodes of genocide, some only a few years behind us. Indeed the current struggle between the Israelis and the Arabs, and the Syrian civil war, are violent and protracted, with unpredictable outcomes. There have been many similar cultural and racial conflicts in recent years, such those in the

Sudan, Sri Lanka, East Timor, and Malaysia (Myanmar) and, even more recently, in Egypt, Ukraine, Sudan, Nigeria, and now Iraq, Syria, Libya and Ukraine. What is more to the point, not many of us would put much money on a bet that similar episodes will not break out somewhere else in the world in the near future.

I have tried above to point out the circumstances most likely to ensure the survival of human *cultural diversity* without the payment of a very high price in human suffering. We have to face the reality of human behaviour, and think very carefully before starting social engineering projects that may well have laudable aims but may also have many serious practical and unintended consequences. No matter what plans the utopian liberals have to engineer without our consent their dream world of one happy and 'rainbow' species of human beings, all the evidence points to the fact that people the world over wish to live most of the time with people like themselves, and they hold dearly to their own culture and identity. 'He who does not learn the lessons of history is doomed to repeat them'.

Another aspect of cultural diversity that has so far not had any attention from the social engineers is the matter of *value*. Discussion about different cultures usually seems to assume that all cultures should be valued equally, despite the appalling practices and underlying value systems of many cultures outside the Western democracies (which themselves are far from perfect). This assumption flies in the face of common sense, and amounts to an example of what I call the 'false equivalence error' in argument. To take one obvious example: the Pakistani men who have been convicted of gross sexual abuse of vulnerable white girls in many of our big cities come from a culture in which gang rape and sexual abuse of young women is common. So why should anyone brought up in the traditional British culture, imperfect as it is, think it would be a good idea to import such callous and abusive men into our country? Not so long ago, liberal intellectuals were saying that we should respect other people's cultures, as if these cultures were of equivalent value to our own. Cultures, including our traditional culture, have evolved slowly over hundreds of years and continue to do so. The struggle for women's rights in Britain is certainly not over yet, and will not be helped by importing men from cultures that, in our eyes, are extremely backward and unpleasant, to say the least. Developed cultures are always fragile and easily prone to retrogressive forces.

Another example is the culture of drug abuse, knife violence and absent fathers in Jamaica, which was imported into London to solve the problem of cheap labour in 1948. It was not very long before that cultural infection spread widely from Brixton throughout our large cities, with all the consequent, severe, social problems associated with drug abuse. That particular corrosive genie has caused a profound amount of human misery, and cannot easily be put back into the bottle. And yet, establishment figures are still, in late 2014, talking about the 'benefits' of immigration, but of course, they mean the financial benefits to their own cabal of rich business cronies. They do not care one jot about the rapid and profound deterioration in our culture suffered mostly by our poorest compatriots.

Over the last few decades in Britain and other European countries a huge and momentous social engineering experiment has being carried out by our politicians and establishment liberals without any real discussion so far about the political ethics of such an experiment, without any clear objective or plan, and with considerable evidence that a high price is already being paid by the poor indigenous population. We must not ignore the ominous facts that indicate that things can only get worse unless we have a serious and open debate. The first step in taking control of our destiny is to restore the freedom of expression which has been ruthlessly curtailed by our political establishment over the last sixty decades.

§

CHAPTER NINE

FREE SPEECH
VERSUS
POLITICAL CORRECTNESS

THE LACK OF FREE SPEECH AND EXPRESSION, which many people in Britain in the last sixty years have complained about in private, is keenly resented. It has always been thought, in Western democracies, that free speech (and other forms of expression) is a crucial component of a democratic society, and the British have for a very long time been proud of their tradition in this respect. Totalitarian regimes, on the other hand, always make great efforts to prevent or abolish this freedom, often with very repressive measures, usually accompanied by the setting up of a state propaganda machine to ensure that only the tyrant's information and views are allowed to circulate. Tyrants are well aware that in order to control a population they need to control information, news and communications, so that free-thinkers and rebels can be made to feel as if they are alone, and so that their own personal views are not shared by anyone else. Indeed, potential tyrants executing an insurrection make an early priority of taking over control of radio, television and other forms of communication, and thus continuing to control rigidly all news.

Many British people now think that 'political correctness' (PC) has, in recent decades, become an oppressive weapon that has been used to stifle free speech, and opinions unwelcome to the Government and its supporting establishment. Most native Britons feel strongly that they are no longer free to voice any dissenting opinion against the establishment's propaganda in favour of the 'multicultural society', and its strong and relentless campaign to welcome mass immigration. No doubt the political correctness movement, which originated in American universities, has rightly made us all more sensitive to the feelings of minority groups and vulnerable individuals who in the past have been unfairly treated, ignored, victimised and stereotyped. This means that we have become more careful to ensure that we do not give unnecessary and gratuitous offence to anybody during daily social intercourse. But the British were already renowned for their politeness long before the 'PC' phenomenon arrived at our shores, and politeness and good manners were the basis of the unwritten code that guided behaviour in social encounters. It was often said that an Englishman was the only person in the world who would say 'Sorry' when someone trod on his toe. The English code of good manners was imbibed with our mother's milk, and children easily learned most of it by the time that they entered primary school, and the rest of it at school. People who transgressed were subject to social disapproval, which was usually sufficient to ensure that most citizens seldom gave offence to others, and particularly to vulnerable persons. Those who persistently used offensive language were usually aggressive male characters who used (and still do) such language mainly within a work situation of similar men, and would often modify their language in more polite society. Anyone who belonged to a group that habitually used offensive language and insults to all and sundry, especially to vulnerable people, would be considered to be poorly-educated and loutish by the polite majority, and would be shunned.

However, the introduction of the 'political correctness' phenomenon and its rapid extension by the intellectual establishment to the censorship and repression of unwelcome viewpoints, smacks of the work of George Orwell's 'thought police'. Many words have been added to produce a pejorative lexicon, such as 'racist', 'fascist', 'Nazi', 'xenophobe', 'homophobe', 'Islamophobe', 'prejudiced' and 'discrimination'. These words were, and are, used in what looks like a deliberate campaign to stifle the expression of any dissent against the received wisdom of the propaganda machine, endlessly telling us, relevant to our current example, that immigration is good for us. These pejorative words were, and are, used as *insults* to blacken the character of anyone who dares to disagree with the propaganda. It should be noted that definitions of the meanings of these words are seldom, if ever, given during any public discussion or debate, but most people assume that the recipient of such insults is a dangerous and disgraceful character, filled with hatred against foreigners, and comparable to the Nazi-holocaust perpetrators. The irony of this situation is lost on the PC brigade — they are acting like Nazis themselves, in stereotyping their debating opponents, labelling them with pejorative terms in a campaign of hatred, and stifling dissenting views. 'O wad some pow'r the giftie gie us, to see oursels as others see us' — to quote perceptive and prescient Robbie Burns.

Few native Britons would, in post-WWII times and now, want to stir up hatred against anyone, whether an immigrant, foreigner or someone else that they dislike or disapprove of. Very few would wish to see attacks on immigrants or would approve of race riots or any other serious mayhem in society. But most still think that they should be able to voice their opinions on controversial subjects, and particularly, one so important as the uncontrolled influx of legal and illegal immigrants who threaten by their very presence in large numbers to destroy their culture. *Free speech means nothing* if it does not mean the right to express one's dissent from the views of the establishment, or any other source of the prevailing or received wisdom. We therefore need to examine the factors that have, in recent decades, produced an atmosphere in which ordinary citizens have come to believe that their long-cherished right to free speech has been suppressed, so that they are not now able freely to express their views on this crucially important aspect of modern life in our country.

First of all, the pronouncements of politicians of all parties have frequently and monotonously made it clear that mass immigration into Britain is a wholly desirable phenomenon, and they have said this with no mention of any possible adverse consequences, as if it were an undoubted, self-evident and accepted, scientifically-proven fact. This same technique of endless repetition has also been used to try to convince everyone that 'Britain is a multicultural society now', which is 'here to stay, and there is nothing we can do about it'. I have earlier examined the specious arguments used to back up these assertions, and found them wanting. However, I am here concerned with the effect on popular feeling of being constantly bombarded through the media by our politicians and their media cronies in a completely biased fashion, so that the impression is given that no respectable counter-argument exists, and that anyone attempting to question the received wisdom of the establishment is an evil rogue or worse. Indeed, in the early days when a few dissenting voices were heard in public, they and their views were immediately rubbished (remember Enoch Powell's 'rivers of blood' speech, and the 'cricket test' idea of Norman Tebbitt?). Thus the extension into British culture of a severe form of 'political correctness' began to inhibit ordinary citizens from expressing their own opinions on immigration.

One hardly needs to point out (I hope) the *overarching arrogance* of people who think that their own opinions are so evidently 'correct' that they have the right to suppress any contrary opinion and dub it 'incorrect'. The constant propaganda extolling the benefits of immigration have frequently reminded me of the aphorism coined by Joseph Goebels, Hitler's notorious propaganda chief: 'If you repeat a lie often enough it becomes the truth.' This assertion has been confirmed by modern psychologists, using scientific experiments that have shown that constant repetition of any word or phrase gives a feeling of familiarity and pleasure, and produces a positive bias in assessment that is completely unconscious. Advertisers and dictators have long realised that the repetition of slogans is an effective method for instilling ideas into the minds of their target populations. Some of us are aware of these techniques and are sceptical of all advertisements and political propaganda. The good-looking dentist in a TV advert who is telling you that 90% of her patients use a certain brand of toothpaste is, of course, a paid actress; the supermarket giant that advertises endlessly that: 'We are saving you money every day', is of course trying to get as much of your money as it can. We may think that only an idiot would believe such nonsense, but we underestimate the unconscious effect that the daily repetition has on our beliefs and actions. The advertising industry would not be as prosperous and all-pervasive as it is if it did not get results.

Personally, I am a firm supporter of free speech in its most stark form, as are many Western, democratic people. It is universally recognised to be a major foundation of true democracy. I agree totally with the view of the English libertarian philosopher John Stuart Mill, who said: *'Free speech or expression has no meaning if you are not allowed to cause offence to other people who have different views. The only constraint should be that one's words should not cause actual bodily harm'*. I tried to publish the first draft of this book in 2002 and no publisher would even look at a synopsis or chapter before turning it down, even though some of them advertised in the *Writer's Handbook* as being keen to publish books on controversial subjects. I contacted Peter Hitchens, the Daily Mail journalist, who wrote: *The Abolition of Britain*.[14] He replied that he would not be able to get a book on such a subject as mine published. It was obvious that publishers were self-imposing censorship out of fear of unmentioned reprisals by Muslim terrorists. I am ashamed to say that I felt defeated, and consequently shelved the idea of publication. My recent change of heart (2012) was triggered by reading Melanie Phillips's book.[15]

---

14   Hitchens, Peter (2002).

15   Phillips, Melanie (2008).

I noticed that her book was published privately, so I started this revised version with a view to doing the same.

The 'multiculturalism' campaign of the Tony Blair 'New Labour' Government propaganda machine (a TV report on 30.08.2006 said that the Whitehall press officers then numbered some 3,200!) was heavily reinforced by the views of its celebrity supporters and establishment figures, who were able to express their views in the media. Such people as church leaders, intellectual liberals and other political commentators who presumably wished to portray themselves as lovers of suffering humanity, all took the opportunity to jump on this morally attractive bandwagon. The 'great and the good' made it clear that they were on the side of the angels, and presumably waited smugly in quiet anticipation of their eventual heavenly reward, as they welcomed hordes of the third world's economic refugees, to say nothing of the ubiquitous enterprising gangsters and other European criminals.

Many of these 'liberal' intellectuals had no hesitation in denigrating the few dissenting politicians who had the temerity to question the Government message. These dissenting politicians unfortunately soon learnt that they had to keep their 'controversial' opinions to themselves, because the political leaders of both mainstream parties began to see the need to start wooing the immigrant section of the electorate. Enoch Powell, one of the 20th Century's most intelligent politicians, was immediately shunted off, after his 'rivers of blood' speech, to Northern Ireland, where he must have quickly had his viewpoint concerning the problems of multicultural societies confirmed, but where he was out of the media limelight, and therefore less able to lead the opposition to the Ted Heath Government's immigration policy.

Periodically, in the early days, one or other politician unguardedly uttered a statement that coincided with native opinion but which was out of line with the propaganda view of the 'multicultural society' and its so-called benefits. Immediately he would be rebuked by his political opponents and their media allies and, almost always, the 'offender', to his shame, would back down with some lame attempt at claiming that he had been misinterpreted, or his remarks had been taken out of context. Thus even those who almost certainly agreed with the majority native opinion were afraid to be labelled 'racist', and they consequently gave yet more credence to the received wisdom by their intellectual cowardice, and learned to keep quiet.

Worst of all, when ordinary people (the plebs!), who had actually experienced the mounting social problems created in their own localities by the influx of many immigrants, expressed their dissenting views and hostility to the Government's settlement policy on radio phone-in programmes, they were frequently rebuked by the celebrity presenters. It was thus, once again, made clear to the public that any opinion running counter to the received wisdom of their moral and intellectual superiors would be suppressed by the very effective weapon of public humiliation.

In addition it was clear, and still is, that people of immigrant racial and cultural groups have been preferentially promoted into television jobs, especially in the BBC, so that they can be seen and heard in these presenter roles, far more frequently than their proportion in the community merits. Are we simple-minded plebs expected to believe that these well paid celebrities are 'doing the jobs that our people aren't willing to do'? Maybe I've misinterpreted this phenomenon and they had to be head-hunted to do these intellectually demanding jobs (!) because we don't have the highly skilled people amongst our unskilled, native population? Or maybe the BBC has been doing the work of the Governments' propaganda machine, not under direct control, but more likely because that organisation is riddled with woolly-minded, Pecksniffian 'liberals' and people with loose morals keen to destroy our culture. The BBC goes to enormous lengths to portray positively the British 'multicultural society' at every opportunity, presumably as a subliminal attempt to get us used to thinking that immigrants are doing all the important jobs, and therefore reinforcing the mantra that immigration is benefiting the nation. If there is a health scare they find a black- or Asian nurse or doctor to be filmed treating a black or Asian child. If the news item is about maternity services, we see a black or Asian midwife helping an immigrant pregnant mother. If a school is in the news, lo and behold, the filmed teacher is an immigrant and most or all of the children are black or Asian. Call me paranoid if you wish, but it is well known that this type of 'real-life' advertising is much more powerful than direct advertisements, which people distrust and tend to disregard. The aim is clearly to make us think that the 'multicultural society' is a fact of life, and to portray the black and Asian immigrants in a positive light, playing an important role in our cultural life. Often a similar pattern can be discerned when an expert or professional has been chosen to enlighten us on some topical problem or event: if at all possible, the one black or brown veterinary surgeon, aeronautical engineer, or expert on some obscure infectious organism in Britain is mobilised to appear on TV, presumably to create the impression that most of the clever, able and professional people are now immigrants and 'we can't do without them.' It seems to me that many of us ordinary voters think that the BBC is a leftish, liberal-biased, anti-Christian, anti-white, anti-British, pro-ethic minority organisation, *as described by many of its current and former presenters*, who have courageously spilled the beans.[16]

The BBC establishment must wish that all the nightly police documentaries on other channels that show immigrants committing most of the crimes could be banned. And most of us natives, who are still able to resist the effect of the daily stream of propaganda, and

---

16   Marsh, John (2012). The Liberal Delusion, pp. 149-153.

who are still lucky enough to live in an enclave of our aboriginal compatriots, fear for the future of our grandchildren, who are likely to be at a disadvantage in the job market because of a policy of positive discrimination in favour of the immigrants. The National Statistics Office told us that in the second quarter of 2014 unemployment fell by 167,000 but *three out of four new jobs went to immigrants*, a statistic that I find alarming, whatever the underlying reasons may be.

Some of us who live outside the big cities and seldom come into contact with these clever immigrants, and who read, watch and discuss widely in order to be able to form a more balanced opinion, have become highly sceptical of the propaganda message that 'we can't do without them'. We do not wish to be lectured, informed and entertained by foreigners all the time on our own nation's TV programmes. We are not expressing some insane and extreme, uniquely British, or paranoid point of view; we are expressing a *universal* human psychological feeling of preference for our own culture and people, as do immigrants the world over when they huddle together in their self-imposed ghettoes. **This is not xenophobia – it is merely the expression of a natural preference for our own culture, our own faces, our own familiar names, and our own people when we are being communicated with in our own country.** Geneticists call this phenomenon 'kin preference', to describe the strong tendency for creatures, including mankind, to look after and defend their close progeny who have many of the same genes.

The Africans, the Indians, the Arabs and most of the colonial countries formerly invaded, exploited and governed by the European imperialists, unceremoniously and recently turfed out their colonial 'masters' to claim their liberty, and to live freely in their own cultures. We are no different, and many of us wish to emulate their example. It seems odd that many people from these liberated colonies, almost immediately after gaining their freedom from their European masters, have decided that they wish to join the very countries whose yoke they have just thrown off, with the expectation of great happiness. Odd that is, unless they are all hoping to exploit us, and are more interested in economic improvement and a life in our culture rather than in their own. As for me, and I would guess for a lot of my compatriots, if I wanted to live amongst Arabs or Africans, Afghans, Poles or Romanian gypsies I would go to one of their countries and (legally) settle there – not to sponge on their hospitality but to pay my way, and benefit their economy. And I would not expect to be treated preferentially, nor would I persist in giving gratuitous cultural offence to my hosts.

It is also more than annoying that we are constantly made aware that we are being given a false impression of the social mix and its effects, by some hidden group of media manipulators. Come back George Orwell now we really need you! Our country is now more like 'Nineteen-Eighty-Four' than that celebrated author would have imagined possible in Britain. We are now living in Airstrip One, threatened with thought-crimes, and bombarded with the propaganda of The Ministry of Truth. Everybody who has not read his two classic satires of the Stalinist USSR tyranny should read them now, in order to get some idea of the depths to which modern Britain has sunk regarding free speech.[17] [18]

Even more potent forces have been at work to inhibit dissent from the propaganda viewpoint. The 'race relations industry' has been, and still is, vigilant in seeing racial prejudice everywhere, and at every opportunity castigates people and organisations as 'racist' and 'institutionally racist', and thus deliberately inhibits debate by the use of these terms of abuse. It has been very successful. Of course it must be admitted that real racism exists in Britain as in

---

17   Orwell, George (1949).

18   Ibid. (1945).

most countries, but care needs to be taken with emotionally laden words such as 'racism', 'fascism', 'Nazi' and 'xenophobe'. Indeed, if a reasonable, rational and fruitful debate is to take place, we must be very careful with all the words we use, especially the ones loaded with emotion, because otherwise confusion and misunderstanding will be the inevitable outcome. I therefore intend later to examine some important words and their usage.

Free speech has been further repressed by the use of the legal system. On 23.10.2011 John Terry, a well-known Chelsea football captain was found 'not guilty' at a Magistrates Court, having been charged with a 'racially aggravated public order offence' aimed at an opposing footballer, Anton Ferdinand. Imagine the scene: two grown men, being paid large sums of money (Terry was earning £160,000 per week at the time) for playing a very physical and highly competitive game, fired up with adrenaline, coming into physical contact as footballers often do, and one feels very angry at what he believes was a foul attack on him by the other. He utters in a spontaneous angry outburst some offensive curse. I don't know what this was, but let us say that he called Ferdinand 'you black bastard.' The legal 'offence' of racist abuse clearly depends on the word 'black'. We know that the victim is black, and it may well be that he is not a bastard or, even if he is, that slur on his parents is not the word that the legal system would object to (I guess). I am amazed that such a natural, spontaneous outburst in these circumstances should be considered to be a *crime*. It is very common when people curse someone, that they use an expletive combined with some physical or racial characteristic that serves the function of distancing the curser from the victim. This serves to stop the obvious retort: 'So are you.' Although Terry was found 'not guilty' by the law, a later hearing by the Football Association Regulatory Commission, using less strict standards of evidence and guilt, found him guilty and sentenced him to a four-match ban and a £220,000 fine.

It seems to me to me that the use of the law to threaten punishment for events of this type is to use a very big hammer to crack a very small nut. I doubt whether anyone else, apart from a few of the other players and possibly the referee, would have heard what was said. The event was trivial in the extreme and, to my mind, Ferdinand should have been man enough to have shrugged it off (as in fact he did immediately after the match) by either giving as good as he got or, better still, ignoring the insult. If one of my children complained of such an event in a primary-school playground I would advise him or her to ignore such taunts, as did my parents. The proper and appropriate reaction should have been the referral alone to the football governing authority for investigation and possible disciplinary action. When one sees on nightly TV immigrants committing serious crimes but being given bail, so that they have the opportunity to disappear, as they often do, one can only agree with Charles Dickens's Mr Bumble: 'the law is a ass – a idiot.' When Muslim protestors against the publication of the Danish cartoons held a parade in London outside the Danish Embassy on 30.09.2005 many paraded openly with placards with seriously racist slogans, such as ' Butcher those who mock Islam', 'Europe you will pay, your 9/11 is on the way' and 'Massacre those who insult Islam'. They were allowed to do so by the accompanying police, *who made no attempts to arrest anyone.* After some MP's protested about these offensive and threatening placards, and the lack of police action, the police arrested and charged five of the protestors six weeks later. Three protestors were given sentences of six years' jail, and one of five years' jail. Clearly the original behaviour of the police in allowing the open display on our streets of slogans inciting Muslims to take part in murder, was not accidental, but would have been the policy at that time determined by senior police officers anxious to exhibit their 'non-racist' credentials.

In October 2014, Ben Flower, a Welsh International rugby player, was seen on TV to knock out an opposing player, Lance Hohala, and then deliberately punch him in the face whilst he was lying on the ground unconscious. This was clearly a case of causing actual bodily harm, but so far the assailant has not been charged with any offence, although the Rugby Union has banned him from playing in eight matches. So it would appear that in the eyes of the law it is more serious to swear at a footballer in a match with a 'racist' curse than viciously to attack a player physically! No wonder people think the law is an ass.

The intention of the British Criminal 'Injustice' system has presumably been to protect immigrants from insults, which might lead to civil commotion or worse. I fear that the main effect is to make foreigners *ultrasensitive*, and is also likely to encourage them to *manufacture offence*. Black people can be seen on the nightly TV programmes which show the police at work, frequently playing the race card: 'You only stopped me because I'm black'. I don't think that black people will ever be happy until they drop the role of victim (as the Israelis certainly have), and develop some pride in themselves. If they do not have any pride in themselves, they can hardly expect us to manufacture it for them. Liberals usually think that the problem underlying racism is that of white people's feelings of superiority and hatred, but they ignore the black people's feelings of inferiority and hatred, which they alone must throw off. There are usually two sides to most human social problems and conflicts, and it is a common mistake to think that all the blame is on one side. Anton Ferdinand should have acted like the lucky man he is to hold such a well-paid job when John Terry insulted him, instead of acting like a spoilt child, as he later did. Another aspect of that incident is the obvious fact that in Premier League football in Britain there is now only a small number of white players. Might this fact cause the fans on the terraces to express racist dislike or hatred because they see foreigners taking over most of these highly paid jobs?

This leads me to think that any chants or gestures of a racist nature from the football fans, meaning that they don't like black players, may well be a result of their natural preference for their own compatriots. Unfortunately the 'beautiful game' has moved from being a contest between teams of local players, which generated strong local pride, to being a massive entertainment industry which is based on the profit motive. Players are 'bought' and 'sold' in an international market, and there is thus no longer any concern for local emotional preferences and affiliations. It could nevertheless still be made a mixture of the two interests by having a rule that say, seven of the eleven players in each team must be native Britons. As it is at the moment, I often cannot remember or pronounce any of the names of the eleven players in many a famous British Premier League team. This certainly has the effect on me of losing interest in watching the games, and I doubt whether I am the only person with that feeling.

The problem of giving 'offence' is being tackled by the legal system and other authorities in a way that is inhibiting freedom of expression, and that results, inevitably, in an increasing resentment amongst the natives of this island. This is illustrated by the detachment from politics, and an attitude of ridicule towards the law. We have recently seen that *gestures* are now being included in the prohibition menu of 'racist offences'. Another footballer, this time a black one, Nicholas Anelka, in 2013 gave a 'quenelle salute', which was thought be a form of reverse Nazi salute, and to give offence to Jewish football fans of the opposing team, West Ham United. I had never heard the word before, nor did I know what the gesture meant. Anelka was given a five-match ban and fined £80,000 by the FA disciplinary hearing for this seemingly trivial offence. However, the FA was the right body to deal with this event.

What will come next, after gestures? We are not far away from making facial expressions and thoughts illegal or banned. The law (and the FA) is becoming much more of an ass than it was said to be by Dickens's Mr Bumble not so long ago. At most football matches the slogan 'Say No To Racism' is prominently shown throughout matches; it is reminiscent of the Orwellian slogan: 'Big Brother Is Watching You'.

Our Criminal 'Injustice' system now deals severely with the trivial 'crime' of giving offence, which seems to be a crime usually committed by white natives, and deals lightly with very serious crimes which seem to be committed disproportionately by foreigners. The Western world in general, and Britain in particular, seems to have gone mad, judging by the way that it is treating its ordinary citizens with severity and repression, and is doing everything possible to avoid prison sentences for serious and dangerous foreign offenders. Here is an example amongst many, of the futile sentences for serious crimes, on a 'cops and robbers' programme on 20.10.2014: the police caught a man after a high-speed car chase, who was then charged and convicted of burglary, dangerous driving, driving without a driving licence and insurance, and car theft. He was given a prison sentence of eight months, which of course in our pathetic Criminal 'Injustice' system means only four months. This expensive police, court and prison fiasco is most unlikely to deter him or any other criminal from repeating such crimes, and the whole performance amounts to a ridiculous pretence of protecting the innocent public. Clearly the police 'interceptors' do a good job, which they obviously enjoy, but the criminals are able to continue to plague the law-abiding citizens and enrich themselves.

On 2.10.2014 we learned that a new unit had been set up in Birmingham by the West Midlands Police to deal more efficiently with foreign criminals on our road network. The unit is staffed with police officers from many European countries who are able to access criminal records immediately after an arrest by the British police at the roadside. Within a few hours of this unit's first operational day, an arrested man was identified as being a serious criminal with a record in his native country. At last some effective steps are being used to deal with at least some of the foreign criminals who plague us, and it is to be hoped that every effort to continue this innovative system will be made and that the ones who are caught will be swiftly deported. Whoever designed and executed this system should certainly be rewarded. Normally the criminals are always many steps ahead of the police and legal system, and we need more innovative schemes using modern technology to try to beat the enterprising criminals. Of course, the criminals are now turning to cybercrime, because they can reap much greater and easier pickings using internet scams, and are more difficult to catch, because they can operate from other countries. Again, this needs cooperation between Britain and many other jurisdictions, and no doubt that cooperation will be difficult to obtain. One such scam has already started taking advantage of people seeking better investment returns on their pension money, quickly following on the introduction of the Chancellor's new pension rules, which allow people to transfer their 'pension pot' to new investment providers. Many vulnerable people have already lost thousands of pounds to overseas scam 'providers' not registered with the Financial Services Agency.

Suffice it to say, at this juncture, that real debate on the issue of immigration had hardly begun in Britain before the EU election of May 2014 as a result of the *de facto* ban on dissenting viewpoints, so that the received wisdom was that immigration was wholly beneficial to the host nation. The severe and inevitable consequence of this effective banishment of the right of free speech was that the largely hidden resentment felt by law-abiding citizens had no proper, democratic means of expression. We must remember, and the political establishment must learn, what they should all along have realised, that the safety valve of democracy is free and unfettered speech and expression, and to repress it is inevitably to store up rising and strong resentment, which will in due course produce a social explosion. In my view, most of the current social problems, including 'home-grown terrorism', must be laid at the door of the recent governments, which should have realised that suppressing free speech is the surest way to get completely out of touch, as it unequivocally has done. This prediction of mine, made before 2004, has been clearly confirmed by the EU election results of May 2014. It would be amusing, if it were not a serious matter, to watch the utter panic sweeping now suddenly through the political class and the liberal intelligentsia in Britain and of most of the EU countries, at the rise of new political parties garnering the protest votes of people disenchanted with so-called 'representative democracy'.

I'm sure that our current Prime Minister, David Cameron, whom we understand is a practising Christian, is familiar with the quotation from Hosea, Chapter 8 Verse 7: 'They have sown the wind, and they shall reap the whirlwind'. His arrogance, and particularly that of his coalition Lib-Dem colleague Nick Clegg, in believing that they are always right no matter who, or how many, may disagree with them, will almost certainly lead to their downfall. They are not atypical in this regard, since practically all politicians suffer from the same psychological disorder of arrogance, and a belief that they alone have the intellect and wisdom that is required to govern. The traditional three major parties of the last century appear to believe that they are destined to rule because they know what is good for us plebs better than we know for ourselves. They play the game of competing with each other to hold all state power, but they have so much in common that voters are now disenfranchising themselves by not voting, because they believe that their wishes are completely ignored.

Our politicians in 2014 have become perplexed at the apparent increasing detachment of the electorate from politics. In the May 2014 EU elections, the turnout was only 34.1%—so *two thirds* of the voters refrained from voting. This figure alone should give rise to great concern, because voting is a precious right in a democracy.

The winning of this right in Britain, which began in 1254 with Simon de Montfort's parliament following the attempt in 1215 by the Magna Carta to limit the King's power, has involved fierce and bloody struggles ever since. If an increasing proportion of the electorate no longer values this right, we are in peril of the power to rule being taken into the hands of tyrants once more.

So out of touch with the wishes of our people were the politicians, even immediately after the crushing victory of UKIP in the EU election of May 2014, that they still did not 'get it', that is, they did not and do not, understand what the electorate want. They are still convinced, as they always are in defeat, that their problem is one of presentation: 'We are listening, but we failed to get our message across.' In other words, 'The voters are too stupid to know what we are doing for their benefit.' It seldom occurs to them that we do get their message but we don't like it. It does however seem now that David Cameron has realised, at last, that the electorate have had enough of the 'benefits' of mass immigration, multiculturalism and the dictatorship of the EU, which he now, belatedly, describes as: 'Too big, too bossy, and too interfering.' It remains to be seen if he can force the EU to change its ways so that his proposed 2017 'in/out' referendum will produce his preferred outcome of 'stay in.' I think he wants too little and has left it too late, and that the electorate will, at the 2015 general election, wreak further retribution on the three traditional parties by electing UKIP's first handful or more of MPs, and more Greens. The voters seem to be, at last, coming to their senses and are realising that our politicians have always ignored the wishes of the people and pursued their own self-serving agenda. If I am right, the hopes of the politicians, that they can hold onto power by making a few small gestures towards the dissatisfied and resentful voters, will be doomed to failure. I do not think that the voters are going to forget what has happened, now that they see that UKIP is not just an ephemeral protest party but a realistic alternative, and a refreshingly innovative political party, with common sense policies and a belief in allowing the electorate to make the important political decisions.

Perhaps we are at an historical turning point, with the prospect of having a new political party that truly does represent the people's wishes. The next chapter will investigate the meaning of some words that have been frequently used in the last few decades around the subject of immigration, in order to ascertain the effect they have had in confusing the issues.

§

CHAPTER TEN

THE TYRANNY OF WORDS

WORDS AND LANGUAGE, spoken, printed and written are meant to communicate facts, ideas, propositions, commands, wishes, requests and even emotional states. This essentially human invention has been a major milestone in our evolutionary history, and it has enabled us to cooperate in large social groups, and to exploit and dominate nature and the world. Language is however an *imprecise too*l and, if care is not taken by the speaker or author, the listener or reader can misinterpret the message. In highly-charged emotional situations in particular, two parties exchanging messages are likely to be using the same words with different meanings. Misunderstanding is therefore likely in debates unless the important words are defined carefully. Sometimes the speaker or author intentionally misuses language in order to confuse the listener or reader, or more commonly, uses vague language to hide his true meaning. It has been said of a young politician that he will not go far if he keeps telling the truth. Clever salesmen, journalists and lawyers are also skilled in the use of words and can easily confuse a listener or produce emotional responses that a victim may not have wished to make.

How many hundreds of times have you heard a politician say: 'We have listened and understand the message'? (or words to that effect). And did they mean it? Apparently not, if they did not modify their policies to suit the voters. The reason for this rather odd behaviour is that they did not want to do what the voters were requesting; they wanted to go on with their own agenda whilst convincing the voters that they were going to obey their requests. Obfuscation is an essential tool of the ambitious politician. When our politicians become aware that the voters are becoming restless about some matter or other, and are demanding action, they talk tough but usually fail to take the necessary and promised measures. Remember Tony Bair's famous slogan 'Tough on crime, tough on the causes of crime'? Another one of his was 'Education, education, education'. This slogan is a perfect example of the politician's art: it sounds good, but it promises nothing. The art of the politician is to sound as if he is going to solve the current problem, as his top priority, but to give no actual details. Another frequently heard sentence uttered by many politicians is: 'I want to make this absolutely clear...' Most people do not usually find it difficult to make themselves understood, but politicians apparently think that they are talking to people of limited intelligence, and they therefore have to give the impression that they are being very emphatic and lucid when addressing the voters. I think that the truth is that they are protesting too much, and are trying to hoodwink us when they utter this phrase. Actions speak louder than words.

However, let us now investigate the meaning of some of the words that are usually used to suppress free speech and to humiliate people who are expressing dissenting views from those of the liberal propagandists. The commonest of these is 'racist'. Now as soon as you concern yourself with trying to think of a definition you will realise that it could mean almost anything, but intuitively it sounds very bad. It could mean the nasty end of a spectrum of behaviour that brings to mind immediately the attitude and actions of the most notorious politician of the 20th Century, Adolf Hitler, and of his willing henchmen. A racist of this type is someone with a burning hatred of a particular race, or even of all races apart from his own. Hitler's racism, as everybody knows, obsessed him and spurred him on to a systematic and industrial project to cleanse Germany and its occupied territories of the Jews, (and other vulnerable groups) who were humiliated, abused, experimented on, dispossessed of home and possessions, and executed in millions in what is rightly called 'the Holocaust'. And history, both ancient and modern, records many other holocausts: those of Ghengis Kahn, Joseph Stalin and Pol Pot, to name a few. It is not therefore surprising that almost everybody in Britain who is called 'racist' in any circumstance, but particularly if they have voiced in public an objection to the continuing immigrant invasion, feels guilty by association and probably stops explaining their views. But it should be obvious to all native victims in Britain of being called 'racist', that they bear no resemblance whatsoever to any real racists, and that this use of the word is only *a form of abuse,* albeit a very uncomfortable one. It should be treated with the contempt that it deserves, because it merely indicates that the perpetrator has no intelligent argument or debating point to make. Indeed, the use of the word is not intended to describe an opponent and her views, but to cause her to stop giving her opinion or viewpoint. In other words, it is an attempt to inhibit the expression of a viewpoint that the arrogant perpetrator does not want to hear. Unfortunately most British natives have been cowed into submission under the constant barrage of public humiliation carried out over the last sixty years or so by the PC brigade of elitist politicians, 'liberal' academics and celebrity opinion-formers.

At the other end of the spectrum of 'racism' most people, of all races, prefer people of their own race or genetic origin but do not have any hatred towards strangers or foreigners. Their 'racism' is of the mildest possible degree, and is a universal human psychological characteristic. It is surely recognised by all races of people that most of us feel happiest with our own compatriots, whom we can recognise with a fleeting glance in a chance encounter, knowing that we are likely to feel comfortable and trusting in their company. Furthermore, people obviously 'vote with their feet', meaning that if they have the money and opportunity they choose to live amongst people like themselves, have similar friends, and tend to marry compatriots with similar educational and cultural characteristics. By contrast, we do not like obviously different people invading our neighbourhoods or national territory, especially in large numbers. The appearance in one's neighbourhood of foreign people with similar cultures, especially in very small numbers, will however be either welcomed, or at least easily tolerated. Most British people, like all people across the globe, will not think that this preference for one's own cultural compatriots amounts to 'racism' at all, and they will be offended if they are so labelled. However, if their protagonist is a skilled, celebrity, media presenter, or an immigrant or liberal sympathiser, and uses the 'racist' term in a hectoring, bullying manner in public, many will feel guilty, and back down or excuse themselves. Other, more timid, people will keep their opinions to themselves, or only voice them amongst friends and family.

Thus this tactic is often repeated by the PC bullies, which of course encourages the immigrants themselves to 'play the race card,' in order to harass public servants such as Local Authority employees who have to deal with important matters, such as allocating social housing or welfare benefits, and in order to create an atmosphere of fear and intimidation. Free speech on the subject of immigration is being suppressed, as it certainly has been over the last six decades in Britain, and the most serious consequence of the loss of this cherished right is that the politicians lose touch with popular opinion whilst the native public become resentful, angry and detached from the system of representative democratic politics. We have seen the disastrous result of this ubiquitous tactic in the Rotherham scandal, where the most appalling sexual abuse was covered up because the Local Authority managers were afraid to take the necessary actions to protect vulnerable young women from the Pakistani perpetrators. They were frightened of being labelled as 'racists', and thereby losing their jobs. And this terrible event is surely only the first of many similar scandals in our Local Authority and Government institutions.

I have laboured this technique of free-speech suppression because it is necessary to make explicit that the adjective/noun 'racist', and its noun 'racism' is used not to communicate an idea or description during an open and rational debate, but as a word of *abuse* to stifle opposing views. The user of the word is not interested in an exchange of opinions and ideas, but is determined to achieve the objective of encouraging the native population to submit without protest to the 'multicultural' project.

Even at all football matches organised by FIFA, the 'Say No To Racism' slogan is prominently displayed all around the pitch, to remind the fans to behave themselves, and not to chant, sing or gesture in any offensive manner that might upset any of the grown men on the pitch, or other fans. Thus George Orwell's slogan: 'Big Brother Is Watching You' still marches on, long after 'Nineteen Eighty Four' was published. And, of course, everyone in the Britain of today knows well that Big Brother is indeed watching them in all public spaces through the huge number, estimated at over six million, of ubiquitous CCTV cameras, which are being monitored so that they can follow anyone's movements. Sadly we need them, as part of the nation's security paraphernalia. It still astonishes me that we can so easily forget how wonderfully free we were in the 1950s, and how quickly we get used to such repressive measures. We are truly living in a police state, but one which is necessary to control the crime epidemic, and prevent a descent into total social chaos.

Words other than 'racist' are frequently used with the same objective, such as 'Nazi', 'xenophobe', 'homophobe', and Islamophobe. Nazi is of course even worse than 'racist', in that it is more explicit in its connotation of Hitler's obsessive hatred and extermination project, and no right-thinking democrat would wish to be called a Nazi. The word 'xenophobe' means a person who hates foreigners, and in these enlightened days few Britons or Western Europeans would think of themselves as hating European foreigners because we all have fairly similar cultures, despite the recent history of many European wars. That is not to say that we are happy to be invaded by large numbers of foreigners who have very different cultures with medieval and revolting practices.

Another word that can be misunderstood because it has different meanings, is 'discrimination'. Humans, like other animals, plants and more primitive organisms, discriminate for the obvious reason that, in a competitive Darwinian world and its multifarious ecosystems, a failure to discriminate between favourable and benign situations, or between benign creatures and dangerous ones, would soon result in the death of individuals and the elimination of an undiscriminating species. We have developed hard-wired brains that discriminate rapidly and efficiently the appearance and intentions of other people in any encounter. In warfare this is very obvious, hence the ever-present question in the frontline soldier's mind of 'friend or foe?' Less obviously, but also importantly in our normal daily encounters, we are constantly discriminating between people, and between the emotional state and apparent intentions of the other person. Our faces, body language and speech are being constantly, and usually unconsciously, scanned and reacted to as we communicate and interact with each other.

Discrimination of this type therefore is second nature to us all and still serves an important survival function. The modern PC use of the word should be used solely in certain legally and accepted social situations, where it is meant to prevent unfairness, and in which most of us agree that discrimination is wholly undesirable in a world where there is much racial diversity, and vulnerable minority groups. In Western democracies, discrimination is outlawed in employment and access to public services, largely because it has been realised that this is essential to promote social harmony. In a political system that relies on majority decisions which affect everyone it is necessary to be sensitive to the needs of minorities who have the same human needs, but sometimes special needs in addition. Thus arises the notion of 'human rights', which are meant to apply to everyone, and are enshrined in law in democracies with the hope that they will be observed globally. Unfortunately some countries are still very backward in strictly applying these rights, and even in the most civilised Western democracies perfection has still not been achieved, the prime example being the equal treatment of women and men in terms of employment opportunities and reward. In Islamic countries in particular, women are subservient to men and sometimes treated barbarically, as with the common practice of gang rape in Pakistan and even in India, with recent appalling examples in 2014.

Nevertheless, discrimination of the universal type is not going to be eliminated because it serves a useful purpose for all of us, and would be considered by most people, if they thought consciously about it, to be a human right in itself. We discriminate when we choose our friends, our marriage partners, our careers, our hobbies, our homes, our neighbourhoods, our clothes, cars and other possessions. These discriminative decisions are what make us into different and interesting people, and they give us a feeling of individuality. In tyrannical societies individuality is repressed, and behaviour, at least in public, is firmly controlled so that displays of robot-like marching en masse are used to demonstrate the power of the tyrant. North Korea is a prime example of this repression of individuality. The natural human need for the feeling of differentness and individuality based on each person's genetic makeup, upbringing and preferences, causes most people, given the chance in a free society, to discriminate in many ways and to rebel against repressive measures. We are social animals living in large groups, but we strive to keep our individuality, which we express by making our own choices in many different ways.

Words like 'discrimination', 'clear', 'independent', 'good,' in the mouths of our politicians have several different meanings and are 'weasel' words; that is, many of them are meant to be comforting and reassuring but their ambiguity covers their true meaning. There is, for the curious and politically engaged citizen, only one sure way of knowing what their politicians are doing or are going to do, and that is to see what they have actually done in the past. It is the discrepancy between the promises and the performance of our politicians that has now convinced a majority of voters that there is little point in voting for one party or another because 'they are all the same', meaning that they do not heed the wishes of the electorate, and they do not fulfil their promises.

This short investigation makes clear that words can confuse as well as communicate meanings, and a common error of opponents in debates is to use mutually exclusive categories, such as 'good versus bad', rather than defining carefully one's proposition and terms at the outset and then accepting that the debate should consider a more graded or numerical scale from one extreme to the other. In most topics or situations, both natural and man-made, a graduated scale is more likely to model reality, and possibly to show that the opponents are not so far apart as they think that they are.

A rigid, oppositional stance is very common in debates on emotionally-charged subjects such as politics, where opponents have a fixed point of view, and where discussion or debate is seldom rational. Protagonists commonly have a hidden agenda, based on a fixed belief system, and are trying to convince their voter audiences by the use of obfuscation and specious arguments. A rational debate needs to start with a proposition or question in which the terms are defined, so that everyone is clear about the subject that is under discussion. To give an example of the level of obfuscation that a poorly constructed question can stimulate, I quote from a popular BBC TV debating programme called 'The Big Questions' in 2104. One of the questions was the disarmingly simple: 'Is immigration good for Britain?

In a popular radio programme of the 1940's one of the expert panel contributors was a Professor Joad, who was famous for his frequent opening statement: 'It all depends on what you mean by…..' Applying this useful appeal for the definition of terms to the above Big Question produces the statement: 'It all depends on what you mean by 'immigration', 'good', and 'Britain.' Of course, no one did say that in the TV programme, and no definitions were therefore given, as usual. So the debate was inevitably heated but completely uninformative. Let us try to explore the question further. Immigration of what *type* of immigrant – Europeans or all-comers, Africans, Somalis, Muslims, Asians, etc?; those with skills which are in short supply in Britain, or poor unskilled workers from the third world?; billionaires who bring in their wealth and entrepreneurial skills and who can be enticed to Britain by being given political honours for cash?; genuine political refugees in danger of their lives in their countries of origin?; welfare and health tourists (economic migrants) who will overburden and impoverish our public services?; professional criminal gangsters?; Muslim extremists? And perhaps the most important question is: How *many* immigrants – one million, ten million, or anybody who wants to come? If you listen to the liberal politicians you get the impression that there is no limit to their high-minded tolerance, and they would let in the population of the whole world, presumably with the aim of sinking the British Isles.

Enough of that difficult definition - let us explore the simple word: 'good'. What *sort* of good?; do we mean that mass immigration will increase our wealth?; (and that word also needs definition, because politicians use an increase in GDP to measure wealth, whereas if we are all to get *wealthier* as a result of immigration we need to increase the GDP *per capita*, which is a very different measure of wealth!). Or does it mean that our culture will be improved or enriched in some way or another?; does it mean that the neighbourhoods and the countryside will be improved by the increase in the population?; does it mean that destroying our beloved monoculture and replacing it with a multicultural diversity that no one asked for nor wanted is a great improvement?; does 'good' mean that the crime statistics will improve, because the influx will consist of superior law-abiding people who will introduce a more moral attitude into our culture?

And finally: 'good' for Britain, but *for whom*? Good for the native men and women who cannot get a job because they have been displaced by immigrants who will work for lower wages?; good for the natives who are in work, but whose wages have been depressed because they have to compete with the immigrants who will work for lower wages?; good for the natives whose homes have been displaced from their neighbourhoods and towns to make way for the immigrants?; good for the better-off natives who have moved away from their neighbourhoods into rural areas or have emigrated to other countries where they can live in little ghettoes of British culture?; good for the poor and deprived natives who cannot move away and have to live close to immigrants and their often-criminal activities, their drug-misuse, violence and stealing that contaminate our culture and our children?; good for the native children who have to attend inner city schools where the pupils speak literally dozens of different foreign languages?; good for the Labour party, which needs poor immigrants who will reliably vote for the politicians who hand out the most welfare benefits?'; good for the big-business owners who benefit from having a cheap source of labour and from having a bigger population to consume their products?; good for the small and local businesswomen who are put out of business because they cannot compete with the lucky big businesses?; good for all our public services which are now overloaded?; good for the young couples who now cannot afford to buy a home for their families because the mass influx of foreigners has pushed up the prices of houses?; or good for the very vulnerable young women in Rotherham and Sheffield who have been horrendously abused by ghastly sexual predators from the Indian subcontinent?

What terrible consequences for our culture are hidden in such a simple word as 'good'. So this Big Question posed by the BBC programme is a fine example of the tyranny of words, taken to the extreme of obfuscation. To call such emotionally-charged chattering a debate is itself to misuse a word; such programmes are pure entertainment, with a fair bit of propaganda thrown in.

This sounds like a long list of required definitions, but I doubt whether it is exhaustive. Anyone who stops to think will quickly realise that the seemingly simple Big Questions are far from simple, and that the tyranny of words is a trap waiting to ensnare anyone without a questioning mind or debating skills. Professor Joad was rightly famous for his opening remarks because he always wanted a definition before answering a question or debating a proposition. One of the reasons why current TV shows ignore the complications of defining terms before launching a so-called debate is that TV is all about entertainment and ratings, in competition with other programme-makers. The programme-makers seem to assume that their audiences have a very poor ability to concentrate, and that therefore things have to be kept simple, and in any case, heated conflicts are much more entertaining than rational debate. In this they are almost certainly correct, because they keep a close eye on the ratings of their own shows and the performance of their competitors. One must keep in mind that whatever TV programmes are portrayed to be doing, such as educating the public or debating important issues, these aims are usually bogus, and the real ones are mostly the lowest common denominator of entertainment in competition with their rival channels. Even the once-admired BBC has sunk to this level as it panders to this ubiquitous form of modern entertainment, and a race to the bottom of public debate. And, of course, the real point of debating the question was to come up with an answer favourable to the BBC's propaganda campaign extolling the benefits of mass immigration and cultural diversity, easily achieved by carefully choosing the participants.

'Prejudiced' is another term of abuse that is aimed at people who might express concerns about the immigration invasion. It may well have a basis in fact because we all tend to form judgements on the basis of partial and inadequate information. How could it be otherwise? If we receive stories of certain types of criminal behaviour being frequently attributed to specific groups of immigrants through the various media sources, we are likely to assume that many such people are guilty of those crimes, without any knowledge of the behaviour of a particular individual from that group. That may be unfair to many individuals in those groups, but most people will be initially wary of such a person, and it is surely ridiculous to imagine that we can stop ourselves forming prior judgements, or that we ought to do so. If the police know that Romanian gypsies are committing most of a certain type of crime in their town, such as pickpocketing or credit card fraud, or that black youths are doing most of the drug-peddling in a particular area, it is only sensible for them to concentrate their efforts on those groups. The available numerical information forms what psychologists call a base statistic, and further information, when and if it becomes available, should be used to modify the targeting. Thus the pejorative use of the phrase loved by a lot of black people, namely 'racial profiling', which they accuse the police of using, may well be an attempt to reduce police effectiveness. In effect it becomes another form of abuse intended to intimidate.

A contemporary example (mid-August 2014) of the latter phenomenon has been seen in the riots in Ferguson, Missouri, USA. A black teenager named Michael Brown was shot six times and killed by a white police officer after the teenager had stolen goods from a convenience store. This event sparked off rioting for more than a week and shops were looted, Molotov cocktails and missiles were thrown, along with gun-shots at the police. It was noticeable that the US TV media presented the killed man as a black 'teenage' victim, and the police officer as a 'racist' white man. The police released video footage of Michael Brown showing him stealing from a convenience store and threatening the store staff. Teenager he may have been, but he was a well-built young man of 6 feet 4 inches height and, therefore, a formidable threat to anyone, including the well-built police officer who shot him, and who said he was being threatened by Brown when he (the policeman) fired several bullets (which autopsy reports revealed were all in the front of Brown's body).

I do not know at the time of typing whether the policeman was justified or not in his decision to fire at Michael Brown, nor does anyone else seem to know. The black protestors say that Brown's friend Darryl Johnson claims that Brown was surrendering with his arms in the air when the policeman fired. Protestors have pointed out that the Ferguson police are predominately white whilst the population of the city is mainly black, and that tensions run high because the police use 'racial profiling'. Some commentators complained that the police chief should not have shown the video recording of Brown's shoplifting in the store, because it was 'inflammatory'. The intervention of Ban-ki Moon, the UN Secretary General was interesting: after a few nights of serious rioting had occurred in Ferguson, Mr Moon said that the authorities in Ferguson should be careful to allow peaceful protesting, which is a right under US law. This caused me to wonder whether he had had any recent eye tests, because all the footage shown on TV was of violent protesting, rioting and looting, which the police could not contain, even with tear gas and riot squads, for quite a while. Apparently a lot of the rioters were opportunists coming to Ferguson from other parts of the USA.

I do not wish to give the impression that I think that all is well between the police and the black population in Ferguson, Missouri, nor do I wish to judge the rights and wrongs of the shooting of Michael Brown. The information that we have at the moment is very conflicting and, because of the emotions aroused and the comments that various people have made, it may not be possible to come to a definite conclusion as to the facts, even after the inquiry which has been set up. What bothers me, however, is that such violent and irresponsible rioting, which appeared to be well organised, should be happening in the USA which is supposed to be a beacon of democracy. Indeed, we heard on 19.08.2014, that another person had been killed by the police during the riots. One would have thought that all the protests should have been peaceful, and that the population of Ferguson should have waited until a proper inquiry had been completed. These events only illustrate that where there are racial and cultural fault-lines in a community, there will tend to be suspicions and hostility sooner or later, and that these feelings may well last for decades or longer, as has often happened in other places and at other times. As for 'racial profiling', what is a policeman on duty protecting the law-abiding population to do if he is instructed to apprehend a criminal suspect? Naturally in a racially diverse population a major indication of identity is whether a suspect is of this appearance or that. It would hardly accord with common sense if the police where not to take account of the racial appearance of suspects that they are seeking to apprehend: 'racial profiling' is just another phrase to indicate that they use major indications of identity based on physical descriptions, as indeed ordinary witnesses of crime naturally do. Some people who dislike 'racial profiling' are surely people who are part of a social group who indulge in crime and who wish to weaken the efforts of the police doing their duty. It seems to me that this is another example of 'manufactured offence' being used as a counter-measure to the efforts of those whose duty it is to maintain law and order.

Ordinary members of the public will form their prejudiced profiles of particular groups, as will Local Authority officials dealing with daily appeals from immigrants for welfare benefits and housing.

Learning from experience is bound to result in a judgement on particular groups who have a relatively common approach to their requests for help, or other such behaviours. Obviously those officials have to abide by the rules laid down by Parliament, which are intended to ensure that all citizens are dealt with equally and fairly, but being human, the officials will, in the light of their experience, naturally form their own opinion about the ways that the rules are applied and the fairness or otherwise of those rules. Members of the public who are natives undoubtedly have come to the conclusion that the rules give unfair priority to immigrants over the heads of local people, and the result is a growing feeling of resentment, which of course most public officials will be careful to hide in order to keep their jobs.

The tyranny of words, used deliberately by politicians and their liberal supporters to suppress freedom of expression and to obfuscate the serious issues around 'multiculturalism', has caused resentful voters to turn away from politics or, more accurately, from politicians. I think that the rise of UKIP as a credible protest party has saved us from more severe and frequent civil strife and stopped the rise of popular extremism, such as happened in France with the recent electoral triumph of the Front National Party (FN) headed by Marine Le Pen. The FN polled over 4,700,000 votes, coming first with 24.86% of the votes for MEPs in France, in the 2014 EU elections. Across Europe in the 2014 elections of MEPs, there was a definite rise of protest political parties, and in some cases, of extremist parties of both right and left persuasions. The message to EU politicians is surely clear: the electorates of the Union have had enough of mass immigration and the problems that it causes, and they want immigration strictly controlled. The utopian social engineers have been defeated, which was probably inevitable, because they rode rough-shod over the views of the electorates due to their arrogant assumption that they know best. In other words, they are elitist, and do not believe in true democracy.

Indeed they use the word 'populist' pejoratively, when they should welcome the views of the people. They are condemned by their own words.

Personally, I think that most native Britons have been too easily persuaded of the so-called 'benefits' of immigration, and have been too tolerant of the loss of their long-cherished freedom of expression. We must hope that the rise of UKIP will continue as more people realise that they have been duped by their politicians and the establishment. The worm is turning at last, but we must hope that it is not too late to avoid cultural suicide or violent protests. The omens are not good, because thousands more young men from Africa, Eastern Europe, Arabia, Syria and the Indian subcontinent are pouring across the European continent and the Mediterranean Sea, most of them hoping to begin a new life in Britain.

It is surely beneficial for our democracy that the British population is now beginning to treat political statements and promises with a healthy scepticism, and that voters are now realising that **representative democracy is a fraud**. The word 'representative', taken at face value is a comforting word, intended to lull us into thinking that all our public servants are working for our benefit and a better life for everybody. A few newcomers to Parliament may well be so motivated, (as is the indomitable and sincere Dennis Skinner, the long-serving MP for Bolsover) but the majority of politicians have been found out to be representing themselves and their cronies. We must remember the expenses scandals that involved so many MPs. We must remind ourselves that they have voted a very comfortable pension scheme for themselves, and have increased their own salaries at a time when they are holding down wages for public servants, and reducing pension benefits for the citizens. And we must remember that senior politicians, of whom Tony Blair is the best example, leave office much richer than when they entered it, and go on to very highly paid sinecures in global organisations such as those of the United Nations, or as advisors to other Governments and powerful, international, commercial companies. According to *The Guardian* newspaper of 23.10.2014, the latest register of MPs' interests reveals that twenty MPs have declared over £100,000 income from second jobs, such as directorships, paid employment and share-holdings. Gordon Brown tops the list with earnings of £492,331 for public speaking around the world, and with expenses of £583,985 for travel, accommodation, staff and research. He says he doesn't get this money personally, and it goes 'to support his ongoing involvement in public life'. Not bad for a Labour politician – he appears to have developed a late belief in private enterprise.

The next chapter will investigate the all-powerful elite known as the 'establishment', because politicians are closely surrounded by other groups who are heavily involved in forming Government policies, and all of them are trying to gain influence for themselves.

§

CHAPTER ELEVEN

THE ESTABLISHMENT

FIRST OF ALL I MUST DEFINE the meaning that I attach to the word 'establishment.' The most important and essential element in a democracy is the governing class, which of course is basically the elected Members of Parliament, who are the representatives of the nation's people. The Government is chosen from amongst his MPs by the leader of the winning political party at a general election, and this victorious party can therefore legislate its programme if it holds enough seats to produce a working majority of MPs. Unusually in modern times, we have, in the current Cameron Government, a coalition, consisting of the majority Conservatives and their junior partners, the Liberal Democrats. And then there is the *unelected* House of Lords, forming the second chamber of Parliament – a collection of bishops and political worthies chosen by party leaders to enjoy the privilege of being life members of the best club in town. All of this you know.

However, we must include under the term 'establishment' other people who are less often in the political limelight but hold a great deal of power without being elected. The Conservative Party is backed by most of the nation's big-business community, many of whose members donate considerable sums of money to the Party, and expect in return, to have considerable influence over the Conservatives in Government, so that their interests are safeguarded. Conservative MPs and ex-Ministers usually benefit from their connections with big-business, and with the Confederation of British Industry (CBI). After retirement from Parliament, MPs, and especially Ministers, are often able to secure well-paid directorships on the boards of big companies. The Labour Party has in the past been mainly funded by the Trades Unions, but this is now being changed, so we are told by the Labour leader, Ed Milliband, and it will in future be funded mainly by party members and some rich donors. The Liberal Democrats (Lib-Dems), and other smaller parties are mainly funded by members and some wealthy donors.

The media, namely the circulated newspapers, and, increasingly, the online press, TV and radio companies, are also very influential components of the establishment, as was revealed during the phone-hacking scandal which involved the Murdoch media empire. The politicians are naturally very keen to please the media moguls, editors and correspondents, because they are only too aware of the media's power to influence the reading and viewing electorate. The BBC has had, and still does have, a major influence in the campaign to advance the social engineering project of 'multiculturalism' and has acted as a highly efficient propaganda machine for the various Governments of the last few decades.

There are also many professional lobbyists, paid mainly by large commercial companies to promote their interests by directly influencing MPs and Ministers. A third group consists of university academics, who study politics, write articles for the press, advise politicians and ministers and often are commissioned to produce reports and surveys or to sit on inquiries. Other groups consist of political advisors, top civil servants, the legal profession and the judiciary. These people also have a powerful influence on Governments. This list is not exhaustive.

None of the above will be news to sophisticated and well-informed members of the public, but I doubt whether most people who are not very interested in politics will realise what a huge effort is being made by a great number of large organisations to influence Government for the benefit of their own private affairs, and for their own profit. Nor will a majority of voters, at least until recently, have realised what a *corrupt system* this all amounts to and what little influence the ordinary voters have. All these groups are part of the 'representative' democratic system of so-called checks and balances, intended to ensure that constitutional power is not in the hands of the Government alone. Nevertheless many of the people who constitute these groups are working together, communicating closely day by day in the 'Westminster village', and come largely from *the same socioeconomic class*, so that, in effect, they continue to hold most power as an establishment clique. I am leaving out the monarchy, who also play a part, but one that has diminished over many centuries and is now largely ceremonial and peripheral.

The striking thing about the establishment is that *they still hold so much power*, bordering on totality, even though we are inclined to delude ourselves that a democratic government is, as Abraham Lincoln said: '... government of the people, *by* the people and *for* the people...' It seems quite clear to me that we are wholly mistaken in thinking that this description applies to our current representative democratic system: the British establishment governs *in their own interests* as far as they can get away with it, as they have always done. They form an elite group who believe that they know what is best for the country, and that they have a divine right to rule. Over the centuries since Magna Carta was sealed by the barons and King John at Runnymede in 1215, (and quickly revoked by the King!), the people have struggled to wrest more power from the establishment, and the struggle continues to this day. Unfortunately, the establishment now controls most of the modern media and news outlets, and thus exerts a powerful grip on the voters' perception of reality.

In saying all this I must, if I am to convince my fellow citizens, provide supporting facts and arguments. I shall therefore follow now with evidence, based on the recent actions of the establishment in bringing about the social, moral and cultural decline that we have experienced in Britain over the last sixty years or so.

The first question to be asked here is: 'Why are the middle and upper social classes who constitute the establishment so strongly in favour of uncontrolled mass immigration, when one might have expected an older and essentially conservative group of native people to be automatically against it? I think that the answer is one that motivates us all for most of the time – namely that it is in *their perceived self-interest*. This, of course, is also the reason that the working classes were automatically against immigration at first, before they succumbed to the propaganda campaign. However, mass immigration was clearly in the perceived self-interest of the establishment. It is quite cheering to realise that these antagonistic British social classes may have had, for a short time at least, one prime motivation in common, albeit with opposing objectives. The difference, however, is that the establishment, especially the politicians and the liberal opinion-makers, are always portraying themselves and their motives as altruistic – a luxury that the working classes cannot afford and which they seldom claim.

We should now go back to the beginnings of the recent mass immigration in order to find out, if we can, why and how the whole process got started, and why the politicians let it happen, and then encouraged it. On 22.06.1948, four hundred West Indians from Jamaica arrived in Britain aboard the ocean liner *Empire Windrush* in search of a better standard of living and took jobs in London, such as bus drivers and conductors. They mostly settled in Brixton, in South West London. This small cohort of immigrants had been recruited by London Transport to fill jobs that natives were apparently not interested in doing. It was facilitated by the 1948 British Nationality Act which gave British citizenship to subjects of the former colonies of the British Empire – another liberal 'good idea' that has had monumental unintended and corrosive effects on our culture. Not surprisingly, but apparently not predicted by the Government, the word spread widely and quickly around our former colonies. From then on, large numbers of West Indians, Indians and Pakistanis, and smaller numbers of West Africans, Cypriots and Maltese, followed to settle in Britain.

Later on, the numbers of immigrants entering the country steadily increased, including many illegal ones, organised by international criminal gangs, as poor people from around the world realised that entry to Britain, with its open borders and its generous welfare benefits system, was a ticket to easily-acquired wealth.

Some of these immigrants have been deliberately lured to Britain by both Government and commercial companies. The original West Indian group was enticed by London Transport to solve, at a stroke, its recruitment problems. The next cohort of Asians were recruited to fill vacant (and dirty) jobs in a West London tyre factory, and they settled in nearby Ealing. The opportunity to recruit cheap, immigrant labour into dirty and low-paid jobs that were difficult to fill with native Britons, was taken up by many other large firms, and thus spread the myth that 'we need them to do the work that the natives won't do.' Of course, there was an element of truth in that statement, but it has become one of the frequently-used glib mantras to explain to the electorate the necessity for the continuing invasion of millions of foreigners. The reason the natives were not willing to work for low wages was probably because they were receiving more cash in benefits.

In addition our Governments have, on several occasions, deliberately mounted campaigns to recruit nurses from third-world countries in South East Asia, and doctors from Pakistan and Egypt, to solve the problem of shortages in the National Health Service – problems of their own making. They are still, in 2014, repeating these immoral, overseas, recruiting campaigns and yet the crumbling NHS is still short of doctors and nurses.

The biggest and most scandalous reason for the continuation of the mass immigration invasion however, was the contribution made by the 'New Labour' Governments of Tony Blair and Gordon Brown. Andrew Neather, a speech writer for Tony Blair, revealed in 2009 that Labour relaxed immigration controls in a plan to 'open up the UK to mass immigration'. As well as bringing in hundreds of thousands to plug labour-market gaps, there was a 'driving political purpose behind immigration policy'. *Ministers hoped to change the country radically and 'rub the Right's nose in diversity'.*[19] Lord Mandelson admitted that '*Labour sent out search parties' for immigrants.* He also conceded that the influx meant that 'the party's traditional supporters are now unable to find work'.[20]

The annual *net* migration figure quadrupled under New Labour during 1997-2009, and by 2010 the figure was 2.2 million. I have no doubt that these clever politicians were mainly motivated to execute this deceitful project when they realised that the majority of the immigrants were voting for their party, because the previous immigrants had quickly discovered that the Labour Party was more in favour of generous welfare benefits than the other political parties. The evidence to back up this suspicion is the fact that at the last general election in 2011 our 'international city', London, voted almost solidly for Labour. Of course, the word of the Labour invitation travelled fast round our former colonies and soon after reached the Eastern Europeans, to say nothing of the opportunist gangsters from everywhere.

The Labour Party has always branded itself, and still does, as the 'party of the poor'. That is no secret: they constantly and proudly say that they represent the poorer section of the electorate, despite the fact that most of their top politicians have never done an honest day's work, and they live in some of London's many mansions. There is no shame in representing the poor, but it means that the Labour Party needs the poor just as much as the poor need the Labour Party. What was scandalous about the Blair and Brown Government's actions was that they made a deliberate

---

19   Mail Online (24.10.2009): Neather: 'Labour deliberately let migrants in…'

20   Mail Online (14.05.2013): Mandelson.

and covert decision to allow and encourage as many immigrants as they could reasonably expect the natives to accept without causing civil unrest.

When people of a different political persuasion demanded a control of the numbers coming into the country, the Blair Government had to reveal that they did not even know how many people were arriving, because they had no means of counting in place. This seemed to indicate that they didn't wish to control the number of legal immigrants, let alone the illegal ones, and didn't wish the public to know the size of the continuing mass immigration. **This devious and underhand decision must surely amount to one of the world's greatest examples of gerrymandering practised by a Western democratic political party.** During the time of the Government of Margaret Thatcher (1979-1990), one of her supporters, Dame Shirley Porter, engineered a policy in Westminster Local Authority to allocate social housing to Conservative supporters in order to ensure that there were more of the latter voting in the local elections, and thus gerrymander the results. This attempt was a scandal at the time, but was clearly in a totally different league from the machinations of Tony Blair and his co-conspirators. It is the first duty of a government to protect its people, and the decision to allow and encourage a continuing mass immigration of poor people into Britain without any control by Prime Minister Blair amounted, in my opinion, to a *scandalous political misfeasance*, although it appears that gerrymandering is not a crime in Britain. He brazenly entered the (2014) public debate on the EU policy of freedom of movement, which allows these migrations to occur despite the efforts of some member Governments to control the inflow, and threw his influence behind that EU policy although the recent elections have indicated that most of the British electorate were, and are, firmly against it. Perhaps he had a private agenda which over-rode any consideration that he should have had for the people of Britain. He declared on TV (June 2014) that he was not a candidate for the open post of President of the EU, but it seems likely that he would soon have changed his mind if he had been offered the post.

Many of our people were, at the time of the Iraq war, and still are, of the opinion that Mr Blair was wrong to take Britain into that war. He has been criticised by many political commentators for that decision, including the veteran Tory MP Sir Peter Tapsell, who called in Parliament for his impeachment 'for allegedly misleading the House on the necessity of the invasion of Iraq in 2003'.[21]

The politicians of the three traditional parties were all in favour of more immigration until the elections of May 2014 sent an unequivocal message to them that the electorate has had more than enough of immigration. Many of the voters who supported UKIP in those elections want full control of power to be firmly given back to our own Parliament, and therefore wish to leave the EU. Despite that message, and that most politicians say they have 'got it', many of them are still saying that 'immigration is good for Britain', and the rise of support for UKIP is 'a free protest vote', and it will fade away at the next general election. They attribute that 'protest vote' to a lack of trust in politicians since the expenses scandal, and to the fact that the electorate think that 'they are all the same.' Another political view is that the severe economic crisis and its austerity consequences have made people very dissatisfied with the apparent impotence of the politicians to raise the standard of living for working folk.

It seems at first strange, that all three traditional parties are so out of touch with the electorate, given that they regularly monitor the results of polls conducted by various academics, and independent polling organisations, and they also manage their own political focus groups. The Labour politicians are still courting

---

21   Huffington Post (18.06.2014).

the immigrants because the latter have a strong tendency to vote for them, as described above, and as was clearly indicated by the large Labour vote in London in the May 2014 elections. They are, however, they are making vague promises that they want a future 'in/out' referendum on staying with the EU, but that *they still want to stay in*. This is a very lukewarm change of heart, forced on them by the recent rise of UKIP support. They are clearly not going to give up wooing the immigrant vote, which is now a major part of their electoral support, and a growing one at that.

The Liberal Democrats made clear during the May 2014 elections that they were the party of strong support for staying in the EU, and were almost wiped out as a result. Nevertheless their leader, Nick Clegg, backed by his other top politicians, has since repeated their policy objective of staying in the EU come what may, and he states their view that they are right, and that they were courageous by being the only party that took that view during the May 2014 elections. Please note that this firm stance clearly indicates that they think the electorate was, and is, wrong; in other words they are *elitist by their own admission!* Liberal they certainly are, but democrats? I don't think so.

The Conservatives, under the leadership of Prime Minister David Cameron, appear to have got the message at last, even if they don't like it, and are saying that the only way for the electorate to get a referendum is to vote the Conservatives back into power at the general election in 2015. However, the referendum that they are prepared to offer the electorate has to wait for 2017, after the PM has had time to persuade all the other EU countries (all twenty-seven of them!) to change the rules and laws by repatriating most of the current rules and laws back to Britain. Before the rise of UKIP, and when the PM thought that UKIP was 'a bunch of loonies', he was against holding an 'in/out' referendum, then slowly changed his mind to: 'A referendum when the time is right.' By which, of course, he meant when he thought he could win an 'in' result. Another elitist wolf in a democratic sheep's clothing. Part of his change of mind has been caused by pressure from many of his own MPs in marginal seats, who are naturally worried about losing their seats to UKIP in May 2015.

So we clearly have plenty of reasons why two thirds of the electorate have lost trust in representative democracy and its politicians: the politicians are seen to be untrustworthy; they are interested only in increasing and protecting their own wealth; they represent themselves and their cronies; they are elitist and think they have a near-divine right to rule; they have nothing but contempt for the bulk of the electorate. They are in effect *anti-democratic*.

We now need to say something more about the media as part of the establishment because they are in control of the news that is presented to the public, and most of us would have no idea what is going on without the essential activities of the various media organisations. So important are they in modern society that any tyrants executing a coup or revolution make a top priority of capturing the radio and TV stations in order to manage all information, so that they can control the population and thus prevent any organised opposition and a counter-coup. Tyrannical regimes, such as the Communists in Russia, North Korea and China, exert rigid control of news and detain or murder journalists who try to uncover the truth and present it to the people. Of course, modern digital technology is now giving ordinary people more alternative channels of communication, but the tyrants still attempt, usually with success, to control those also.

Media channels are important in democratic societies because the electorate receive most of their information through the national media regarding the activities of their Governments and politicians. In Britain, the BBC has had until recently a world-wide reputation for reliable news, investigative journalism, drama productions, and art and science programmes. It therefore has had a major influence on current affairs, on Britain's reputation in the world, and on the spread of the English language and culture. It is still living on its past reputation for impartiality and balanced reporting, but this reputation has been comprehensively lost over the last few decades. It has recently been mired in several appalling scandals: for example the high salaries and retirement pay-offs of senior executives, and the Jimmy Savile sexual-abuse activities on BBC premises over some forty years. Day by day, in 2014, we have had news that the police are investigating allegations of sexual abuse against more BBC celebrities. It seems clear that many senior managers at the BBC and in some NHS hospitals, who gave free access to Savile over such a long period, must have known what was going on. It seems possible that another protective paedophile ring was operating in both organisations. There have been many different 'independent' inquiries into the facts of the scandal, but very little has yet been made public, and no heads so far have rolled, although some senior managers have retired. It looks as if we shall never know the total truth, and no doubt someone hopes we shall forget about this scandalous betrayal of the duty of care that has occurred within two of our hitherto famous and trusted public bodies. The long delays in producing the reports of the investigations into the scandals is a sure sign that the BBC and NHS establishments are hoping that people will have lost interest in these appalling betrayals of trust. There is something very rotten in the state of modern Britain.

My immediate concern is the part the BBC has played in acting as a propaganda machine for Governments that have promoted the 'benefits' of the uncontrolled immigration invasion that now threatens the very culture that the BBC once promoted under its famous chief, Lord Reith, its first Director-General. It seems unlikely that this propaganda campaign has been controlled in any direct way by the politicians. It seems much more likely that it is an important component of the multicultural, social-engineering project that has been espoused at the BBC by its liberal intelligentsia since the end of World War II. The executives are part of the liberal establishment and move in the same social circles as other media journalists, political academics and the politicians. The BBC appears to have operated a strong policy of affirmative action in relation to its recruitment of news presenters, so that Asians and black people have formed a considerable proportion of new recruits since about 1960. Moreover, when any expert is filmed or interviewed it seems that immigrants are shown disproportionally. Joseph Goebels, Hitler's Minister of Propaganda, was world-famous for his propaganda skills, but his reputation has surely been comprehensively eclipsed by the BBC.

It is clear that the starry-eyed liberal intellectuals in Britain, who I'm sure are prone to think of themselves as the conscience of the nation, convinced themselves that the country should welcome all the world's poor and underprivileged masses, especially those who had 'suffered oppression under the British Empire'. They saw the chance at the start of the immigration invasion, of facilitating a grand, social-engineering experiment, in which people of diverse racial, religious and cultural origins would live happily together in a 'multicultural society'. The BBC acted as the project managers, with a pervasive propaganda campaign that continues to this day. Constant repetition is clearly meant to induce unconsciously in the minds of the unsuspecting viewers the messages that 'immigration is good for Britain', 'we can't do without them', and 'Britain is now a multicultural society.'

Some of the liberal intelligentsia also seem to be suffering from post-colonial guilt, as illustrated in BBC programmes about the British Empire. The programmes have tended to be full of criticisms, and short on the undoubted benefits that accompanied the admittedly unfortunate, colonial exploitations and cruelties. Such programmes as one presented by Jeremy Paxman seem to have no awareness of the mistake of rewriting history from a modern moral outlook. Do the BBC liberals think that the African and Indian economies and cultures would be as far advanced from their previous undeveloped states as they are now, if the 'scramble for Africa' by the European powers had not occurred (in a far different moral climate from our current one)? Of course, many of them are still relatively undeveloped, and in Africa many are governed by authoritarian regimes and have slipped backwards, but they still have the advantages of the English language, of railways and other infrastructure, of British economic connections and aid, but are bedevilled by corruption, tribalism and armed conflicts. The trans-Sahara trade of black people from West to North Africa probably began before 1,000 BC.[22] Muslim slave-trading was endemic in Africa centuries before the European colonialists arrived, and, although the latter took advantage of it, they were soon assisted by the natives who captured the slaves from other tribes, and sold them to the slave traders. Britain was eventually in the forefront of the abolition movement, with Quakers being early opponents of the trade in the mid-18th Century, and the Royal Navy then policed the Atlantic in order to stop the trade. Those BBC celebrities who fancy themselves as historians should try to achieve a balanced presentation, instead of rewriting history in the light of their 'liberal' delusions. Times have changed, and they are changing very rapidly, and past circumstances and moral attitudes are not always relevant to current problems.

The BBC may be thought by some to be only promoting the liberal views of most of our native people, and therefore spreading the attitudes and views which are part of British culture. After all, most kind, friendly, tolerant, well-educated and rational native British people think of themselves as being liberal. But like most things, as I have mentioned before, there is a wide spectrum behind this categorical notion, and we should be careful of overstepping

---

22   Thomas, Hugh (1997). The Slave Trade, p. 44.

the sensible mark. The idea that all cultures should be respected is patently nonsense, if we are to have any idea of values. Moral relativism has been debated over thousands of years, but is now largely discredited in modern Western philosophy. *Respect has to be earned*, whether for an individual or a group, and our tolerance should be limited, if our culture is not to be destroyed. Naturally we think our own culture is the best, or at least it is the one that we like and wish to preserve. Probably most Britons would, if it were put to them, agree with the categorical imperative of Immanuel Kant, the famous German 18th-century philosopher: 'Act only on that maxim which you can at the same time will to be a universal law.' That maxim is a modern philosophical version of the old proverb: 'Do as you would be done by', or the earlier Biblical commandment: 'Thou shalt love thy neighbour as thyself.'

The BBC is now seen to be in no position, after its recent scandals, to be the national authority on morals or tolerance. It protected for about forty years Jimmy Savile, reckoned to be the country's most prolific sexual abuser of young girls. Senior employees at the BBC must surely have known what he was regularly doing on their premises, and neglected their duty of protection of the vulnerable star-struck young girls. Many of their popular entertainers are homosexuals, who are of course prominent in the entertainment industry, and these people are pushing the boundaries of what is acceptable entertainment, so that the repetition of smutty jokes, gestures and remarks becomes normal 'fun'. Some of us have no problem with homosexuals engaging privately in consensual sex of a kind which we would find disgusting, and we certainly approve of their being treated equally under the law as citizens in all public situations, but we don't think that the BBC should be promoting the decline in morals that is today so widespread, by allowing entertainment shows to be dominated by material with explicit or implicit sexual material. This once-admired iconic institution has now become the national engine of cultural and moral destruction. No doubt there are many homosexuals who live a blameless life in a permanent loving relationship, or even in celibacy; unfortunately there are others whose activities involve many other sexual appetites, and who seem to be bent on converting vulnerable youngsters to their own life-styles. In November 2014, the BBC aired a programme with the title: 'Prostitution: Where's the Harm?' That title, and the programme, indicates the depth of moral decay that the BBC has now reached, in what looks like a deliberate attempt to destroy our moral code. Who benefits? The answer surely is those people with abnormal sexual appetites who wish to feel part of normal society, just as alcoholics feel more comfortable in a group of people who drink heavily, and are uncomfortable if anyone refuses to comply with their requests to 'have a drink'.

What some of us do not approve of, is the strong tendency of TV celebrity entertainers to flaunt their abnormal behaviour in public, as if they are trying to convert us to their life-style and their often-promiscuous ways of life. That attitude is no different from that which we apply to heterosexual people. Sexual activities are better treated as private matters, or in carefully devised educational programmes. Unfortunately many young people, brought up on a TV 'education', think that any behaviour is now acceptable, including getting drunk regularly to the point of paralysis, and fighting in the city centres at night.

Moral relativism, or non-judgemental respect for other people's religious or moral codes is now largely discredited. There may be few universal moral absolutes, but most Britons do not approve of the dictates of Sharia law, nor of the domination of women as if they were chattels owned by men. Muslims obviously have different moral values from most Western democrats, and some of these values we abhor, but others we might incorporate with benefit. The onus, nevertheless, is on the immigrants who want to settle here or in other Western countries to embrace *our* values and customs. If they wish to live under Sharia law then they should stay or settle in a Muslim country. The British liberals, who seem to believe in moral relativism, and think that it is acceptable for immigrants to practice a religion and culture which gives grave offence to us, and which preaches the overthrow of our religions and culture, are living in cloud-cuckoo land. The encouragement that they give to the Muslims will result, sooner or later, in a rebellion on the part of the long-suffering and over-tolerant British population, and possibly in serious civil commotion.

The lawyers play their part in the establishment, ostensibly to act as guardians of our liberty, and as a check on an over-powerful executive. But of course many of them also have their eye firmly on the opportunities for personal enrichment. The EU Human Rights laws have enabled some of them to defeat time and again the Government's attempts to deport dangerous criminals and terrorist Muslim preachers, such as in the case of Abu Hamza al-Masri, imprisoned in Britain over some eight years for terrorist acts, and eventually extradited to America in 2012. These lawyers enrich themselves seemingly without any concern for the well-being of the country and its society. Although the lawyers are supposed to be one of the independent checks on Government, in Tony Blair's Government some of the parliamentary lawyers were his long-time colleagues from the days of practicing in their common law chambers. So much for 'independence', a political weasel word amongst many.

The political, liberal, legal, journalistic, commercial and academic elites who constitute the British establishment have thus combined powerfully in their arrogant and different self-serving ways, to destroy the British culture. This they have done, and are still doing, against the express wishes of the majority of natives, by encouraging mass immigration in the guise of the idealistic idea of forming a multicultural society. For many of them this idea is a cover for their true motivations of self-enrichment and self-aggrandisement, and for others it is part of their objective of promoting lax morals. The Conservatives are looking after the commercial and big-business interests, including the provision of a constant supply of cheap labour; the Labour Party are looking after the poorer section of the community, which has been greatly expanded by the entry of a mass of immigrants whom they have bribed for their votes with welfare benefits on their immediate entry to the country; the Liberal Democrats are idealistically committed to their utopian dream of a multicultural society; the BBC and other liberal journalists are managing an efficient propaganda campaign to convince the tolerant and easy-going British population of the benefits of mass immigration; many of the lawyers are opportunistically driving the human rights industry; and all these and other parasites are totally unconcerned at all the terrible and mounting problems that uncontrolled immigration is undoubtedly inflicting on the poorest section of the native population. And, of course, all of these establishment figures who live in London mansions are greatly benefitting from the spectacular rise in the value of their homes due to the influx of wealthy foreigners. No wonder the Lib-Dem idea of a tax on mansions soon expanded from the original £1 million trigger to £2 million; after all, they wouldn't want to pay too much themselves. In any case, clever accountants quickly moved to shield the wealthy from any such mansion tax.

This strange combination of self-serving, elitist groups constitutes the political and intellectual establishment which controls the country under the pretence of representative democracy. How does one explain how such strange bed-fellows as the BBC's favourite liberals Polly Toynbee and Yasmin Alibhai-Brown on the one hand, and arch-Tories such as David Cameron and George Osborne on the other hand, are united in championing the destruction of our culture? The liberals believe they are high-minded social engineers constructing a utopian society, whilst the Tories are taking the opportunities for personal gain presented by 'New Labour's gerrymandering policy of encouraging the mass invasion of immigrants. Although their motives are worlds apart they, and others, are united in their arrogance and their elitist belief that they are born to rule, and that the plebs are too ignorant to know what is good for themselves. Whilst promoting the idea of equality for the foreign invaders, they have shown no respect or concern for the culture of our own working-class, which they have practically destroyed. Many working-class communities have been displaced from their long-occupied territories, for example the London East-Enders displaced to Essex, who are now voting for UKIP as a result of their rising anger at the politicians who have comprehensively let them down.

The mass immigration and colonisation of Britain, which from several different motives has been rapidly started by the political and intellectual establishment and which was quickly stimulated and controlled by avaricious criminal gangs and lawyers, immediately ran out of Government control. Even when the pressure for control continued, so that they had to set up a system of counting and control, it was soon clear that the system was flawed, and in any case they had no way of knowing how many illegal immigrants were entering the country. At the time of writing there are still people overstaying visas, 'students' being trafficked into fraudulent 'colleges', women being trafficked into prostitution, others into slavery as cheap house-maids, and no one knows how many illegals are entering through our ports in containers. In other words, the numbers still entering the country are not known and the management of the process is in the hands of organised, criminal gangs. And this after about sixty years of so-called control measures, and with the current Cameron Government proclaiming that it is doing its best to limit the numbers. Apparently, the ridiculous rules of the European Union even now (mid 2014) ban border-control officers from asking potential immigrants how long they intend to stay in Britain! So we still don't know what the numbers of immigrants entering our country are, and all the talk about strict controls is rubbish for public consumption. It is clear that the Home Office, which is responsible for border control, is still 'not fit for purpose' some eight years after John Reid gave it that label.

The unintended effect that this momentous social experiment has had, and is having, on the social fabric of Britain, does not seem, throughout the period of continuing invasion, to have been of any concern to the establishment. The invited waves of immigrants were obviously introduced into the country to solve the problems of politicians, and managers of large businesses who wanted cheap labour. I have little doubt that the day-to-day 'crisis-management' style of most democratic governments will continue. They operate with short-term *ad hoc* policies, reacting to crises, often of their own making, whilst reassuring the electorate that a constant flow of new 'initiatives' will 'address' the problems. Their motives have been the management of labour shortages, keeping down wages and, of course, profit. The real needs and wishes of the long-suffering population are totally disregarded. This is fine for these establishment 'movers and shakers', but what about the serious and disturbing consequences now being visited upon that section of the population least able to deal with the social problems, namely our own native poor and deprived people?

Let us now examine the specious reasons that the establishment politicians and intellectuals have so frequently given when questions are asked about the immigration of large numbers in such an uncontrolled fashion:

'We need the skilled immigrants to maintain our public services'.
Answer: This is a fallacy and a lie. The Government and its public agencies should plan ahead (as they had to do, and did, in the

past), and should ensure that enough people are trained for the various professional and technical jobs, and that they are paid enough money to maintain recruitment at the right level. The once world-famed British Civil Service had the staff and the means to be able to plan ahead, and their recent failure to do so is a dereliction of duty (unless they were following orders from the politicians). In addition, it is totally immoral to steal expensively trained people from third-world countries struggling to improve their own public services. If it is countered that some of these third-world countries have a surplus of trained people, then that should give our politicians cause for shame, because they have clearly failed to do as well as the Governments of the third-world countries. It is also shamefully wasteful of our own labour capital to deny our own young people the training for the skilled jobs that they aspire to do. A good example is that of doctors. There used to be, when I trained, about one hundred school leavers with the required A-levels applying for each place in our medical schools, whilst now we have to recruit thousands of doctors from abroad because of the shortages caused by the influx of mass immigration which has overloaded this and the many other public services. Clearly we should be training most of our own doctors, as we have traditionally done. The rapidly rising population, due largely to increasing longevity, mass immigration, and the rising birth-rate, has not been matched by the required investment in more medical-school places. Similar problems of skill shortages are seen across the board, such as in nursing and engineering. Not so long ago, we pioneered the industrial revolution, and ruled about a third of the world, and now we can't even produce enough nurses, doctors, engineers or other professionals to run the country efficiently. Mrs Thatcher helped to bring about shortages of trained engineers and tradesmen by discouraging the long-established and vital apprenticeships, which the Cameron Government is now having to re-establish. We only need thousands of skilled immigrants because of the gross incompetence of our Governments. Anyone who thinks that the problem is caused by a lack of intelligence or motivation in the British natives must explain how we managed until the last few decades to play a very large part in inventing the modern technological world.

'*We need immigrants to do the jobs that our own workers will not do*'. *Answer:* that is the wrong solution to the problem. There are several, better, potential solutions. It is possible to develop technological solutions, such as driverless underground trains or better robotic farm equipment, to do the work of many unskilled labourers. If this is not immediately possible then the wages of unskilled labourers should be raised, and people should have to pay higher prices for the services provided – or go without them. In any case, the immigrant and better-motivated foreign workers imported to do the low-paid work soon aspire to be earning higher wages and move on to other jobs, so that another tranche of immigrants is then needed. Finally, native people who collect state benefits for being chronically unemployed should be forced to choose between working or having no money. It is hardly likely that people will do low-paid work if they can get the same or more for being unemployed. It is not sensible to blame the unemployed: the ridiculous benefits system devised by 'New Labour' has been the driving force behind the problem of long-term unemployment. Native poor people have been trained by Labour's scandalous benefits system to depend on the state, and have become totally demotivated to work for a living. The solution of ensuring that benefits for being unemployed do not equal or exceed those for working, is at last currently being tried by the Cameron Government, to a chorus of criticism from the current Labour opposition and from many of the Liberal Democrats. Unemployment as a life choice should never be rewarded above the level earned by the unskilled working population; that's a rule based on scientifically-proven behaviour modification, on anyone's sense of fairness, and come to that on common sense. The trouble these days with common sense is that it's not very common, especially in political circles. The agricultural sector of the economy, which relies on seasonal cheap labour from Eastern Europe for fruit-and-vegetable picking, should either invest in more sophisticated machinery or pay better wages, and consumers should then have to pay the consequential higher prices for their food or go without what they cannot afford. But the essential part of the solution is that which the Cameron Government is now beginning to introduce, namely to ensure that living on benefits is not a more lucrative life-choice for able-bodied persons. Unfortunately they have not yet gone far enough down this road: the new benefits cap is equal to the average wage, when it should be lower than the 'living wage'. Not only that, the unskilled workers are not paid enough from the point of view of fairness – everybody who works should not have to receive benefits as well in order to live a decent life, and the employers who offer only insufficient wages should not be subsidised by the state. The 'living wage' sounds as if a family can live comfortably on it, but it really means that they would die if one had to live on less, and it should be increased.

'Immigrants make a huge contribution to our economy'.
Answer: A few may well do if they have fled from persecution and brought their wealth and entrepreneurial skills with them. A moderate number of highly skilled professionals may also do so, but for Britain to pillage poorer countries of thousands of highly skilled workers is clearly immoral as described in answer (1) above. The unskilled poor majority do not make a useful contribution to our economy. Not only do they keep wages low, but they consume

expensive services and many send money back home. This oft-repeated assertion also seems to show that our Government is concerned mainly with the economy, and that the consequential destruction of our social fabric, culture, and our previous peaceful and civilised way of living is apparently of no account to the establishment. I'm sure that a lot of people would welcome a return to the culture of Britain in the early 1950's even if the economy were to grow more slowly. It might well be that people would think that the cost, which might not be high, would be worth it. But, more importantly, if we did not have this mass of alien cultures in our midst with all the consequential crime, conflicts and threats of terrorism, then police, social services and security services would be costing a fraction of the present sum, and the economy might even be much better than it is now. It seems very strange to me, that despite all the propaganda about the benefits that huge numbers of immigrants bring to our economy, it has never in my long memory been in a worse state and it looks like continuing in that state for the foreseeable future. The credit crisis cannot surely be the only reason why the dreadful austerity measures are not producing real results, when we have all these immigrants bringing us such wonderful economic benefits. Somebody has either got his sums wrong or is lying. It is also noteworthy that the repetitive political assertion that immigrants benefit our economy has never to my knowledge been accompanied by the comprehensive calculations that should prove the case. That in itself gives the lie away.

I am no economist, but I am very sceptical of the complicated statistics that some researchers use. The old cliché comes to mind: 'There are lies, damned lies, and statistics'. And of course the politicians do not ever produce any figures to back up their monotonously repeated 'benefits' message. So I think we can get a fairer idea of the benefits of mass immigration if we do a thought experiment, working from the simplest scenario to the more complicated ones as a scientist would do.

Imagine a cohort of one million immigrants, and let us start by assuming that they are just the same as a similar cohort of the natives in all respects. Our hypothetical cohort will be demographically identical with the natives, and will work in the same proportion of skilled and unskilled jobs, and have the same needs for services and benefits. The nation's GDP would rise as a result of these factors operating in an expanded population, but the GDP *per capita would stay the same* as before. In other words, the average income of the natives would not rise, and the immigrants would earn the same average amount, but the country would become more heavily populated, with all the consequential problems such as more traffic congestion, more crowding on trains and other facilities, a housing crisis, and great pressures on the NHS and the education service. And of course *big-businesses would benefit* from the increase in numbers of customers, which naturally would delight the owners. However most of the small businesses would be owned by immigrants, and serving immigrants, many of whom would be sending money back to their relatives in their countries of origin.

If the original assumptions I have made are not valid, as I think would be likely, we must take account of the possible reality scenarios. We know that most of the immigrants are on average poorer and less skilled that our native population; that many send back money to their families abroad; that many of them are illegal and therefore have to commit crime in order to pay back large sums to the criminal gangs that trafficked them to Britain; that many of them are drug peddlers, pick-pockets, fraudsters of credit cards, driving licences, passports and who knows what other documents, pimps, slavers, car and metal thieves, 'cash for crash' experts, and terrorists – to mention only some of the criminal activities that have resulted in Britain becoming the criminal capital of Europe. The cost of all this crime and the security measures that the state and businesses have had to adopt to attempt to control it, must amount to a monumentally huge financial burden that no government has attempted to calculate. And the number of immigrants known to have invaded our tolerant society is not one million but upwards of six million, plus all the unknown illegal ones, and more are still being allowed in. So the politicians who continue to utter the specious mantra of 'immigration benefits to our economy' are clearly lying, and they must know that they are lying. What's more, their statistical measure of immigration is the *'net'* figure that subtracts the number of natives who are leaving the country in droves *with their wealth*. They use this 'net' measure to hide the *true* figure of immigration, which should be only the number of people *coming into the country to settle*, and this would be somewhere in the region of double the net figure. Governments are experts at deception and obfuscation, and all their statistics are suspect.

Another deceitful ruse used by the proponents of the slogan that 'immigrants benefit our economy' is that they equate the migrants entering the country with those leaving, as if freedom of movement is mainly just a zero sum game, that is: we gain some and lose some, so why worry. However for someone like myself, who is acquainted with a number of friends who have retired to Cyprus, it is clear that most of those Britons leaving are taking their savings with them to buy a retirement home (the Cypriot authorities demand to know their financial resources, along with the number of any dependents), whilst most of the migrants coming into Britain are poor and expect to be provided with a publically-funded house for themselves and their dependents, and free health and educational services. Clearly the only reason that the politicians keep mouthing the mantra about the benefits the immigrants bring, without ever giving us a thorough accounting document which would include all the costs, is because they know that mass immigration is a negative-sum game, that is: we import immigrants that cost us money to support, and export the Britons who take their wealth with them. So, not only are we supporting, the immigrants who need public services, but, in addition, wealth is leaving the country along two routes: the amounts that the immigrants send home, and the amounts that the retired Britons take with them.

An item that is not mentioned in the accounting of economic benefits, is that of health costs. Before the mass immigration started some diseases had been almost eliminated from the native British population, such as tuberculosis and rickets. Since the immigrant invasions these diseases have now increased greatly. Tuberculosis is endemic amongst people from the Indian subcontinent, and rickets is now common again, because dark-skinned people do not get enough exposure to sunlight in Britain to be able to produce the vitamin D required to produce healthy bones. These and other imported diseases are therefore a serious cost on the NHS. In addition, many of the retired natives living abroad get free health services provided for them by their host countries, the cost of which is paid by the British Government! So any accounting exercise that equates incomers with leavers is pure moonshine. This is yet another example of the 'false-equivalence error' in argument.

But we must include the rich immigrants in our accounting exercise. These represent a very small cohort, but obviously bring some of their wealth into the country, mainly into London, where they buy up their mansions, and thus contribute to the spectacular rise in house prices. Some of them have been involved in Tony Blair's 'cash for honours' scandal, and they now are part of the London establishment, wielding power over us in the House of Lords. Others have invested money in businesses and wield commercial power. It is difficult to assess what these activities do for our economy, but this positive contribution is most unlikely to counterbalance the negative contribution of the millions of poor immigrants and the thousands of criminals. But it does of course benefit the establishment figures who own London mansions with steeply rising values, and the politicians who expect their wealthy immigrant friends to help them woo the immigrant vote.

Even that overall, financial, negative sum leaves out of the accounting the distress that overpopulation causes us and all the noxious effects on our culture of so many criminal activities. Strangely, the politicians always talk of the 'benefits' to our *economy*, as if they are obsessed with money above all else, whilst the poor natives are preoccupied with the *dreadful effects on our culture*. But then this isn't really strange, because the financial benefits are gained by the establishment figures, whilst the noxious effects are, as always, visited upon the powerless, deprived, poorest natives.

One final thought on the Conservatives' oft-repeated assertion that leaving the EU would result in our losing several million jobs because of the loss of access to the European market: if that assertion be true how is it that the two most prosperous (and democratic) European countries, Switzerland and Norway, are not full members of the EU? Both countries have had referendums on the matter of joining, with negative results from their electorates. And both countries have free-trade agreements with the EU, and adopt whatever other EU arrangements happen to suit them; and both countries have their own strong currencies. Why then should Britain not be able to mimic their successful example? Big question. The reason that these two countries have adopted this arrangement seems clear enough: *the people decided the matter for themselves,* against the recommendations of their politicians.

'The immigrants enrich our culture.'
Answer: I do not remember any clamour from the general community during the decades since the 1950's for the 'enrichment' of our culture, and I find this assertion patronising and insulting to a high degree. This vague statement, I suspect, was a desperate

attempt from the supporters of mass immigration to drum up some native support when they began to realise that social problems were already beginning to surface. It is noteworthy that we do not currently hear this assertion very often, because the propagandists have at last realised that our 'multicultural society' is in serious trouble, and their glib slogans now have a very hollow ring. It is noteworthy that none of the intellectuals who uttered this mantra has offered an apology for their arrogant pronouncements.

In any case, why should anyone think it is necessary to have mass immigration in order to enrich a culture? Even a few travellers, back from foreign parts, a few immigrants or foreign visitors, can import the exciting, desirable or previously unknown memes into another culture if there is a demand or potential niche for them, as has happened hundreds of times in the past. How do these clever intellectuals think that the hamburger or Mozart's music, Gauss's mathematics, French cuisine or Dostoyevsky's literature got to Britain? Did these enriching, foreign, cultural items or memes, along with all the others, arrive on our shores with invading armies of millions? Indeed, in the modern age of miraculous and all-pervasive information technology, of world-wide trade, and cheap trans-global travel, it would be impossible to *avoid* coming into contact with other cultures, and thus the spread of efficient and desirable memes. That is why people have coined the phrase 'gone viral', meaning that an idea has spread within hours across the globe! Unfortunately, the reverse of enrichment has been the result of the foreign invasions. Our hitherto harmonious, gentle and democratic culture has been infected with many most undesirable memes, such as terrorism, Sharia law, slavery, and all the plethora of new criminal activities too numerous to mention. We now know that the 'multicultural society' project was not planned and executed with the objective of cultural enrichment in mind, but was the 'New Labour' gerrymandering project, described by Baron Mandelson, in order to achieve a deceitful political purpose.

The sort of people, who advance such spurious arguments in an effort to persuade the general public to welcome the mass immigration that is destroying our culture, are not only the politicians and the profit-seeking businessmen who are always looking for easy answers to the problems that they have responsibility for, and have failed to solve. Some of the establishment are people who love to take the moral high ground in all debates, and who deceive themselves that they are advancing the welfare of humanity in general. Sometimes such people make useful contributions to debates, and to the causes that they espouse, but in other cases they may be hugely unrealistic, and may expect people in less fortunate circumstances than themselves to be sympathetic to their point of view, even when this might put the latter at a serious disadvantage. Above all, they are blind to the reality of the consequences of their utopian schemes, because they are so convinced that their high-minded motivation must surely result in good outcomes. To face the reality of a disastrous outcome would be to destroy their wonderful self-image, and therefore cognitive rigidity results in denial. It is noteworthy that all these self-righteous opinion-formers, who bang on endlessly about the wonderful benefits that multiculturalism brings, are middle class and elitist, and they *all live far away* from the displaced communities of our underprivileged poor natives who suffer all the noxious social consequences.

If you think I exaggerate the liberal tendency to dream of unrealistic utopias and to be blinded by their own failure to face the awkward reality of the human condition, then caste your mind over the events which occurred in 1920, when the British Government sent a party of twenty-five people to Russia to investigate the effects of the Russian Revolution. The party was led by Bertrand Russell, the most famous liberal intellectual of the 20th Century, who, along with the other liberal intellectuals during that year, was enamoured of the Russian Communist State. To Russell's credit he became more sceptical during the visit, but the others swallowed completely the utopian but false presentation that they were shown by the Communists. They were apparently blinded by their desire to see a wonderful society actually in action and thus totally failed to use their intellectual powers to exercise a little scepticism. They were not alone at that time and this episode illustrates the human failing of not wanting to face reality. However, two decades or so later, another realistic intellectual, George Orwell, was writing his devastating satires of the USSR, namely *Animal Farm* [23] published in 1945, and *Nineteen Eighty Four* [24] published in 1949. They are both still classics which everybody interested in politics should read, especially now that his skilfully portrayed horrors have been brought to life in Britain.

I consider myself, surprising though this may seem to some of my readers, to be a liberal humanist. I may of course be deceiving myself, and I must leave my readers to judge, but I divide liberals into two categories: the realistic and the unrealistic. It is in my experience a very common psychological failing in many people, to be unable to face reality, and this is usually a seriously dangerous mind-set, that any addicted gambler might have to grapple with. Some politicians often say, with a touch of self-admiration, when talking of a difficult problem: 'I'm always an optimist'. That strikes me as a confession of borderline mental illness, because unpleasant events should surely be treated with a careful assessment of the difficulties of solution, and unrealistic optimism may well result in disaster. The liberals whom I have so far been talking about are the unrealistic ones who embarked on the utopian social project of replacing our harmonious culture with a so-called multicultural one, without it seems, any investigation of the far from harmonious multicultural ones that history and a few current examples easily provide.

---

23   Orwell, George. (1945).

24   ibid. (1949).

Unfortunately they wield most of the power in Britain, and are incorrigible to a high degree, hence their belief that anyone with a different viewpoint is a scoundrel.

In the present context, morally hypersensitive but unrealistic liberals continue to put forward the idea that anyone who claims to have been persecuted in their own country, or is in search of a better life, has an automatic right of asylum in Britain. This viewpoint seems to ignore the possibility that it would give the right to settle in Britain to possibly hundreds of millions of people across our seriously disturbed world. It also begs the question of what constitutes a right. Surely rights should stem from a consensus viewpoint in the community as a whole, not from the views of a self-appointed intellectual elite nor from 'human-rights' lawyers. A majority of the native population of Britain has not to my knowledge ever expressed this unrealistic view.

The only legitimate right of entry in order to settle in Britain, or in any other country for that matter, should be through the granting of that right by the tight legal procedures of the appropriate Government agencies after proper application and approval. The 'New Labour' Government of Tony Blair admitted that about 80% of immigrants were in the country illegally, and that they did not know the true figures. Their later figures were likely to be gross underestimates, given that they were probably motivated to hide the truth, and official figures estimated that Labour added above three million to the British population, and other commentators think that it might have been as high as 5.5 million. At the same time, nearly a million people left the country, many saying that they 'no longer could recognise the country'. John Reid, Home Secretary in Blair's cabinet in May 2006, admitted that the responsible agency for border control, the Home Office, was 'not fit for purpose'. It didn't seem to me, in the light of the immigration fiasco, the discharge of dangerous criminals from prison without proper assessment, and the loss of control of the crime epidemic, that it was fit for any purpose whatsoever. Faced with large numbers of determined people trying with great persistence to get past our hopelessly inadequate border controls, it looked as if the Home Office Ministers and their civil servants had given up the struggle, and hoped that the immigration problem would just go away. And of course, the politicians and their big-business and Trades Union cronies were benefiting from the invasion.

One cannot help thinking, that if the politicians and the lawyers had been living in the rundown city centres where the poor immigrants started to settle, and if they themselves had suffered, from the start, the consequential social problems endured by the poor underprivileged natives, a very different plan of action would soon have been a priority. But then, of course, they would never have been living in a rundown, deprived community in the first place, and, even if they had, they would just have moved away. I hope that readers will pardon my cynicism. It seems to me to be an absolute scandal that one small section of the community could make a decision to engineer the monumental social change that has destroyed our culture without any attempt whatsoever to consult the electorate – and *in a so-called democracy.*

The behaviour of the establishment needs a little more analysis before we move on. The fact is that even in a Western representative democracy the politicians and their wealthy friends, the movers and shakers of society, have the power to take effective action which they so easily manage to commandeer in their own interests, but have no personal stake in the problems of the masses. Prime Minister Tony Blair loved to strut the world stage (he still does) and consort with other world leaders, enjoying the publicity, the power, and the use of force to interfere in other countries' affairs, whilst only occasionally devoting his talents and efforts to the social problems that had largely arisen at home during his watch. He was perhaps devoting much of his time and effort to the objective of enriching himself, as do most of our politicians.

According to some sources, he has eight homes; he is a multi-millionaire with an estimated wealth of £20 million (some say £50 million, he says £10 million); he is paid large sums for being an advisor to JP Morgan (a US Investment bank), and to Zurich International (a global insurer based in Switzerland); he owns his own consultancy firm, (Tony Blair Associates), with a plush office in Mayfair, advising the Governments of Kuwait and Kazakhstan – according to Nick Wood, CEO and founder of Media Intelligence Partners. As Mr Wood says: 'Blair has the breath-taking effrontery to accuse Nigel Farage of deceiving voters by fuelling grievances about immigration'. This model lawyer-politician, who to this day denies that he deliberately encouraged mass immigration despite the confessions of members of his cabinet,[25] [26] is supposed to be a man of the people, whom he betrayed. He appears to me to be a man with no conscience or scruples, and his political misdemeanours are without recent precedent.

No doubt when he finally retires, he will move away from overcrowded city centres to an idyllic rural setting in Britain, or perhaps, more likely, migrate to a desirable and expensive part of Europe or further afield to spend his declining days in one of his mansions, writing more self-congratulatory memoirs. His deceitful political and subsequent record, plus the uncovering of the MP's expenses scandal, has undoubtedly made most of the British electorate extremely cynical about our political establishment, but I suspect that the current revelations of scandals in high places are only part of the hidden story.

The 'race-relations industry' also deserves a mention because, once started, it rapidly became part of the establishment. It is a web of organisations and a favourite device of government

---

25   Mail Online (24.10.2009): Neather: 'Labour deliberately let migrants in…'

26   Mail Online (14.05.2013): Mandelson.

for handling the thorny problem of integration. The articulate members of the immigrant population have been co-opted into the establishment in two different ways, complementing each other. As previously mentioned, the wealthier members, who no doubt, at least in some cases, have bought their way into political favour, are elevated to high and powerful positions, including membership of the House of Lords, whence they can influence Government policy and new laws on behalf of the immigrant population. David Cameron appointed Baroness Sayeeda Warsi into his cabinet to help win over the Muslim vote but soon found, to his cost, that her allegiance may have been to her co-religionists overseas rather than to his cabinet, as was revealed when she resigned her post in August 2014. The reason for her resignation was because she objected to Cameron's 'failure to condemn the killing' of the Muslims in the Gaza strip by the Israelis – a reason that many of us, incidentally, would support. This incident highlights a serious problem of a multicultural society: the 'society' is fractured along various fault-lines, so that any important decision of Government is going to upset one or another of the various national groups, making the nation weak and divided. Western democracies may well become ungovernable, especially when faced by serious problems involving foreign policies.

The other way of courting immigrant voters is by appointing immigrant activists into quangos such as the Commission for Racial Equality, and by promoting the selection of immigrant candidates for election, at first in largely immigrant areas, and then across the country. This seems very liberal and generous-spirited but gives the immigrant population an increasing influence in social policy, which it naturally uses to advance its power further, and to ensure that the flow of immigrants continues. One has only to view some of the TV 'debates' on immigration, with audiences packed with young, second-generation immigrants, not unexpectedly, enthusiastically shouting for more immigration, to realise that the natives are rapidly losing control of their own country.

Suffice it to say at this juncture that I consider that the politicians and their supporters, in conjunction with the big-business members of the establishment who connived at importing cheap labour from the beginning, and still do, are guilty of starting and maintaining a momentous social experiment on a grand scale with scandalous indifference to the horrendous consequences. This irresponsible experiment, which now threatens to destroy the social fabric of a country that previously had a highly enviable record of peaceful stability, has brought much misery already on its poor working class people who, not surprisingly, express their resentment sporadically in violent protest. Where and how this process will end no one can be sure, but the lessons of the history of cultural conflicts do not encourage optimism.

It is clear however, at the moment of writing (June 2014), that the current Cameron Government has realised that all is not well with the haphazard project of creating a 'multicultural society', the change of heart being largely in response to the terrorist attacks in London (7th July 2006), the foiled attempts to blow up airliners flying from London to the USA (August 2006), and the multiple riots in London and several others of our large cities in August 2011. These horrendous riots were sparked off by the police shooting dead a black youth (Mark Duggan) carrying a loaded gun, and the subsequent street protests in the London borough of Tottenham. For about five days there was looting of shops and arson of homes and businesses. The riots quickly spread to other boroughs in London and to other large cities. About 3,100 people were arrested, and more than 1,000 were charged. Five people were killed and sixteen injured, including the deaths of three Asian youths who were trying to protect their community when they were run over by a car driven by a black youth. 3,443 crimes were recorded across London. It was estimated that the cost of property damage was about £200 million, and the cost to the Metropolitan Police was more than £34 million. The general opinion of commentators and researchers was that this was basically a criminal, opportunistic event, and 'a defining contest between disorder and order', organised with the use of modern social media. Severe penalties were handed down from the Courts to the convicted criminals, in an effort to send a message that a reign of terror such as this must be stopped and further riots prevented. A disproportionate number of the rioters were young, black men, with Jamaicans being the largest group amongst the jailed looters.

Researchers pointed out that the causative factors appeared to be opportunism, perceived social injustice, deprivation, and frustration at the way that minority communities were policed. The critical factor however, was the density of youths. Riots, war, and regime-change are, according to the researchers, associated with the age group of fourteen-to-twenty-four year-olds, the so-called 'youth bulge theory'. Communities with populations of more than 20% of this group run the greatest risk of frequent and severe political instability.

Many people referred to the fact that the rioters were predominantly black, but one commentator, Christine Odone, writing in the Daily Telegraph, linked the young rioters to the lack of male role models: as with the overwhelming majority of youth offenders behind bars, 'gang members have one thing in common - no father at home'. Another commentator quoted statistics of the dreadful social problems of boys brought up without a father present in the family. They are 75% more likely to fail at school, 70% more likely to become drug addicts, 50% more likely to become alcohol addicts, 40% more likely to have serious debts, and 35% more likely to be unemployed and on benefits. In recent years, the rate of children murdering children has tripled; 70% of young offenders come from fatherless homes; in 2008 some 11,000 children were treated for drug and alcohol addiction; and the rate of teenage pregnancies in Britain is the highest in Europe. US President Obama has also pleaded with black fathers to stop deserting their children, because of similar problems in America. However, it is not only a problem of black fathers, but is a growing world-wide trend from about the 1980s. In Britain, about 25% of families with dependent children are single-parent families, including those where the father is the carer. It certainly seems from these statistics that the problems arising from our unruly youths and unhappy children are not going to be easily managed without a long-term and very well-thought-out programme of family support, and a serious educational programme in schools aimed at family responsibilities and child care. The use of the legal system to punish offenders, the labelling of 'scum' and dealing with 'anti-social behaviour', are not by themselves going to cure these serious and deep-rooted care-deprivation problems in our society. We have broken down our moral code and traditional child-care in families with the decline of religion, and put in its place the ridiculous, toxic and untried mix of 'tolerance' and 'permissiveness' called 'political correctness'. We have indeed sowed the wind and are now reaping the whirlwind.

Apparently our politicians, like the rest of us, are alarmed at the fact that the Muslim terrorists in our midst are 'home-grown', that is, they are, in the main, young men born in Britain as second-generation immigrants and educated here. It seems that our Government has had to recognise that previous efforts at integration of all young Muslim men into British society have failed. Unfortunately there are no signs yet that the Government has abandoned its conviction, following that of the previous Gordon Brown Government, that the 'multicultural society' is the best model for the modern British community.

The most hopeful sign so far was the statement by two Ministers in the Gordon Brown Government (2007-2010), during their proposed new 'Great Debate', that 'political correctness' must not be allowed to interfere with the voicing of different opinions.

Lifting the lid on the oppressive censorship in public affairs and the media that had been stifling free speech for the previous five decades appeared to be a most welcome development if they had meant what they said. Unfortunately, no debate followed, but the announcement did begin, albeit tentatively, the process of airing some contrary views.

The essential requirement for a successful and open debate is that the Government and the 'liberal' intelligentsia *listen to the voice of the electorate,* and entertain the unpleasant possibility (for them) that their views on immigration may not be shared by many, let alone the majority, of native, British people. Thus, for a debate to be productive, the establishment must listen to its critics as well as to its supporters, something it is not very good at doing. It would also be helpful if it recognised that it is not just the problem of a few terrorists in our midst that needs a solution, but the underlying problem of severe, cultural conflict as a consequence of the mass migrations that are destabilising so many Western countries as well as Britain.

In the modern context of the so-called 'multicultural society', the political establishment should heed the advice of Oliver Cromwell (in a different context): 'I beseech you, in the bowels of Christ, think it possible you may be mistaken.'

§

CHAPTER TWELVE

THE DEMOCRATIC DEFICIT

THE COALITION GOVERNMENT of David Cameron and Nick Clegg has promised to hold an 'in/out' referendum in 2017 on staying in the European Union, if the Conservatives are re-elected in May 2015. The PM has always backed staying in the EU, and that viewpoint reminds us that the Confederation of British Industry (CBI) backed the decision to stay in the European Economic Community (EEC) in the first-ever referendum held across the UK in 1975. This was a successful *post hoc* attempt to obtain support from the electorate by the Edward Heath Conservative Government, after he had taken us into the EEC in 1974. The nation was divided as expected, but support was obtained for the 'Yes' vote of 68%, with 32% voting 'No', on a 65% turnout. That is, only 44.2% of the electorate voted to join the EEC (aka the Common Market). Referendums are not yet legally binding on British Governments because of Parliamentary sovereignty. However no Government would be likely to overturn a firm referendum result because of the political risk of upsetting the electorate – but a succeeding Government would not be bound by such a referendum result. In other words, the British electorate still does not have direct powers to command a Government on any issue once it has been elected. The voters have to rely on their 'representatives', the elected Members of Parliament, to undertake all the decisions, routine and trivial or monumentally serious, such as going to war, which greatly affect all of us.

Referendums are rarely held in Britain on a national basis, (there have been only two so far), and then only when the Government in power thinks it would be desirable for its own ends. Thus Prime Minister Cameron has always been in favour of staying in the EU, backed by his big-business cronies, and only started thinking of holding an in/out referendum since it became obvious that the electorate was becoming more Eurosceptic. He then announced that he would hold a referendum 'when the time is right', by which of course he meant: when he was sure of getting the result that he wanted. The rapid rise of UKIP, whose main objective is to take Britain out of the EU at the earliest possible moment, has made the PM change his policy to a definite referendum date of 2017, once he has been able to negotiate with the EU for a 'repatriation of powers to Britain'. It seems at the time of writing (mid 2014) that he is unlikely to be able to get the EU to agree to any serious repatriation of powers, according to the several statements of the unelected EU hierarchy, which is still bent on an 'ever closer union of member countries', which logically would end in a United States of Europe. It is not only the British electorate that has become more Eurosceptic: in the May 2004 European Elections many other member countries returned more Eurosceptic MEPs, including France with majority support in that country for the far-right *Front National* party of Marine Le Pen. That was not only a clear message from the French electorate that they want no more immigration, it was an indication that extremism is on the rise, with all its dangers of civil unrest. It was also the inevitable result of the French politicians, like our own, having failed to keep in touch with public opinion. When free speech is suppressed, democracy is threatened, extremism flourishes, and civil unrest is eventually a certainty. The ordinary voters have at last realised that they are being ignored, and their tolerance has reached its limit.

The current preoccupations of the electorates and the politicians of the EU member states, including Britain, highlight the widening gap between the voters and their Governments. It is generally agreed that voters are now thoroughly disenchanted with their politicians, as witnessed by the falling turnouts at elections. It appears in Britain that some 60% of the electorate cannot now be bothered to vote at elections, a matter of grave concern, because voting is the crucial activity that upholds the validity of democratic Governments. Many politicians are themselves concerned, but do not seem to understand fully the reasons for the voters' disenchantment with politics, or, more correctly, with politicians. In Britain, they do realise that a contributory factor has been the long list of scandals over their expenses, which has revealed that many of them are corrupt in a straightforward, personal financial way. But they do not seem to be as aware of the fact that the electorate view them as self-serving, arrogant elitists with very little respect for the masses. This voter mind-set has only recently begun to register in the awareness of many politicians, but it has been developing over the many decades since mass immigrations began.

A prime example of this serious 'image problem' for politicians is that of Tony Blair. So delighted was he to welcome the immigrants that his Government even let in Muslim terrorists, despite being warned of their activities and threats to our country by the French security services. **In effect he was carrying out the world's most outrageous and monumental example of gerrymandering:** he was stuffing the country with millions of people, most of whom could be guaranteed to vote 'New Labour' for ever! He then compounded this arrogant and self-serving democratic misfeasance by taking Britain into the Iraq war alongside George W. Bush, on a very dubious pretext. Only now (August 2014) are we seeing the full, disastrous consequences of that foolish and illegal act. While Iraq now seems to be threatened with both Muslim tribal warfare, and also being broken up by the conquering Islamic State barbarians, Mr Blair is nowhere to be seen, despite his job as the UN Special Envoy to the Middle East. (Correction: on 22.09.2014 he appeared on the BBC 'Today' programme to give us the benefit of his vast experience of world affairs and military expertise - he thinks we may have to send our troops into Syria at some point in the war against the Islamic State barbarians). I hope our current PM is listening carefully to the arrogant man who still thinks he is the President of Britain, having failed in his ambition to be the President of the EU.

We all know, and the politicians often remind us, that the first duty of a Government is to protect its citizens. Tony Blair and his cronies in effect engineered the mass invasion of foreigners into Britain, causing horrendous problems for his successor politicians and our long-suffering population, and it seems to me that he was therefore guilty of one of the most serious of political crimes, namely gerrymandering on a grand scale. He and his fellow conspirators should surely be behind bars. But we all know that the poorest of our citizens can easily fall foul of the law for trivial reasons (such as causing offence by using the wrong word!), whilst the people at the top of our political establishment can usually escape punishment for the worst of crimes.

When the mass immigrant invasions began in 1958, there were protests and street marches, often organised by workers and Trades Unions who were fearful of losing jobs to poor immigrants willing to work for low pay. There was also a number of 'race-riots' as native Britons protested on the streets, but these were quickly snuffed out by the judiciary, by handing down harsh sentences to the protestors. The Trades Unions also quickly stopped protesting. One cannot help thinking that all this sudden repression of popular protest was directly engineered by the Government of the day, which soon began a propaganda campaign to convince the masses of the great benefits that the immigrants were bringing. Of course, the liberal intelligentsia were quick to join the propaganda campaign because they realised that this was a wonderful opportunity to encourage a utopian, social-engineering project on a grand scale. They doubtless had many different motivations, some having a religious conviction that all God's children should live in harmony together, whilst others were keen to cause a breakdown of the established British way of life, and its suffocating (for them) moral code. The BBC was also quick to act as the propaganda machine extolling the spurious immigration benefits. Worst of all was the general effect of the relentless propaganda from the BBC, which produced an atmosphere of extreme political correctness, and abuse of those brave enough to protest, so that free speech and expression was eliminated in a very short time.

Not only were many of the ordinary natives seething with resentment at the scornful arrogance of the establishment in suppressing their right to protest at the undemocratic demolition of their culture; they were later treated to the declaration of war on Iraq by Tony Blair on the basis of poor evidence of Sadam Hussein's programme of 'weapons of mass destruction'. Blair had his own agenda, as his later behaviour shows. He was determined to strut his stuff on the world stage alongside US President George W. Bush, which did no harm to his future career as a 'world leader' and éminence grise, so that he could later earn large sums of money lecturing and advising lesser politicians. He was still appearing on television in early 2014, advising us all on the 'war on terror'. Does he ever think of the thousands of soldiers and civilians with grievous injuries sustained in Iraq, or that the current near-disintegration of that sad country has anything to do with his decision to join the invasion? Iraq is now in the throes of an extremely serious insurgency by IS (or ISIS — Islamic State of Iraq and al-Sham). The USA has had to persuade the divisive Shia Prime Minister of Iraq, Nouri al-Malaki, to resign in favour of a more moderate Muslim prepared to share power with the other Arab tribes. The effective and fiercely extremist IS invasion of Iraq from Syria has threatened to occupy the whole of Iraq, and its advance has only been halted by the use of airstrikes mounted by the USA in support of the Kurds. The diabolical beheading of the American journalists James Foley and Steven Sotloff, shown to the world in videos, has shocked the world, but is only one example of their medieval barbarism, as they have killed hundreds of innocent Yasidi Christian civilians in their advance into Northern Iraq. I wonder what Mr Blair thinks, as he counts this year's income, of all these horrendous consequences of his earlier decisions?

My conclusion concerning the severe disconnect between voters and politicians that is now apparent in Britain and other European countries is that people are at last beginning to realise that **representative democracy is a fraud.** It represents only the politicians and their wealthy cronies, who are now, as the governing class has always done, enriching themselves as they wield the power that they believe is their right. Our ignorance of what they are doing and our blind tolerance of their shortcomings, is largely due to the fact that they control the information sources that have deceived us for so long. Ever since 1215, when the barons tried to restrict the power of King John, there has been an everlasting struggle in Britain for liberty, and for control of the Government. Despite the struggles and the millions of deaths of people fighting for liberty, we are only half-way to the goal of 'government of the people, *for* the people, and *by* the people.' **We have a democratic deficit of monumental proportions,** which has allowed our politicians to carry on doing more or less as they wish, because we have misinterpreted the meaning of the word 'representative': a word that has fooled us into thinking that we are in control of our own destiny. **'Representative democracy' is, in fact, elected dictatorship.**

The current Cameron Government, faced with the financial collapse perpetrated by the greedy 'bankers', has carried out an austerity programme which most of us think has been unfairly borne by the poor, whilst the rich have got much richer. The wealth gap between rich and poor has thus continued to widen in Britain, although there is plenty of evidence that the most happy and harmonious countries have the smallest income and wealth gaps. Of course, the 'bankers' (they are more properly called 'opportunistic entrepreneurs'), whose outrageous and avaricious activities caused the financial cataclysm in the first place, escaped with their loot as members of the establishment usually do. When the establishment turns its wrath on convicted criminals amongst the members of its cosy club, it is not for the commission of the latter's crimes but because they are foolish enough to get caught, thus letting down the club.

All these social calamities are the result of political decisions that have been taken against the wishes of the majority of the electorate, who now believe that all the three traditional parties give them no real choices, because they all make promises before elections that they have little intention of carrying out. In addition, scandals in high places, including that of the politicians who have fiddled their expenses, have been brought to light by brave whistle-blowers and investigative journalists, and this has also rightly caused much voter cynicism. Our 'representative' democracy allows the political establishment to do as it pleases, once the small problem of election is out of the way. The corruption, which is now evidently widespread, is mainly hidden because of the fact that many of the establishment groups are scratching each other's backs, and have a mutual interest in sharing the power that enables them to enrich themselves. Lord Acton's aphorism is a well-worn cliché, but nevertheless none is more apt in our modern political system: 'Power corrupts, and absolute power corrupts absolutely.'

The current chronic preoccupation of the Cameron Government, following the May 2014 European election and the rise of Euro-scepticism, is the question of whether enough concessions can be negotiated with the EU, so that the PM can claim that he has been able to repatriate considerable powers back to the British Parliament. He is aware that many native voters are wanting an immediate and drastic reduction of more immigrants entering the country, and that this can only be achieved, if the EU rule of freedom of movement, and the EU Human Rights Act, are not part of British law. David

Cameron has now changed his view about an 'in/out' referendum, which he has promised for 2017. The Conservatives have made it clear (to themselves) that only their party can deliver that referendum. That is not so: if the Conservatives win the general election in May 2015, but without a working majority, they will have to cooperate with a minority party or parties, to form another coalition Government. If UKIP were to gain more than a handful of MPs they might well join a coalition Government on the basis that the referendum must be brought forward as soon as practicable. In other words they may hold the balance of power in another coalition Government.

In any case, Mr Cameron's hope that he will be able to negotiate any meaningful concessions from the EU is most unlikely to succeed, according to the statements being made by the EU unelected establishment. They have made it very clear that Britain cannot remain in the EU on a 'pick-and-mix' basis. They are still wedded to 'ever closer union' which, logically, means a United States of Europe, and that is anathema to many of the native British public. Mr Cameron is hoping that he can achieve a referendum result that will satisfy the British voters but will allow Britain to stay in the EU, which is what most of his big-business backers want. He is between a democratic rock and an elitist hard place. If there were no democratic deficit in the British political system, the choice would be made by the electorate, as should all decisions with serious consequences for the people.

The changing stance of Mr Cameron on the matter of an 'in/out' referendum makes it clear that he and his cronies think that all important decisions should be made by those in power, and that only the fewest possible concessions to public opinion should be made, and then only when an election is in the offing. Not only that, every possible opportunity to further a propaganda message should be used to get the voters to agree with the establishment viewpoint. In the rest of 2014 and in early 2015, there will therefore be a determined effort to win over the electorate to the Conservative view by every means of persuasion at its command, including the usual pre-election items of bribery. Most of the press will be on the side of the Government, so that a proper and balanced debate will not be put before the people. Such a lopsided debate is another example of the democratic deficit: the people can be fooled by a relentless propaganda campaign, especially when the issues are complex and difficult to understand. So far we have heard mostly the mantra: 'millions of jobs will be lost if Britain withdraws from the EU', obviously intended to frighten the people into wanting to stay in the EU. The opposing view – that trade with the EU is declining in importance and we can trade with all the rest of the world, including the Commonwealth countries, is not heard. The BBC Daily Politics show, with its childish graphics and mugs, tends to trivialise most subjects, and seldom invites UKIP spokes-persons, (unless to ridicule them), although it is now the third party in terms of voter support.

It is not likely that Governments in representative democracies, including our own, will therefore use referendums very often, because they see them as unnecessary, and more importantly, as diminishing their power. British politicians always argue that once a Government is elected it is their job to govern, and therefore they have the right to make decisions on behalf of, and sometimes against the wishes of, the majority of the electorate. The MPs, supposedly our representatives, have to obey the party whips rather than their constituents.

This attitude has been clearly demonstrated in the matter of immigration policy, a subject which is of the greatest importance to the native electorate. **It is therefore absolutely astonishing to realise that at no time in the last fifty or so years has any British Government done anything to consult the native people as to whether they are in favour of turning the nation into a so-called 'multicultural society'. This amounts to an unprecedented democratic deficit, and a political scandal of the highest order.**

We now (mid–2014) have the terrifying prospect of some five hundred to one thousand 'British' Muslim jihadists from a barbaric war in Syria and Iraq returning to our country. The difficult task of identifying and coping with this threat falls to our hard-pressed security services, which will need more funds and recruits. These 'home–grown' terrorists will return as *battle-hardened and dehumanised* young men, full of hatred towards our citizens and culture, and ready to terrorise our population. Who, in 1960, could have predicted such an unimaginable cultural calamity being inflicted on our hitherto peaceful, and harmonious society? It is hardly an exaggeration to call the state of our current dysfunctional society *the approach of Armageddon.*

If that is not enough to digest, we know that nothing effective can be done even at this late stage to stop the invasion of more European immigrants and the refugees fleeing from Syria and Iraq, owing to our membership of the European Union. If ever there was a critical need for an immediate referendum then surely the 'in/out' of the EU is it, if this nation and its culture is to be saved from certain, cataclysmic destruction.

We have been *colonised* by massive alien groups from across the world who have been encouraged to invade our Sceptered Isle by self-seeking and cynical politicians with no concern for our culture and our way of life. **In effect we must be the first and only human society deliberately to have committed cultural suicide.** Historical anthropology informs us that human societies have always fiercely resisted territorial invasions unless immediately overwhelmed by superior numbers, and yet we in the Western democracies in general, and in Britain in particular, have supinely allowed our dreadful, self-serving politicians to connive at the destruction of our precious culture. We must at last realise that our representative democracy is 'not fit for purpose' and must be replaced by one designed by the people.

And still we have to endure the constant reiteration by the gloating liberal intelligentsia of the risible mantra: 'Britain is now a multicultural society'. We have to endure looking at foreign faces in the streets and on TV, and at ridiculous foreign garb such as burkas; to put up with hearing foreign languages and accents in shops, and on the telephone; to seeing our towns desecrated with mosques and foreign shops; and to accept being discriminated against in our own country. Britain may be described correctly as 'multicultural', but a society it certainly is not. It is now a collection of ghettoes, many of them full of people who hate us, and who make it clear that their objective is to take over the rest of the country, and to impose their medieval Sharia law on the nation. We cannot blame them for acting out their noxious beliefs, but we can blame the self-seeking establishment for appeasing them, for encouraging them, for discriminating in favour of the immigrants, and for destroying our culture. We can also blame the voters' apathy on the actions of the establishment, especially of the BBC, for repressing opposing views for decades and thus destroying our right to free speech and expression. The 'Bombay Broadcasting Corporation' carries on flooding its daily programmes with black and brown faces in its objective of making us white Britons get used to the 'fact' that *this is no longer our country*. The BBC doesn't 'get it' any more than the politicians, and their propaganda efforts are having the opposite effects to their hopes, and are helping the recruitment of right-wing extremists. The mass of foreign faces on our TV screens, which is presumably intended to get us used to the loss of our culture, has had the opposite effect on me. I doubt if I am alone in the feeling that somehow we have to reverse the colonisation of our country, and take away forever the power from the elitist establishment which has engineered our social catastrophe.

Let us look again at just some of the risible notions put forward as axioms of the propaganda campaign. There was the patronising idea that we need a mixture of all the world's poor to migrate here in order to enrich our culture. The British population did not to my knowledge ever ask for such a cultural enrichment, so who took the arrogant decision to make this monumental mistake? The 'impoverished' British culture in need of this remedial action is the culture of Alfred the Great, the Venerable Bede, Isaac Newton, William Shakespeare, Edward Elgar, the engineering titans who invented the Industrial Revolution, Michael Faraday, Frank Whittle, and the culture which has given the world its railways and the incomparable English language – to mention only a small random selection of the nation's cultural icons and achievements. This idiotic notion of cultural enrichment was surely given its *coup de grace* by the pathetic remark of the late, unlamented, Labour intellectual politician, Robin Cook, when he extolled the virtue of Chicken Tika Masala as a typical example of what immigration was doing to enrich our culture!

We are also frequently told that we cannot manage our affairs without the continuing importation of a large mass of unskilled workers from the third world and Eastern European countries. It cannot have escaped the notice of many natives that we had managed quite well before and after World War II; that we have a large pool of our own unemployed and poorly-skilled workers who should surely have priority for training and employment opportunities; that these 'essential' immigrant workers from the third world had, by comparison with Britain, not made a very good job of managing their own countries; and that they have brought with them many serious criminal problems, many of which are now seeming to be insoluble. Not only that, we know that the motivation of the political establishment and their business cronies is to maintain a stream of labourers who will work hard for low wages. And if and when some of them settle here, they soon aspire to having better-paid jobs, and also bring over their families who are a burden on the national welfare services.

Perhaps the most compelling argument in favour of at least some controlled immigration is the moral one: we should give asylum, as we have always done, to some of those people who are fleeing from genuine persecution in their own countries. The 'open-door' policies of Britain and the USA in response to the Jewish exodus from Nazi Germany in the 1930s is often cited. I do not think that this is a good comparison to the present problems for a number of reasons. The persecution and genocide of the Jews in the 1940s was of almost unprecedented barbarity and cold-blooded determination, and we knew that the victims had nowhere else to hide in conquered Europe, and that no external pressure would have succeeded in halting the Nazi plans. We were one of a few surrounding and nearby countries to which the Jewish refugees could safely flee. In addition they were people who had lived in Europe for a long time and were therefore relatively easily assimilated into our similar culture, especially since the numbers were not overwhelming and the immigration episode was limited to a short and finite period.

By comparison with the above historical immigration episode, persecuted people in modern times, from Asia and Africa, would surely find a more agreeable host culture in neighbouring lands. In fact it seems strange indeed that people in danger of losing their lives in their own country should journey at great expense and mortal danger across the world to another continent, to try to settle into an alien culture rather than into a neighbouring and similar one. Such considerations have unsurprisingly led to the common belief in Britain that most people of other racial and cultural groups ostensibly seeking a safe haven here are in fact 'bogus asylum seekers' or economic migrants, demanding to be given housing and benefits, and experience has not dispelled that belief. Remember the risible statement of David Blunkett, the 'New Labour' Home Secretary: 'Britain is not a soft touch.'?

As far as immigrants from Eastern Europe are concerned, there is probably not much cultural dissonance between most of them and us to make integration a great problem. However, the large numbers (in the hundreds of thousands) entering Britain in a very short time, following the accession of their home countries into the EU, naturally has caused another burden for our public services and more social instability. This is due to the fact that Britain is seen by the economic migrants as a preferred choice compared with many of the other Western European countries, most of which have adopted stricter controls and quotas for entry and have made less favourable benefits available to the newcomers. Unfortunately the Easter European immigrants have included many serious criminals.

We have learned, in June 2014, from the Office of National Statistics, that Britain's population is now the fastest-growing in the EU, and is expected to rise to seventy-four million in the next 25 years. The rise is due to high levels of continuing immigration and an increased birth rate, and it is estimated that it will rise by 10 million by 2038. The pressures on the NHS, housing, schools and transport will obviously increase far beyond the current already unsustainable level. The estimated figures will be larger if, as is certain, people live longer than they do now. Last year the population passed 64 million, and Britain is now the second most populous country in the EU after Germany. Just over half the extra 400,000 rise last year was due to *net* immigration (equal to a city the size of Bristol), and the remainder of the rise was due to the rising fertility rate. The latter factor is also largely due to the immigrants, who are mainly in the key child-bearing age groups. Migration Watch made the obvious comment that this pattern of immigrant population increase is 'unsustainable', whilst Population Matters commented that 'Economic growth does not improve living standards, and we would all be better off with a stable or falling population'.

Unfortunately, and despite the fact that these obvious remarks, and similar ones, have been circulating for decades, the British politicians and the unrealistic liberals ignore this common-sense set of facts and the obvious consequences. Even more unfortunately, now that politicians are aware that the natives are getting very restless indeed, the figures show that they are completely impotent to protect our borders and our country because of the rules of the EU. One might well think that they would change their minds about staying in this utopian failed experiment that controls, to our serious detriment, most of our rules and laws, and opt for a return to full parliamentary sovereignty. But no, they still want us to stay in the EU to achieve their own hidden objectives, but they think that they will be able to extract enough repatriated powers to fool the electorate that all is well.

It is clear (August 2014), that hundreds of thousands of migrants from Africa, Egypt, Syria, Iraq and other troubled areas of the planet, are swarming into Sicily, Southern Italy and other routes, and are overwhelming their services. There is no possibility that these migrants will stay where they land, and they will inevitably move west and north across Europe and many, if not most, will make for Britain. We have to face reality if we wish to hold onto our culture and our way of life, however much we may feel sorry for these people, who are now becoming a modern, human plague (these words will upset the PC brigade, but they seem to be appropriate). I will tackle the subject of morality in a later chapter, because it is important that we make rational decisions and do not let our emotions push us into disastrous policies which, in the end, will benefit no one.

Suffice it to say at this juncture that the democratic deficit is being used by the establishment, as usual, to pursue their own objectives and interests, and the poorer native Britons are sleepwalking into the dire consequences which they alone, as always, will certainly suffer. They are not all blind nor are they all stupid, but their typically British tolerance, and their remaining deference to the authority of the establishment, combined with a relentless propaganda campaign designed to convince them that they are benefiting from mass immigration, have left them powerless, unhappy and demoralised. It is unfortunate that UKIP has taken so long to achieve the status of a credible, alternative, political party, but that delay is not the fault of the UKIP faithful activists. It is due to the near-total control of the media wielded by the establishment which has served to hide the truth. The recent rise of UKIP has panicked the three traditional parties, and they will do everything possible in the period before the next general election in May 2015 to rubbish UKIP policies, and to denigrate and slander the UKIP candidates. Politicians faced with a possible loss of power will use all the dirty tricks they can devise to destroy the threat of their opponents.

Why is this the most likely set of tactics that the three traditional political parties will adopt? Because they wish desperately *to hold onto their power at all costs*. They have done their best over the last few years to ignore the wishes of the electorate, and therefore to squeeze out any new protest party. When they have been unable to ignore a rising new party protesting about mass immigration they have tried to stop its popularity by calling them 'racist', and thus frightening potential supporters. The 'first-past-the-post' system of electing Members of Parliament is *specifically designed* to make it very difficult for new parties to gain a foothold in Parliament, let alone in Government; any new party can get the support of 30% or more of the voters across the country in an election without returning a single MP – another instance of the democratic deficit. First-past-the-post forces a rising new party to have to concentrate on key constituencies where it can develop a strong support, with a chance of winning a seat. This degree of support is only likely if the new party has managed to return a number of local councillors, who can then gain more publicity in their local area. This is helped by the increased publicity given by local newspapers, which are more likely to be free of the control of the national establishment and are eager for local news.

All of these features indicate that the democratic deficit in Britain maintains a powerful set of mechanisms for frustrating the views of ordinary people, and for enabling the traditional political parties to hold onto power whilst apparently defending the flawed system of representative democracy. The inevitable result is that in countries with such political systems, slowly but surely the electorates are losing interest in voting, and a gulf of indifference is arising between the electorates and their political establishments. People are not now detached from politics, as is often said, but, in reality, they are most certainly detached from their politicians. Thus the often-heard statement from the 60% of ordinary people who now do not bother to vote: 'There's no point in voting – they're all the same.' In other words, there is little choice between the traditional parties, who are pursuing their own similar agendas and ignoring the wishes of the people, who suffer the consequences of a deteriorating and dangerous destruction of their culture.

In effect, the democratic deficit is having such a profound effect on our freedom-loving country that it is the main underlying cause of the cultural suicide that is being carried out by our self-serving establishment in the name of the spurious and dangerous 'multicultural society' – an oxymoron if ever there were one.

We have to ask therefore: How is it that so many countries have adopted this dangerous model? The answer is surely obvious: most if not all adopted the 'multicultural' model by *force majeure*. That is to say, by accident, by compulsion exerted by invasion or warfare, or by devious political manipulation, as in the examples above and in Britain. Our 'multicultural society' was begun by an unintended consequence of the decision to import cheap labour for

London Transport, and the process was accelerated by 'New Labour's treacherous policy of encouraging mass, uncontrolled immigration.

One serious aspect of the failure of our politicians to control mass immigration is that Western democracies have *an in-built self-destruct mechanism*. Politicians can set up a train of policies designed to ensure their own survival in power, including a policy of positive discrimination for the invaders which results in an eventual democratic takeover of the host country. That is, if the natives do not realise in time the seriousness of their imminent predicament, and opt instead for some form of overt resistance, such as mass street demonstrations or civil commotion.

Of course, this stark future may be warded off by realistic and timely changes if the current voter apathy is replaced by a realisation that power can be wrested from the three traditional parties, and returned to the people. The first awakening in Britain seems to be occurring, as voters are turning to UKIP, the only party that is determined to exit from the EU as soon as possible. Such an outcome would immediately return parliamentary sovereignty to Britain, and effective control of the nation's borders would then be a priority, so that we can slow the dangerous population increase, and the increasing proportion of foreigners. UKIP holds out the only hope, not only of returning political power to our own Parliament, but of handing it on to the population where it rightly belongs, and thus bringing about a 'velvet revolution'.

Many people will say that this assessment of the present and imminent political situation in Britain and Europe is over-pessimistic, and of course 'racist'. To the constitutional optimists in the establishment – the utopian and religious idealists who will say that we should find a way of living together in peace and harmony, I say again: *Look at the evidence*. Look at the present and past reality. Look at the experience of Northern Ireland, of Yugoslavia, of Israel/Palestine, of Central Africa, of Syria, Afghanistan, Iraq, Ukraine and even America. The era of Western civilisation is under dire threat of coming to a sudden close, as has happened to many other civilisations throughout history. The barbaric and well-organised actions of the Islamic State in Syria and Iraq are surely a signal of the struggles to come in the next few decades, and it appears at this time (August 2014) that the initial responses and reactions of the European and American nations are weak and divided. We are living through a period of history which may turn out to be one of cataclysmic change if the threat of Muslim extremism and imperialism is not met with a united, effective and overwhelming response, in order to maintain and improve on the hard-won victories in the struggle for freedom and true democracy. Above all we must not be complacent and forgetful, and think as we go about our daily lives in comforting neighbourhoods in Britain, that things can go on like this for ever, and that someone else will deal with the problems far away. In today's world the miseries of many suffering peoples will surely be soon visited on us if we do not act vigorously to help them throw off the yoke of barbarism, and the ever-present activities of evil men.

We should remind ourselves that democracy was invented a long time ago in pre-Christian Greece in different circumstances and for different purposes. The original Greek city states were very small communities with a relatively homogeneous racial, cultural and well-informed electorate, depending on disenfranchised slaves for labouring. Their enfranchised citizens voted in a system of Direct Democracy on all important decisions and thus had majority control of their executive Government. Their establishment would have been in close, daily contact with the free citizens. In very recent times, in modern Western democratic nation-states, voting rights have been gradually extended to almost all adults, but voting is for representatives who, once elected, have the right to make all decisions, conforming usually to their party viewpoint. This system amounts to an elected dictatorship of professional politicians who represent only a minority of the electorate, and who use their power to enrich themselves and their financial supporters. They usually do mainly as they wish, largely ignoring the wishes of the electorate, which most of the time they manage to do because they control most of the media, and this allows them to produce the political narrative which confuses and pacifies the bemused voters. This flawed system has a built-in democratic deficit which has enabled the elite to take all day-to-day decisions away from the electorate, and which has resulted in the current disconnect between Government and the governed. We have thus had a so-called 'multicultural society' imposed on us against our wishes, in the manner of a tyranny.

Little thought by our establishment has been given in Western representative democracies to the recent unforeseen circumstances in which our countries have been continuously invaded by alien cultures. In contrast to the Greek city-states, we are in imminent danger of being outvoted by these invaders as their numbers grow rapidly, and thus their power will soon allow them to take over democratically our system of Government. We are already seeing this process in action, in that the Muslims living in large ghettoes are given special privileges, including Sharia law (approved by some of our lawyers!) and faith schools, and are demanding more concessions. Indeed, the process of power transfer, in this case initially hidden, was illustrated in the Trojan Horse scandal in Birmingham schools in 2014.

If you think I am an extremist, pessimist, alarmist or a modern Jeremiah, you may be in danger of wanting to shoot the messenger, rather than facing up to the message. *Try to face reality*. To give a very recent example manipulated elsewhere by the use of a 'democratic' takeover, look at the use of this simple technique used by Vladimir Putin to take control of the Crimea in Ukraine. He previously pulled off a similar takeover in the 2008 war in Georgia, when the Russian military and Russian passport holders occupied and declared the independence of Abkazia and South Ossetia provinces in Georgia. These examples point to the cynicism of dictators such as Putin, whom we ignore at our peril. What did this 'democratic' enthusiast do when the Muslim Chechens wanted independence from the Russian Federation not many moons ago? He sent in the Russian military, and ruthlessly and violently suppressed them as 'terrorists'.

'Independence' movements will soon threaten other Western democracies from within. The problem is that democracies believe in the rule of international law, and their political parties tend to join coalitions of the righteous which are militarily weak and are slow to act, whilst dictators are cynical, ruthless and greedy for more power and territory. The latter also maintain much greater military resources which they are ready to use for threat and for territorial gain. As always, the tyrannical predators are on the prowl for weaker prey. We must be realistic if we are to survive, and we must remember that the price of freedom is eternal vigilance.

Unfortunately, representative democracies are even more disadvantaged in the modern, global, survival-conflict because the self-serving financial greed of the politicians who hold the reins of power means that their top and fundamental priority is not, as it should undoubtedly be, the protection of the state and its citizens. The democratic deficit means that the powerless citizens are at the mercy of the enemies within – the invading immigrants on the one hand, and the cynical politicians that encourage their invasions on the other hand.

The only sensible conclusion we can draw from this sorry scenario is that **representative democracy is a fraud**, and the sooner we get rid of the present system and its political masters, and replace it with a Direct Democracy that mimics that of the ancient Greeks, the much better off we shall all be. The struggle for freedom is still a work in progress and we must complete the job while there is still time. In a Direct Democracy, such as the admired and long-functioning democracy in Switzerland, there is no democratic deficit, because the citizens are the ones who make all the important decisions, and the politicians do as they are told – they are the servants of the people, not the masters.

We must help the disillusioned voters to become more aware of their slavery, as a first step to gaining our freedom, our dignity and political control. If the people of Britain are to re-engage with politics, and they must if they wish to control their own destiny, and protect their priceless culture from extinction, they have to give a resounding 'out' vote in a referendum on EU membership. But first of all we must urgently exert as much pressure as we can on our reluctant political masters by increasing the vote for UKIP in all the elections up to and including the general election in May 2015. This is the only realistic course open to us that will make the politicians realise that the voters mean that 'business as usual' is not an option available to the Government, and that they must bring the referendum forward to 2015.

§

CHAPTER THIRTEEN

MEN AND WOMEN

I EXPECT THAT YOU ARE MILDLY SURPRISED at the title of this chapter, but I think that there is a something important to investigate in relation to this aspect of culture, which paradoxically is so familiar to all of us, but is not really noticed and certainly not much commented upon. We all know that there are psychological differences between the two sexes, and that this can be seen even in very young children. Although some people like to think that the differences in infant play and behaviour are forced upon children by their parents' expectations and treatment, such as the use of pink and blue dress and the different sorts of toys bought for girls and boys, many parents who try to combat these 'prejudices' find that their children still have different play preferences if allowed to choose freely. It is further assumed, by some, that the different behaviours and preferences of the two adult sexes are mainly caused by different, prejudiced expectations and educational experiences. In other words, the two sexes would be turn out to be equal in most respects if treated in the same way from birth.

However, the truth is that males and females are psychologically different from soon after birth, and evolution has hard-wired their brains, and produced different hormonal systems, so that they tend to behave differently. I must hasten to say that I do not think that females are less intelligent than males, nor do I think that they should be deprived of any opportunities or experience, and certainly they should not be paid less than men when doing the same jobs, which is another scandal long overdue for remedy. In fact, I think that in the modern world females are much more adapted to the pressing needs of large-group living than men are. I go so far as to class myself as a radical feminist, and you will learn why further on.

By saying that men and women are psychologically different, I do not mean that the differences are absolute, with a clear separation of traits between the two sexes. In a population there will be, for many psychological traits and behaviours measured on a continuum, an overlap in the middle of perhaps about 10%. In this middle group males and females will have a similar set of traits, and thus be less strongly differentiated from the opposite sex. Beyond this, most adults exhibit fairly clearly different thinking, behaviour and attitudes so, as one psychologist put it: 'Men are from Mars, and women are from Venus.' But not always!

Anyone who gives the slightest attention to the parts played by men and women in the modern world must surely agree with me that men are the root of most evil. The vast majority of crime and violence, including warfare, is carried out by men, who are naturally aggressive, risk-taking and highly competitive. That is not to say that these characteristics are always harmful, and of course, they were evolved under the conditions of small-group living in our ancestral tribes, where survival depended on hunting dangerous animals and fighting neighbouring tribes. Even after civilisation and farming in settled larger groups began, and into modern times, most of these male characteristics were, and still are, useful in many occupations. Nevertheless, men cause most of the seriously harmful problems that bedevil the world, and which show few signs of disappearing. Of course, many men have managed to control their emotional, aggressive tendencies, and behave in a rational and caring way, but it is not as easy as we would like to believe to override our emotions. Many of our decisions, which we think are rationally based, have been shown experimentally to be biased and emotionally driven. In addition to the above male traits, we must not forget (as if we could!) that males, of nearly all ages, have a built-in propensity to want to copulate frequently and promiscuously, often with no concern for their female victims nor for their offspring. It is a common picture on our TV screens to see hundreds of malnourished women in third-world countries surrounded by even more, small, malnourished children - and hardly a man in sight. Can one doubt, that in a heavily overpopulated world, we need somehow to modify the male propensity to rape and to produce children irresponsibly? As I have described earlier, children need fathers to care for them as well as mothers, and, to do this successfully, males must be taught to restrict and control their natural sex drives.

We were told by the BBC in 2007 that in Britain 85,000 women were raped in 2006, which means an average of 230 each day, and most of the aggressors were former or current partners.[27] Yet only eight hundred men, or one in a hundred, were convicted of this distressing crime in that year, and an average of two women were killed each week by former or current partners.[28] Rape is still common in Britain, and in countries like India and Pakistan gang-rape is very common. It is also the case that some women are violent in domestic situations, but, nevertheless, men are more violent and commit more violent acts more frequently than women do. Some women committed barbaric acts in the Nazi concentration camps, but they were in a small minority in a situation organised and controlled by men. Women are now being recruited into front-line combat duties in many armed forces, but I think that this innovation is driven more by the need for enough recruits for our modern, volunteer forces than by the desire of women to take part in the horrors of battle. It is a development which we should all totally regret.

Women also evolved for millions of years in our ancestral, small groups or tribes, and modern women have retained hard-wired brains through the much shorter period from the invention of farming and settlement in large societies. They are just as intelligent

---

27   BBC 1 (12.11.2007).

28   British Crime Survey 2006-2007.

as men, and now are taking up all the opportunities which modern education, commercial enterprises and scientific work are offering. They have shown that they can do most things as well or better than men, excepting those few activities that still require heavy muscle power. They do however, have different psychological tendencies, which are surely much better adapted to modern conditions. Women on average are less aggressive, more risk-averse, more co-operative/compromising and more nurturing – characteristics that had obvious survival value during the evolutionary period of hunter-gathering, when their major role was producing, nurturing and protecting their offspring.

Now some people will say that I am trying to push women back into the home-making role where men think they should be. I hope and believe that I am doing no such thing. However, I do think that modern society, and some feminists, have made a mistake in applying psychological pressure on women in Western democracies to abandon their nurturing role, and to take up 'proper' work outside the home, on the grounds of achieving 'equality' with men. If that view be correct, women are paying a high emotional cost as they fight their natural feelings of wanting to care for their children, or having to delay their pregnancies whilst they compete with men at work. Many of the children are also paying a cost, because they are ferried about from home to paid 'child-care', and do not have their birth-right of constant maternal care in their most important and formative infant years. I cannot help feeling that the pressure on women to go out to work is based not on what is good for mothers, infants and society, but on the need of commerce for (cheaper) wage-slaves, just as the armed forces need more volunteer soldiers in combat roles, and just as women were recruited into the factories and agriculture during WWII.

Of course I may be wrong in thinking that I am putting forward a rational argument when maybe I'm driven by some emotional aspect of my personality. That possibility is of little relevance to my argument, because rightly, individual women will do as they wish, given the opportunities. My expectation here, however, is that any hostile contrary comment about my views will be made by middle and upper-class women, who form the bulk of the vocal feminist movement, and are obsessed with their 'glass ceilings', and who seem to have little awareness of the situations in which poorer women live. It is one thing to be able to achieve professional success in the commercial market place after having a university education, and then to enjoy the privilege of being able to employ a house-maid to do the domestic work, and a nanny to look after the infants and children. It is quite another to bring up several infants whilst having to live on benefits, or doing menial and poorly-paid work, and the shopping and housework as well. And all that with no partner, or a very unsatisfactory one, for many 'single mothers'. Our society has a very poor record of recognising the plight of poor mothers (and fathers) and their dire need for help with child-care. It is not therefore surprising that there are many 'troubled' families, much child and domestic abuse, and lots of delinquent children.

However, I have strayed a little from my main thesis, which is that modern society needs men to be educated and trained to adopt female psychological traits, instead of the present opposite trend to pressurise women to adopt the undesirable traits and behaviours of men. The opposite trend is clearly motivated and driven by the needs of commerce, manufacturing and the armed forces. Those enterprises are the beneficiaries of this trend, whilst children, mothers and society pay the price. I cannot help thinking that the slow progress in giving working women the same pay as men for the same work is due to the fact that the beneficiaries not only need recruits, but *cheap* labour.

My view that men should be trained to adopt some female psychological traits, as opposed to the prevalent opposite trend, is based on the fact that our large, modern communities need to control and eliminate aggression and violence whilst concentrating on compromise, cooperation and nurturing. We know from long-established ethological studies that animals of many species are very aggressive towards their conspecifics when their territory is invaded.[29] We are animals, and indeed show many of the same behaviours as other animals. One only has to experience one's own feelings when sitting in a motorway traffic jam or when 'cut-up' in slow-moving traffic by some impatient driver, to realise that one feels much calmer when one has plenty of space to oneself. The modern phenomenon of 'road rage' is due mainly to the frustrations of our crowded roads, coupled with male psychological traits. Young men have the highest motor accident rates and fatalities. Our cities are also overcrowded, and the majority of people now live in large cities where aggression and violence are common problems for both citizens and the police. City dwellers are more prone to drug and alcohol abuse, which are more likely among people stressed by overcrowding and pressurised working practices. We therefore need to be able to control male aggression, competitiveness and risk-taking, so that these traits are exhibited only when useful to society, or when taking part in leisure activities such as sport, regulated by formal rules.

If female traits were highly valued and practised by men, we would have more cooperative and nurturing behaviour and less violence and warfare. If all our politicians were women they would not be dreaming of national honour in battle and looking for the next opportunity for another war, as some of our male politicians do, (when in a tight spot politically there is nothing like a war to unite the nation, and give the national leader prestige, as every politician knows). What mother would want to send her sons to war? A few perhaps, but not very many in any civilised country.

---

29   Lorenz, Konrad, (1966) pp.27-30.

Many objectors will say that Margaret Thatcher and Golda Meir were both considered to be 'iron ladies', and were more aggressive than men, but, of course, they were working in the competitive world of male politics and had to be more aggressive than their male colleagues in order to succeed.

In addition to the need of children for maternal (and paternal) care, the elderly constitute a large and growing group of our population that require physical and emotional care of a much higher standard than is currently available to most of our citizens. The current arrangements of the publically-financed elderly-care-system are a national scandal amounting to the bare minimum of physical care, and often to neglect and abuse. Standards should be equivalent to those of the best private-sector residential homes, many of which have very high standards. Elderly people should not be cared for by a largely foreign staff, nor should their social, intellectual and emotional needs be neglected. The carers should be adequately paid to attract well-motivated recruits, carefully selected, trained and qualified, and of both sexes. It would be worth trying to hand over the service to private-service providers with a good track record, such as some currently operating in the private sector. Most of the care of the elderly should not be isolated from society and other age groups, and many of their activities should be in public places and involve frequent contacts with various volunteers.

I have earlier in this book accused unrealistic liberals of utopian dreams and of not facing reality, and yet I am here suggesting what may seem to be an unrealistic programme aimed at bringing about a fundamental change in human behaviour. But the social reality (and cultural change) that I am trying to address is the one which stares us in the face – namely the frightening amount of aggression, abuse and neglect in the world in which we live, both domestic, national and global. It is surely obvious that, as British, European and world populations rise inexorably, we shall have more conflicts for resources and more warfare in the continuing struggle for survival.

Most of the modern world's problems are caused by men, whose Darwinian-evolved brains have left them with dangerous, aggressive tendencies, and an irresponsible compulsion to produce an excess of offspring. Unfortunately we are pressurising women to act like men, at a time when civilised life in large conurbations and global overpopulation require the nurturing and compromising psychological traits inherited by women. We therefore need women to be more in control of political, commercial and family power, and for men to learn their social sensitivities and behaviours from women. We have had male domination for at least several millions of years, since before our ancestors came down from the trees in Africa, and the world is not yet in a stable state for civilised living. Any scientist doing an experiment in human sociology would surely think that enough data has been collected over that period, and that it was now time to do the opposite experiment and try a few million years of female domination, to see whether the same result would occur, or, as seems likely, a much better outcome. My bet is that it would not need many decades of female domination before the data would indicate a considerable improvement in the form of much-diminished violence, aggression and warfare. Of course, if that experiment quickly showed this expected outcome, and if males were being trained in childhood to adopt female psychological traits, conditions could then be relaxed and a more equal division of power allowed.

Men commit most of the crime that infests our communities, and indulge in violent behaviour towards women and children, as well as to other men. The gang leaders are usually men, who will turn their skills and efforts to any foul criminal activity that will bring in easy money. Gang rape is common in many Muslim countries where, in any case, women are still dominated totally as chattels belonging to their husbands. And we should not forget that rape and child abuse is common in Britain and all countries, although much of it is still covered up by the powerful establishments. Of course, women can be criminal and violent, but in general, women are more conciliatory, more compromising and more risk-averse even in these modern times, when they are being encouraged to take up violent sports such as boxing. What wonderful cultural progress we are making, when some women are now being encouraged to punch another woman's head and brain in a so-called sport that should be discouraged for all of us!

Most of the so-called 'bankers' who caused the financial collapse that has impoverished the rest of our innocent citizens were men. What is more worrying is that they got off scot-free, when they all should be serving long prison sentences. Presumably they have been protected by other men in our establishment. One of the most unfortunate developments in recent years is the introduction of women into the armed forces, originally to do logistical and medical work in order to 'free men for the fighting'. Inevitably this change moved quickly to the current 'progress' towards equality, so that women are now able to train for frontline combat. It seems clear to me that the reason for this move is not to award women with the equality of opportunities that they deserve, but is a cynical solution to the shortage of recruits in our now volunteer forces.

Of course male characteristics such as risk-taking can be useful, for example in the police and rescue forces and in deep-sea fishing. But risk-taking, in male motorists for another example, which one can observe every day on the roads, and which is backed up by the accident and insurance statistics, is taking an unnecessary toll of deaths and injuries. Women are far better drivers than men from the point of view of reducing road accidents which, after all, are not really accidents, but the consequence of bad driving and risk-taking. Some will say that in politics the women leaders are no different from the men, or are even worse than the men, but that is not a valid argument because the women leaders were operating in a man's world, and had to be more aggressive and competitive than the men in order to reach the top spot. Golda Meir was described as the 'Iron Lady' in Israel long before Margaret Thatcher earned that epithet (from the Russians!).

So our societies would surely benefit hugely if we were to work rapidly towards a situation where women were in the *majority* of positions of leadership, in politics, commerce and all other areas of collective organisation, so that their natural psychological traits would become the dominant force for the vital changes that we need for modern urban living. In education it is important that more men should be teaching at primary levels to provide role models – but in female-led schools. At secondary level more women should be prominent as heads of departments and headships. Sport is the civilised outlet for male aggression, carefully channelled under a system of rules which encourage fair play, as recommended decades ago by Konrad Lorentz in his book: 'On Aggression'.[30] We are fortunate in Britain in that the legacy of the London Olympic Games of 2012 has stimulated a strong interest in sport.

The capitalist economic system has served us well in overcoming the need for constant, hard, physical labour, and to provide us with basic necessities, at least for some of the world's population. It has been highly successful in producing food, shelter, technological and manufactured goods, but it is now also producing harmful side-effects which threaten our very existence, such as climate change and overpopulation. It has been woefully unsuccessful in spreading its benefits fairly across the globe, or even amongst the citizens within the most developed nations. In fact, recently it has been widening the gap between the haves and the have-nots, as technology and

---

30   Lorenz, Konrad, (1966), pp.241-243.

automation carries on eliminating labouring jobs and even many professional jobs. It is now making a diminishing contribution to human happiness, which requires more time for relaxation, and for people to choose their own preferred activities, both physical and social. The relentless pressure to acquire money and goods has become a harmful obsession, and we all need a more balanced life-style, and the time and opportunity to achieve it. Politics should also start taking account of the obvious fact that the obsession with constant economic growth is unsustainable. Unfortunately this obsession is fuelled by the male striving for power, and is not likely to change while men are predominant in powerful positions.

Now is the time for radical solutions to be tried, in an effort to stem the growing tide of horrendous extremist violence, civil and cultural wars, and to maintain and spread the benefits of real democracy. The replacement of male domination and its aggressive habits with the natural traits, behaviours and attitudes of women is long overdue. The objectives and practices of capitalism must be modified, to take account of the pressing modern need for more compassion and humanistic concern for the suffering victims of male aggression, and of the global need for economic stability to replace unsustainable economic growth. Runaway capitalism is producing more wealth for fewer people, at a time when we need to spread the wealth amongst the people both inside countries and between countries. These fundamental changes will not occur whilst males dominate politics, Government and commerce. Women of the world unite!

§

CHAPTER FOURTEEN

LEADERS

IT IS ACCEPTED BY ALMOST EVERYONE that all organisations need leaders, otherwise nothing would get done, at least not what people would want done in their name and interest. It seems obvious, that without leadership in our crowded world, chaos would reign and evil would triumph. If communities of like-minded normal people did not appoint leaders to organise and execute agreed policies for the benefit of us all, then despots and criminals would soon take over and organise for their own evil benefit. Indeed even in our hugely complex nations and states, the criminals are better organised, and usually many steps ahead of the police and the legal systems. We therefore need strong leaders in order to make the complicated decisions required in our very large and complicated communities. It seems clear to us all that nation-states need the leaders that we call 'politicians', to organise and control the multifarious activities that such states must have. Even pack animals, such as our ancestors the apes, and our greatly valued companions the dogs and their ancestors the wolves, needed leaders to organise the packs in order to succeed in carrying out their hunting survival activities.

Despite this need for leaders in complex communities both small and huge, there are obvious problems that leaders tend to produce. Leaders, both animal and human, expect, by virtue of their important role, to be given preferential treatment when it comes to sharing out the spoils. Leaders, or top dogs (alpha males), expect to get the best of everything, and often have little concern for the weaker members of the pack. Human societies, nevertheless, have slowly developed over evolutionary time empathy for their weaker members, probably as an extension of the necessary nurturing feelings for infants, children and the elderly. That extension seems to have been weaker for the elderly, for the obvious reason that they would have been seen as less valuable contributors to survival activities, and, in tribal communities, the elderly may well have been a definite and unsustainable burden in times of hardship. Nevertheless, the elderly were valued in the past for their knowledge and wisdom, but in our modern societies with rapid technological changes requiring new skills, the elderly are losing their traditional place in society. In addition, the increased longevity of most people and their burden of health problems is producing a crisis in the state-organised care services that are replacing traditional family care.

In modern societies, the problem of leaders is getting out of control; they want not only reasonable preferential treatment, but expect *ex-cathedra rights to a very unreasonable share of their community's wealth.* The problem has been tackled by various rules intended to limit their power. Thus most organisations have formal, written rules that define the duties, and limit the powers of politicians at national level, CEOs of companies, and even the chairmen of small clubs. At the lower level, where the chairmen (and other officers) are unpaid volunteers, the problem is usually one of finding effective and willing people to do the job. At CEO level, and even more so at politician level, the problem is that the rules limiting power and rewards are very often broken or subverted in various ways, owing to the strong temptations of having access to large sums of money, and to the natural greed of talented and powerful people. This problem is a serious one in representative democracies, but worse in despotic Governments and in other hierarchical organisations such as religions. It is noteworthy that the high priests, in some religions, minister to the poor but live in palaces. The Pope has one of the world's largest congregations of mainly poor people yet lives in one of the world's richest palaces – the Vatican. When do you think we shall see a female Pope?

In Chapter Two we tried to understand why it is that humans seem to be born with brains that are hard-wired to believe in, and worship, supernatural beings or gods. We came to the conclusion that this inbuilt 'programme' or 'app' has evolved over millions of years as a survival trait, that ensures that tribal members follow their leaders and worship their dead leaders, in order that the essential survival skills were handed on, and to explain the chance workings, mysteries and hazards of their world. Leaders and dead leaders thus were a positive and necessary part of successful tribal organisation. The example of ancient Egypt, in which the Pharaohs became gods, and thus bolstered their earthly power, seems to support this conclusion. We are still stuck with similar brains, and the tendency to worship gods and leaders lives on, despite there being no scientific evidence to support the idea of supernatural beings influencing life on earth. For my money, if I had to choose a supernatural being, I would revert to my childish belief in Father Christmas, who brought me toys each year and only required me to be good for a few weeks before delivery.

I'm sure that most British voters today will agree that, even in Western democracies like Britain, our leaders fail us, because the constitutional controls on their use of power are feeble and totally inadequate. That is hardly surprising, because the leaders make the rules themselves. Gerrymandering is not a crime, almost certainly because the main traditional parties practice it when they can get away with it. The CEOs and chairmen of the banks have recently caused a monumental financial crisis that has hurt the poorest in our society to a grossly inequitable degree, whilst the crooks have got off scot-free. The politicians have been discovered to be fiddling their expenses, and most of them are corrupt, and enrich themselves at our expense. They do not represent us, but themselves and their backers.

My contention is that the time has come to consider carefully *our over-reliance on leaders,* who tend to be untrustworthy, devious and self-serving. We must develop a healthy scepticism of the statements and promises politicians routinely make, especially just before elections. We must also develop much more robust control of their decisions and actions, and ensure that we still have a free press that can investigate any suspected wrong-doing. During the recent debate after the phone-hacking scandal at the News of the World, and the following Levenson Report (November 2012), there was a fierce struggle between the press and the Government regarding legal curbs on the press and their methods of investigation. It remains to be seen whether the balance of power is now set at a reasonable level. *We must have a free press* because it alone, in many cases, has been able to uncover serious wrong-doing in high places.

Leaders are by nature competitive, aggressive, confrontational and power-hungry – and usually male. The larger the organisation that needs a leader the more likely it is that competition for the role will be fierce and ruthless, even if superficially the candidate may be suave, charming and highly educated. This is particularly the case in politics, where no holds are barred, and where there is usually no shortage of competitors. Power is the ultimate aphrodisiac, and wealth is the currency of male sexual attraction in our modern world, as it was in ancient cultures. If we look at historical leaders such as the pharaohs of ancient Egypt, we see the incredible wealth and power that was the prerogative of the leader/god. When looking at the pyramids – the magnificent burial tombs of the Pharaohs, intended to assist their passage to the after-life as a god – we have to marvel at the immense amount of labour that the leader could monopolise in order to maintain his power status. Over the last few thousands of years, ordinary people have had to struggle towards their freedom from domination by tyrannical leaders and we are not yet free. We shall not gain our freedom until we realise that we can manage *without leaders*, or at least without leaders who do not accept the primacy of the ordinary people who create the nation's wealth. We have to realise that leaders will appropriate as much wealth as they can whilst in power, and that the rules we presently have to circumscribe their power in our 'representative' democracies are 'not fit for purpose'. Even if we have the luck to have elected a leader who has only the selfless motivation to serve the people, he is likely to become corrupted by all the self-serving politicians around him. It is difficult to stand out from ones' colleagues and their values, and very easy to become corrupted.

The British electorate has now distanced itself from the politics of its leaders, as a result of the voters' perceived impotence to control the politicians who ignore the electorate's needs, wishes and hopes. But the recent Scottish Referendum has surely pointed the solution to this problem of the democratic deficit. The Scottish electorate has been electrified and the referendum turn-out was 84.6%, - the highest turnout in any British election. This wonderful example of the solution to the politicians' puzzlement over how to engage the electorate, has confirmed for me the fact that people are engaged in politics *when their votes are meaningful* and they know that the result will be their choice, and that the resulting action is mandatory. This example of the power of the referendum must not be forgotten nor allowed to lapse as a freak event.

We should now embrace the political system of Direct Democracy perfected over some 160 years by the Swiss. This system has the overwhelming advantage that *all important decisions are made by the electorate,* and their politicians have to carry out the wishes of the people. It is noteworthy that the Swiss have not been engaged in any wars for some five hundred years, have a policy of strict neutrality, have not joined the Euro, have their own strong currency and are prosperous. It is not surprising that very few people in Britain have ever heard of this political system, because our politicians are the last people who wish to advertise its merits, because they naturally want to hold onto the present system that has served their interests so well. But the genie of the referendum is now out of the political bottle, and we must ensure that it is not put back – in politics there must be no more 'business as usual.'

§

CHAPTER FIFTEEN

The Elephant in the Room

THE CONSENT OF THE PEOPLE is taken for granted in our Western representative democracies, and the politicians will rue the day when that consent has finally ebbed away. The platitudinous slogans that they have continued to utter since the May 2014 elections indicate that they have not yet come to terms with 'the elephant in the room', namely that the citizens are beginning to realise that a political revolution is necessary. Power is seldom given up voluntarily, and the people must rouse themselves out of their current despondent apathy, and take political power into their own hands. The 'great and the good' have been discovered to be frauds, thieves and corrupters. How are the mighty fallen!

For the members of the British ruling class, the recent but continuing drip-feed of bad news about their immoral activities, and their abuse of power, constitutes a calamitous fall from grace. From the point of view of the electorate however, these discoveries amount to an epiphany – a revelation of the truth. This epiphany may well lead to a healthier and more open society. The politicians frequently refer to 'the need for transparency', and love to precede their sentences with 'I want to make it perfectly clear that...' We now know that these platitudes usually constitute political code for 'lies'.

The most important conclusion of this investigation is that all the misery that has been heaped upon the natives of Britain in the last few decades has been caused by the political establishment acting without the electorate's consent. We have been comprehensively duped by an elitist cabal, and, in the process, we are having our precious culture destroyed. Therefore essential and urgent actions have to be taken in order to stop, and then reverse, our cultural decline.

The task of establishing a true democracy will certainly be difficult, for a number of reasons: too many voters are now ignoring politics because they have become apathetic, and feel that they have no influence on public affairs; the 'first-past-the-post' system of electing MPs makes it very difficult for any new party to gain seats in Parliament, even when it is backed by about 30% of the votes across the nation, as in the case of UKIP. First-past-the-post means that any new party must start by gaining local council seats in areas of maximum support, build up a local group of activists to campaign for more support, and then target the local parliamentary seat. All of this with the other essential task of building up a large amount of cash to fund the huge election-campaign expenses. The three traditional parties that the new party must oppose are long-established and well-funded. A formidable extra difficulty is that publicity, which is essential to get across the new party's messages, is often mainly in the hands of the traditional parties. They have long-standing relationships with the newspaper editors, and, in particular, with the radio and TV media moguls who control the amount and content of most media coverage.

It has been noticeable that the BBC practically ignored UKIP since the May 2014 EU elections, and up to the successful by-election result in Clacton – despite UKIP being ahead of the Lib-Dems in most election results and polls. It will therefore be a formidable task for UKIP to make further progress in terms of what will matter in the May 2015 national elections, namely breaking into Parliament with more than a handful of MPs. If this new party nevertheless manages to do this, despite the obstacles, we have the exciting possibility that there may be a hung Parliament, presumably with a Conservative victory but having no overall majority, which is necessary for an effective legislative programme. UKIP could then join in a coalition with the Conservatives on the understanding that an immediate 'in/out' referendum be held, to obtain the consent of the electorate to stay in the EU, or to leave at once. Such a scenario would, I'm sure, be popular with the public who are now very Eurosceptic, and who wish to have control of their own laws once again, and, in particular, of their own borders and thus their own immigration policy. I also feel sure that once the public use a referendum, with a mandatory command to the Government, they will be in favour of extending the use of this democratic weapon, and thus slowly edge towards the Swiss style of Direct Democracy.

If all these possible momentous changes come to pass, and the electorate act to curb the power of their political masters at the next general election, the process of renewal of our nation can begin. If not, British civilisation will be doomed, and cultural suicide will soon be completed.

§

CHAPTER SIXTEEN

CONCLUSIONS

THE IMPORTANCE OF CULTURE cannot be denied. Its importance however is often overlooked in stable societies, because we grow up in our family culture, and it becomes part of the social world that we take for granted, just as we take gravity for granted in the physical world, although both have to be learned in infancy. Most humans prefer to live amongst people who are like themselves in appearance, behaviour, language, history, religion and basic values, that is, who share the same racial origins, socio-economic class and culture. This psychological trait has arisen because it has survival value; we feel safer amongst people whom we can instantly trust.

In Chapter Two the contribution of religion in most cultures was explored. This contribution arises partly because we seem to have brains fashioned by Darwinian evolution to be hard-wired to worship ancestors, and to need an explanation for the great uncertainties of life and death. In addition, as culture became more complex in larger societies, religions had a great influence in the adoption of moral codes of conduct, and have also helped to provide comforting social rituals and pastoral care. The rise of a scientific explanation for so many of the unknowns previously 'explained' by the supernatural God, or gods, of early civilisations has led, along with the rise of marvellous technological progress, to a decline in religious belief in the West. Unfortunately those cultures that are based firmly on religious faith have proved historically that this has been a mixed blessing. Those adherents having a strong conviction that theirs is the only true faith, and that the religions of different faiths are wrong, often indulge in conflict and warfare with other religion-based cultures. Sadly for modern British natives, who had reached the point in 1960 where most of the population had no or very little religious faith and were living in a harmonious, relatively homogeneous, secular society, we have now become colonised by masses of immigrants who are strongly devoted to various medieval religions and their alien practices.

Human societies value highly their traditional, personal, family, tribal and national territory, especially if it has been held over a long period of time. Thus invasion of personal and family privacy is liable to arouse hostility and conflict. Invasion of tribal and national territory is usually also fiercely resisted, and, even in our somewhat enlightened times when we expect nations to obey international law, most countries still have to maintain military forces ready to ensure that they can protect their citizens and territory from other predatory groups.

Social class is not usually mentioned when culture is being discussed, but it clearly illustrates many of the features of the wider cultures of societies. Although many political commentators think that social class is now not important, it is obvious that there is still a wide gulf between people of different social classes, based on very different upbringing, education and wealth. Indeed, the traditional political parties are supported largely by voters of different socio-economic classes, and their policies reflect their supporters' interests. The middle-class may well have expanded greatly since the industrial revolution, but the rich upper classes and the poor lower classes are still miles apart in terms of wealth, education and life opportunities. The wealth gap between rich and poor in Britain has widened in recent decades, and this wide gap not only seems to be extremely unfair, but also produces social disharmony and even poorer health across *all* social classes. A degree of equality is better for everyone.[31]

Politicians usually talk in terms of mutually-exclusive categories, and seldom think or debate in terms of numbers. In the case of

---

31   Wilkinson, Richard & Pickett, Kate (2010).

a cultural threat from immigrants bent on settling in a strange country, the relative numbers are crucial to the outcome. Small numbers of strangers from other cultures are usually perceived by most people as non-threatening to the host culture, at least initially, and until they are demonstrably a real threat. Just as we travel to other countries for study, holidays, business or sporting events, we welcome foreign visitors, but expect them to return to their own country after experiencing our culture. When an influx of foreigners bent on settling into a previously stable community is seen by the host natives to be massive, uninvited, illegal, out of control and organised by criminal gangs, then the host population becomes quickly very hostile, whether the governing body is concerned or not. The increase of immigrant numbers in Britain and Europe is also being fuelled by their higher birth rate over that of their native hosts, because the immigrants have bigger families, and their age group is initially, largely in the peak years of fertility. This fact is also alarming to the natives because it will, by itself, result in an increasing proportion of foreigners to natives.

Britain is overpopulated already, and the sudden rise of the population is causing severe strains on all public services. It is not only Britain that is suffering from this population increase; overpopulation is now an urgent problem for the whole planet, and little or no awareness of this horrendous problem is being shown by many politicians and businessmen, who are more preoccupied with short-term affairs, especially with economic growth. The latter obsession seems to stem from an intense desire for personal enrichment, for which end population growth is a relatively quick route, but this comes at the expense of a declining standard of living for the poorest in society who suffer the inevitable consequences of the increase in overcrowding.

The social changes that have occurred in Britain in the last six decades as a result of continuing mass immigration have been monumental, rapid and corrosive. Most of our large cities are now occupied partly by obviously alien peoples, who live parallel lives in ghettoes that border on being 'no-go' areas for our police forces, as well as for the natives. London, according to the BBC, is not our capital city any longer, but an 'international city', in which native Britons are now in a minority. Not unnaturally, the people who have been displaced from the towns and neighbourhoods now occupied by foreigners, especially the poorest native citizens, greatly resent the unimaginable changes that have been forced upon them. Whole communities, which were stable over many decades and generations, have been displaced and destroyed.

Change and stability are two opposing features of all complex organisations, and must be carefully balanced for success. The changes in Britain's social fabric over the last six decades have been far too rapid. The native culture has been destabilised, public services heavily overloaded, and long-established communities have been destroyed. The actions of the guilty politicians have gone unpunished, and the people have stopped voting in large numbers, which threatens our democratic way of life. Far from these changes succeeding in making us more tolerant of foreigners, they have convinced a lot of hitherto-welcoming Britons that we need to be free of most of the foreigners and their destructive influence on our hitherto-stable culture.

One of the social changes that has caused the most hostility and destruction of our culture, is the horrendous crime epidemic that arrived with the immigrants. The Afro-Caribbeans brought with them a violent, machete-, gun- and drug-riddled culture; the Muslims brought their medieval religion with its domination of women, forced child marriage, gang rape, female genital mutilation, its jihadist terrorists, Sharia law, and a mind-set which desires to dominate the whole world; the Eastern Europeans have brought manifold criminal enterprises organised by gangs. All of this has caused Britons untold misery and enormous expenditure on policing, prisons and the undreamt of ubiquitous security measures required to try to control this epidemic. We now live in a police and criminal state, with a constant fear of crime and terrorist atrocities.

Cultural diversity is the utopian, social-engineering objective of many of the liberal intelligentsia, who think that we should all live together in a wonderfully harmonious earthly paradise, wherein different racial, religious and cultural characteristics will all be equally desirable. Unfortunately, this phantasy picture of the 'multicultural society' lacks both historical and contemporary hard evidence. Indeed, surprisingly, many of the worst and most protracted conflicts seem to arise amongst close cultural groups, such as the various Christian sects (Protestants and Catholics), and Muslims (Sunni and Sharia), to say nothing of the history of the recent, horrendously brutal wars between European nations. Muslim immigrants are a particular, severe and continuing threat to our culture, because of their large incoming numbers, their higher birth rate, and their religious belief that they are fighting a holy war against infidels. They *intend to take over the host countries in Europe and the world*. We have already experienced horrendous terrorist acts carried out by young, Muslim men in Britain, most of them 'home-grown', and more atrocities are undoubtedly being planned. It is noteworthy that many of the activists for 'multiculturalism' are people who seem to have lax morals, whilst being in favour of equal respect for all cultures and codes of conduct, including of course their own. They are constantly attacking our moral code for their own ends, because they wish to portray their own immoral behaviour as alternative life-styles of equal value with the traditional ones. One thing stands out from the views of the proponents of the 'multicultural society': *they are so elitist* that they think the rest of us should have no choice in this important matter of culture. In other words we must submit to their social-engineering experiment whether we want it or not. Those of us who can remember the relatively peaceful, harmonious, and mainly mono-cultural society in which we lived before WWII do not wish to embrace their phantasy dream world, because we can easily draw the unfortunate comparison between now and then. The realistic model of 'multiculturalism', in the sense of preserving the world's different cultures, is surely for most cultures to occupy the different territories in which they arose, such as those of Japan and Iceland - or even Britain before WW II. Britain now is more like a human zoo than a society. It is not surprising that we have a crime epidemic, nor that the favourite strategy of the 'liberals' to deal with it, is to decriminalise as many criminal activities as possible. We thus seem to be in the end-state of imperial decline, when cultural suicide is being engineered by a powerful, destructive and immoral cabal.

The intensive and prolonged propaganda campaign carried out by British Governments and the BBC rapidly suppressed free speech, and protests about the mass immigrant invasions. This campaign was originally based on the 'political correctness' movement, but was rapidly used by our politicians and their cronies to inhibit any real debate regarding immigration. Protestors were humiliated by the media pundits, and abused as 'racists', and all opposing viewpoints were rapidly shut down as a result. Many people became very angry at the loss of their hard-won freedom of expression, and the politicians consequentially lost touch with public opinion. In the meantime, the BBC, in particular, carefully selected and managed the so-called 'debates' that were broadcast on TV, and showed immigrants in news clips as often as possible in a positive light. The frequently-repeated mantras, such as 'Britain is a multicultural society now', tried to convince the public that this objective of the liberals was a wonderful social change. and is already irreversible.

Many words have several meanings, and in the TV so-called debates about immigration, no one ever bothered at the beginning to define any of the words in the propositions or questions being discussed. Thus confusion reigned, and many participants were angry with their opponents on the basis of the inevitable misunderstandings. Language is used for communication, but such is the tyranny of undefined words that public-broadcast debates were more like arguments between aggressive opponents spoiling for a fight, than the rational discussion of different viewpoints of equal validity. As a result, to this day there has not been in Britain a carefully argued debate, about the benefits and costs of the continuing and uncontrolled immigration of millions of foreigners into our small island. Even now, when the effects of mass immigration are at last being tentatively aired, there is still not true freedom of expression.

The political establishment has pursued its own agenda, as it always has done, of enriching itself and its cronies, with little concern for the consequences of its policies on its citizens, especially the poorer ones. The three traditional British political parties are very similar, in that they all think they have a near-divine right to rule; they are all elitist; they all support the 'first-past-the-post' election system which has the effect of making it very difficult for newer parties from getting a foothold in Parliament; and when in power they all pursue policies which are aimed at pleasing their supporters and financial backers, rather than the majority of the electorate. The political establishment is supported by most of the media, especially by the BBC, which has acted as its propaganda machine, by the lawyers, the liberal intelligentsia and by other opinion-formers. There has recently been a steady disenchantment of the electorate with the politicians, due to the expenses and sexual abuse scandals, corruption in high places, and to the fact that the voters are now more aware that their concerns over the continuing mass immigration and its consequences are still being ignored by their political masters.

The most scandalous, outrageous and previously unimaginable behaviour of the recent 'New Labour' Government has been the encouragement of the mass immigration which threatens to destroy our culture and our nation, without the slightest attempt to consult the electorate. This example of a democratic deficit has resulted in the *colonisation* of our country, and amounts to what is probably the first act of deliberate *cultural suicide* in the history of mankind. Not only has the electorate not been allowed to express their opinion on this momentous social change, they have been bullied into submission by a fierce and relentless propaganda campaign. The voters are now so used to the fact that they have had no say in this important matter that over 60% of them no longer think it worthwhile to turn out to vote at elections. Representative democracy is therefore now viewed by the voters as being *fraudulent*, but the politicians are carrying on as usual, despite being aware that they have lost touch completely with the nation's citizens. The three traditional political parties still say that we need more immigrants, although they are aware that our public services are heavily overloaded. They apparently cannot see the blindingly obvious connection between the increasing population and the pressure on all our public services. We should be *reducing* the population, and then most of the urgent problems would be much easier to solve - as well as saving our beautiful countryside and its wildlife from further destruction.

Overpopulation and climate change represent some of the most profound problems that the human race is likely to have to face in the next few decades. Politicians do not seem to be addressing these problems effectively because they are always preoccupied with local and short-term issues. Overpopulation is already causing severe problems with public services in Britain, and the continuing mass immigration, and the high birth rate of young immigrants, is going to make this situation beyond remedy unless effective control of our borders is soon established.

Males are the cause of most violence, crime and warfare, and their long-standing domination in human affairs should be replaced by female domination, which can be expected to reduce conflict, and to promote compromise and negotiation as a more civilised method of settling disputes of all kinds. Men and women have different psychological traits. Male aggression needs to be replaced by female nurturing, compromise and empathetic concern as the predominant civilised human interaction.

Muslims in Britain, Europe, the Middle East and other parts of the world are involved in what amounts to a well-organised holy war or 'jihad' against the Western democracies and their religions, and the extremists amongst them are trying to establish a new Muslim Caliphate. They are making much initial progress in Iraq and Syria by acting barbarically, and thus causing a wave of terror that allows them quickly to take new territory. The Western democracies appear to lack a firm resolve to stop this enterprise, with the possibility of us having to experience many decades or more of very barbaric conflicts, and to witness the spread of terrorism to Middle Eastern countries, Northern Africa, Europe and to America. Britain will not be excused, and if the young, British Muslim extremists who have taken part in the jihad organised by IS return to this country, we shall have more terrorist acts in our communities. We have to face the unpleasant reality that we are now involved in a *global religious and cultural war* that is going to be the major conflict of the 21st Century.

The current attempt by the American-led coalition of Western and Arab countries to repel and contain the barbaric 'Islamic State' operating in Iraq and Syria is likely to last for decades or more. This localised, barbaric war is preoccupying the US-led coalition, but in reality, it is just one small part of the global conflict. The difficulties that the coalition is having in making any progress are a warning sign that the Western democracies, which now have little appetite for more wars, are losing the fight with the Muslims, who are using very effective terror tactics. Not only are they taking territory, they are causing huge humanitarian crises that the Western and surrounding countries have to try to alleviate. The overall picture seems to indicate that the Muslims will win unless a global effort is made soon, to defeat them whenever and wherever they are operating.

Britain is likely to have severe problems in dealing with many of the estimated five hundred British jihadists who are involved in this barbaric enterprise, when they attempt to return to Britain. Some of these 'home-grown' terrorists have already threatened to take part in bomb incidents when they return to our country. We have clearly replaced, over the last fifty years or so, our hitherto-harmonious monoculture with a typically fractured and fault-ridden 'multiculture', as a result of the devious and self-serving actions of our political establishment. Unfortunately, multicultural countries are gravely weakened when it comes to having to defend themselves against any aggressive and warlike external cultural groups, because of the enemies within. The so-called benefits of diversity are about to morph into the grave problems of internal strife.

It is clear from the actions of our politicians and their establishment cronies that 'representative democracy' is not for purpose. We therefore need to replace it with a true democracy, in which the people make all the important decisions by referendums that the politicians are obliged to execute. The example of Direct Democracy, as long-established in Switzerland, should be adopted as soon as possible, and the first practical step to that objective, which will be fiercely resisted by our politicians, should be an increased support for UKIP, and an early referendum on withdrawing from the EU.

§

CHAPTER SEVENTEEN

THE GREAT PROJECT

WE NEED AT THE OUTSET TO BE VERY CLEAR what our objectives are, before we decide on the necessary strategy to achieve them. The fundamental change that many of us natives want is to return to the Britain of civilised behaviour, and to a gentle, polite, caring and relatively *homogeneous culture*. If any reader is not acquainted with that culture, I recommend again that he or she reads the picture painted in Bill Bryson's book: *Notes From A Small Island*.[10] His description is of Britain in the 1970s, not so very long ago, but what must seem to a young or middle-aged, modern, British city-dweller like some sort of phantasy. The impression that one gets from reading his account is of a stable, calm society at peace with itself. Of course, the same picture might easily be thought to portray a dull, slow, stuck-in-the-mud community, completely out of touch with all the exciting technological and cosmopolitan social changes going on in the developed, go-ahead countries – but those in favour of a more dynamic and fast-changing world sometimes mistake change for progress.

British culture is a product of the collective wisdom of generations of natives, by which I mean the descendants of people of mainly-European stock who have occupied these islands for many hundreds of years. Naturally they think, as do most peoples the world over, that their territory belongs to them by virtue of a shared long occupation, hard toil, a common history, and a culture that has arisen spontaneously, and is the means by which the peoples are welded together like an extended family. Culture, as we have seen, is the social glue that enables the community to live in harmony based on trust, and to enjoy life with many opportunities, and relatively little fear, suspicion or conflict. Of course, there are differences of belief that are tolerated, problems that are easily managed by negotiation, or, if need be, settled under the common law, and there are regional eccentricities that provide interest and local pride.

Our major objective should be to restore our culture to suit our native community, and to eliminate most of the serious problems that have been recently visited upon us. We must not shirk from unpleasant decisions, just because we are used to being tolerant and easy-going. As the old proverb has it: 'One can't make an omelette without breaking eggs.' Although the political establishment led by Tony Blair in effect encouraged the mass invasions of immigrants, and subsequent politicians, utopian liberals and the BBC suppressed opposition to these invasions, we must acknowledge that the British public quickly accepted their loss of free speech and expression and failed to protest with vigour. I cannot really understand how it was that the nation that fought two horrendous wars to keep our island free of foreign domination, and to uphold the values of democracy, succumbed so easily to a propaganda campaign that used verbal abuse and public humiliation to silence protest, and thus allowed our culture to be threatened with destruction by foreigners. Untold harm has been caused by public servants being afraid of being called 'racist', and no doubt the currently exposed examples represent the tip of a very big iceberg.

So another important objective is to *restore free speech* and other forms of expression. There is no need to cause gratuitous offence to anyone, and indeed such actions are not helpful to this or any cause. We must all start to give voice to our views without feeling guilty or being called 'racist'. No doubt many people will express their feelings of 'offence'. We are talking about the ordinary natural behaviour of *expressing our preferences*, which is common to most humans, regardless of racial origin, religion or culture.

I am probably at one extreme of the spectrum of preference for one's own people. I am quite happy to see and interact with individual foreigners, and I certainly do not want to hurt anybody. I consider myself to be a realistic liberal, but not in any circumstances to be a utopian liberal, who thinks that all people are the same, and that everyone is entitled to act as they wish. I am fed up with looking at foreign faces on TV in my own country. It turns me off the programmes, and I now often visit other channels, such as the English Al Jazeera one, because at least their programmes are more detailed, and seem to be less biased than much of the childish rubbish and propaganda on the BBC. I spent most of my life with no feelings of antipathy towards foreigners, but the recent influx of so many immigrants from alien cultures, the horrendous crime epidemic, the positive-discrimination policies, and the ridiculous and relentless propaganda in favour of multiculturalism, have now caused me to dislike them *en masse, but not as individuals*.

We are not only too tolerant of foreigners and immigrants, we are now being governed by them in increasing numbers, and this trend will continue unless policies are changed. Some lawyers are proposing that Sharia law should be recognised for Muslims; halal butchering is allowed to appease the Muslims, and the banks give special mortgages to Muslims. Mosques despoil most of our towns, but the natives did not vote for the jarring spectacle of these foreign religious buildings.

Our political establishment must be punished by the new 'People's Army', whose duty it surely is to *do away with 'political representatives'* once and for all time. They are indeed 'all the same', in the important sense that they all usually ignore the views of the voters. We need to embrace Direct Democracy, and take all the important decisions ourselves, starting with the one in May 2015, when we have the opportunity to send an unmistakeable message to the three traditional parties, that we want a velvet revolution which will put power where it belongs – in the hands of the people.

The 'first-past-the-post' current system of electing MPs is a formidable obstacle, designed as it was by the governing class to prevent new political parties from gaining a foothold in our Parliament. The fact that only about 30% of the electorate is now bothering to vote means that we have to concentrate on wooing the demoralised non-voting section of the population. If only a third of this alienated 70% group can be persuaded that their vote will count, it seems likely that we could have a hung Parliament, with probably the Conservatives winning the most votes but having no working majority again, and therefore having to turn to another party to join in a coalition. For a suitable coalition partner they would not contemplate the Labour party, and it is highly likely that the Liberal Democrats will be wiped out. The Greens and others will probably not have enough MPs to form a realistic partnership. That scenario would then give an opportunity to UKIP, which is likely to be the party with the most numerous minority group of MPs as alternative coalition partners, if it can improve on its results at the last MEP elections.

UKIP made spectacular gains in the 2014 European and Local Authority elections as a result of their main objective of an early departure from the European Union. A large proportion of the native electorate is now firmly Eurosceptic, due to a late but increasing awareness of the great loss of British Parliamentary power that has been the cause of our failure to control immigration, and even to deal quickly and effectively with dangerous foreign terrorists and criminals. It is tragic that we have allowed our Governments over the last few decades to shackle themselves with laws and rules formulated outside our territory by unelected professional bureaucrats in Brussels, all in the name of 'free trade' and 'ever closer union'.

It is true that UKIP will have an uphill task to gain enough MPs in 2015 to be the only realistic coalition partner, because the BBC and most newspapers are still doing their best to rubbish UKIP and its policies, and to give it no positive or impartial publicity. In addition, as a new and rising party, it does not have the financial resources of the other parties, although it is attracting more members and donations from some wealthy backers. I therefore hope that sympathetic readers will join the party as paying members, and become the new activists to be the foot soldiers needed to do all the hard work of canvassing and leafleting. This opportunity of causing a velvet revolution in British politics must not be missed.

Most readers will probably not have heard of Direct Democracy, and the reason for that lamentable ignorance is that the establishment, including all the political commentators, pundits and politicians, seldom mention it. I hope that many of my readers will at least make an effort to acquaint themselves with this remarkable alternative form of democracy, which the Swiss have been practicing for about 160 years! The quickest and easiest way of learning all about direct democracy is to get online with Wikipedia.[32]

At this point, it may be that those readers who have learnt about Direct Democracy will balk at the thought of voting on referendums maybe ten or so times each year. But this potential deterrent is maintained because we still have *an archaic system of voting*. Anybody who watches TV game-shows, and even current-affairs programmes, will know that the presenters often ask viewers to vote on various topics, and the results are given within minutes. Why are we still travelling to our local schools for elections, using voting papers stuffed into boxes which are then transported to halls where they are put into piles and counted? Some will argue that an electronic system would be open to fraud, but that probably goes on now with the paper system, and it is surely possible to devise an electronic system at least as secure as the paper one. After all, most of us are using electronic banking, and many well-off citizens complete their self-assessment tax returns securely. It seems highly likely that an electronic election voting system would be cheaper

---

32   Wikipedia: Direct Democracy, 2.2 Switzerland, 3. Democratic
        Reform Trilemma, 4. Electronic Direct Democracy.

to manage, and it might well bring back a lot of the present non-voters, who could vote at home, and thus improve the validity of the results. A healthy democracy must have an active and engaged electorate, and therefore surely needs voting rates in at least the 60% to 70% range. The example of the referendum for Scottish independence, indicates without a doubt that voters are galvanised to vote when they realise that their votes are going to count, and that *they* are in control of their country's future, not the politicians.

The first major step to regaining control of our own country is therefore to vote for UKIP in May 2015 in large numbers, especially in the marginal constituencies that UKIP must and will target, in order to get enough MPs to make it the only realistic contender for becoming a coalition partner. Of course, every opportunity in the meantime to elect UKIP county and local councillors, and to recruit new members, must be taken in order to build up a momentum amongst the electorate. Local newspapers are usually more likely to give the party publicity than national ones which are dominated by the traditional parties (apart from the Daily Express, which supports UKIP). Activists and ordinary members should write letters to their local papers, to counter the dirty tricks of the other parties and to inform the public of UKIP policies.

One lie that is often peddled by UKIP's opponents, especially the Trades Union Congress and the Confederation of British Industry, is that 'three million jobs will be lost if we leave the EU'. This is total nonsense, because exports to other countries and the EU are based on commercial decisions, not political ones. Our products being exported to EU countries now are ones that have been chosen because they are better or cheaper than the competition, and that will not change. Of course, our imports from the EU likewise will continue to flow. The EU is in recession and our trade with the EU has been in slow decline for years. Britain exports more to other parts of the world and this trend will also continue. UKIP will encourage trade with the rest of the world, and especially to the Commonwealth countries as we used to do. Trade agreements between us and the EU can just as easily be forged as those between the EU and other expanding world markets, such as China, India and South America. Britain's overseas trade does not depend on the whims of the bureaucrats in Brussels, but on the demand of consumers across the globe for the products that we produce and they prefer.

We should also face down the slur of 'racism', which is freely used as a dirty trick by the other parties, who use this as a term of *abuse* and never explain what they mean by the word or its noun/adjective 'racist'. UKIP has a strict policy of demanding that new members sign up to declare that they have not previously been a member of a racist political party. Of course, it is possible that some people will lie and slip through the net, but they will sooner or later be found out and rejected. The opposition claim that UKIP is a 'racist' party because it states openly that it is *against mass immigration,* and wants to have a points system for foreigners wanting to settle in the UK - like the one operated by Australia. I hope that no one is fooled by the use of this abusive language from people who think that they alone have the right to rule. The British public is at last beginning to realise that we must be in control of our own borders, as we used to be before we joined the undemocratic European Union. UKIP is not against immigration or foreigners, but has the common-sense policy of wanting to control the numbers, and the sorts of people that are likely to benefit Britain. Why should anyone think that this is not what any country would do? Do you allow all and sundry to enter your home? Of course not. Does that make you a racist? Of course not. Then if, as is likely, you also value your neighbourhood, region and country, why should you not have a say about who is allowed into your long-held territory? Do you want to see your neighbourhood turned into a colony of Pakistanis or Poles just because a devious cabal of businessmen and liberal intellectuals have decided undemocratically to encourage mass immigration for their own benefit? Of course not. Why do I think that I know how my native compatriots feel about these horrendous incursions into our territory, towns and neighbourhoods? Because I see with my own eyes that the natives move out as soon as the invaders move in. We are indeed being colonised, and as the process continues, we shall lose all power and ability to control our country. And of course, the poorest Britons will be left in small, powerless ghettoes, living like the Aboriginals in Australia and the Native Americans in the United States, whilst the wealthy Britons, including the intellectuals who have engineered this cultural suicide, live in London mansions or have left the country to enjoy their wealthy lifestyle abroad. To go on allowing an unlimited number of foreigners to enter the country and settle here, is a recipe for cultural disaster, and there is only one reason that Britain has allowed such a disastrous policy: *because it benefits the establishment* who have encouraged it. Go and look at Brixton, Ealing, Bradford, Great Yarmouth, Rotherham or parts of Birmingham, and see if you notice, amongst the squalor, the foreign shops and the women dressed in black burkas, any wealthily-dressed intellectuals enjoying the diversity. And ask yourself, where have all the natives gone? Many with enough money have already left the country, and the poor natives have been displaced into the periphery of the towns in squalid ghettoes. If we can only galvanise the apathetic, poor, working-class into voting for UKIP, we can still save the situation from getting worse by the day, and begin to reclaim our native territory. A referendum on 'in/out' of the EU would almost certainly electrify the voters in the same way as happened in the Scottish referendum.

Assuming that in time, hopefully in 2015, we manage to leave the EU and thus once more govern our own country, as do the Swiss and the Norwegians, we can start to do what the native population wants. We will be able to control our borders, select which people we wish to admit for settlement, and protect our citizens and our culture. One of the greatest improvements of Direct Democracy (DD) over the current so-called representative form, is that voting is for *individual policies,* and not for TV personalities. Particular policies are therefore debated responsibly before people vote in a referendum, the result of which is mandatory. In other words, the Government must legislate according to the result. The media organisations are therefore encouraged to debate issues in great detail, and the voters become much better informed. They are also much more likely to vote and to be engaged in the political debates, because they realise that their votes really count. Another important benefit of DD is that *it does not split the nation into two oppositional groups* of 'left' and 'right', but unites it by what seems, to most people, to be a fairer system in which they can have influence on all important issues. They can not only veto Government proposals for new laws, they can also campaign for their *own* laws through the 'popular initiative' via a petition for a referendum.

Britain is heavily overcrowded (if you assume that people need wonderful countryside for leisure activities, for wild life habitats, and for more agricultural land) so we will need a *population control policy* as a major objective. The first priority should be to stabilise the current number, which was just over sixty-three million at the last census in 2011, and then do everything possible to reduce the population to something like the 1939 figure of about forty-eight million. This is a difficult problem to tackle, but that is no reason to avoid tackling it. The current size of the British population is unsustainable if we want to protect the countryside, the wildlife, and relieve the enormous pressures on all our public services. There is more to life than getting richer (especially when the wealth is so unfairly distributed). *We all need space* to avoid the queues, the traffic jams, the pollution, the tower blocks and more urban sprawl into the Green Belt, and we need the parklands and hills for leisure enjoyment, and the farmlands that could make us more self-sufficient in food production. In fact, we need much less obsessive emphasis on growing the economy (which is an unsustainable objective) and more on increasing and improving leisure time with our families. Our politicians are often saying 'we need more housing' (or roads, railways, airport runways, schools, nurses, doctors, midwives, etc), but never 'we need fewer people', which would solve all the other problems and give us all a much better standard of living.

Why do the politicians always want *more* of everything? Because that is the easy way for their big-business cronies to get rich quickly. Although the capitalists make much of the benefits of competition, in practice they would sooner eliminate all the competition, and have lots more customers, including by the quickest and easiest method of letting in the immigrants. The thing that the population want more of is surely *space and leisure time* and a reduction of overcrowding of all our public services. No, I'm not a 'xenophobe' and I don't hate foreigners. I just want *a much smaller number of them and a lot fewer criminals* – numbers matter. Even the prisons would be heavily overcrowded if the Criminal Injustice System was not letting so many criminals off with just a caution and an apology.

We therefore need a *very strict policy* for new settlers, like the one in Australia, so that we only allow entry to new applicants with the exceptional skills that we need. Skilled specialists can be hired from abroad on time-limited contracts, as is done in the rich Arab countries. We should train almost all our own doctors, nurses, engineers, and scientists, just as we always did in the past. But we need to do much more than that if we are to reduce the population. We will need to reduce the birth rate, and to encourage late newcomers to return to their original homes. The state should stop rewarding all our citizens for having children. Yes, that means no state benefits for having children. If that means that many couples with both partners working cannot afford child care, so be it. They will have to do what we always did in the past: either choosing to have no children, or mother (or father) staying at home until the children are in school, or both parents going to work if they can afford child care. This is obviously a tough policy, and no doubt would be unpopular with many people, but it was like this before benefits were introduced, and before mothers were pressured to take up work. It could be argued that we might have a bonus for this policy in that we might have fewer delinquent children and less antisocial behaviour. More children would be cherished and loved, and would have more parental attention, which is a far better way of bringing up children, especially in their first few years, than buying them loads of toys and electronic gizmos and paying for child-care because the parents have little time for looking after their own children .

So perhaps you think I'm a backward-looking male chauvinist pig? I don't mind that, and you are entitled to have your own opinion. All I know is that we have a very difficult set of problems with no one appearing to want to solve them. Building more houses, more roads and railroads, more runways and, above all, constantly being obsessed with growing the economy is not part of the solution but *a large part of the cause of the problems*. Unfortunately, we wage-slaves are trapped in a mind-set that the politicians have created with their propaganda in order to succeed in enriching themselves. We must create a better world based on *more equality of income and wealth*, and a concentration on co-operative living and helping each other. Have you ever wondered why we bring up our children in a family culture that is basically Communist ('To each according to his needs, and from each according to his ability'), and then teach them, as they mature into adults, that they have to fight for a living in a highly competitive capitalist world, where some succeed in getting exceedingly wealthy by stealing from the masses who live in poverty and misery? What a strange world we live in, where we all accept the old cliché, 'the poor are always with us', despite the fact that we live in a rich country. We should ask instead: *'Why are the greedy rich always with us?'* The reason for this apparent conundrum is that the rich people with the power *need* the poor, indeed they *create* them; the churches accumulate wealth which they get mainly from the poor; the left-wing political parties (including the so-called Communists in Russia and North Korea, and the Labour Party in Britain) need the poor to provide them with their wealth and power; and the Conservative Party needs the poor as wage-slaves working in their capitalist economy. We should be totally ashamed that, over the past few decades, the wealth gap between the rich and the poor in Britain and between countries, has got much, much bigger. The statistical measurements and comparisons are complicated, but *a few figures give an alarming insight*: the eighty-five wealthiest people in the world have total assets equal to the combined wealth of the poorest 50% of the world's population (or 3.5 billion people!). The three richest people in the world own more than the combined assets of the poorest forty-eight nations![33] Wow! How can these levels of economic inequality be justified? And whatever happened to the capitalist 'trickle-down' theory? The wealth flood is definitely going in the opposite direction. The increasing income and wealth gaps seem to indicate that this weasel phrase would be more accurately replaced by the 'squirt-up' theory.

The solution to the long-running conundrum of the 'poor being always with us' despite the increased wealth being produced, is not to try again the failed Communist system, which, in practice, is just another fraudulent way of convincing the masses that their masters are working for the common good. We should continue encouraging entrepreneurs whose ideas, determination, organisational skills and hard work have been the basic driving force for our modern capitalist world, but keep a reasonable control of the income and wealth inequality gaps. My view is that a CEO should be content with a total income of about twelve times that of the lowest paid of his

---

33   Wikipedia: Economic Inequality: Notes 1, 2, 3: Extent: Notes 17, 18, 19.

workers. If the lowest paid worker gets £15,000 per annum, why should he not be satisfied with £180,000? If he is greedy for more, he should have to pay his workers at the bottom more to increase his own pay, and that would surely be a better and more equitable system. We would also have a happier and better motivated workforce if most large enterprises gave workers a financial stake in the firm, as some already do. The Government could encourage these schemes through the business tax regime. This is not a pipe dream: there is plenty of evidence that such arrangements lead to better working relationships, better productivity and happier societies.[34] The obstacle is, as always, that the people in power are never going to give up their power voluntarily, so we have to take it away from them.

To tackle poverty we need to *reduce inequality of both income and wealth*. In the Nordic countries the income–inequality–gap is less than half of that in Britain, although their GDP *per capita* is greater than ours; so reducing the share of the richest would not appear to damage the economy, as the wealthy claim. In Denmark and the Netherlands the richest 1% of the population take 6% of total incomes, whilst in Britain 13% is taken by the richest 1%. It is not surprising that the economy benefits from the workers at the bottom of the pay scale receiving a bigger share, because they are the ones who will spend most of their money on daily necessities, whereas those at the top will either hoard most of their ill-gotten gains or spend them abroad. The Government should also tax the wealthiest progressively, so that we can increase the incomes of the poorest people. It would obviously be better if this attempt to close the economic inequality-gap were to be coordinated across all the world's countries, because heavier taxes in one country would only drive the mega-wealthy to flee with their wealth to other countries that would entice them. Another tactic could be to exempt from tax all wealthy donations to any of a list of good

---

34   Wilkinson, Richard & Pickett, Kate (2010).

causes, so that the wealthy can have the kudos and self-satisfaction of being benefactors. We also need a massive and prolonged campaign *to shame* greedy, mega-wealthy people. Someone in America was quoted as saying: 'When I had forty-two billion dollars I was no happier than when I had forty billion'. There would seem to be a law of diminishing returns operating here, and I imagine that, if anyone pursues the acquisition of wealth for a lifetime, it just becomes a useless and evil habit.

To get the population down, we must take drastic action. We do not need any more poor immigrants. The members of the CBI and the Conservatives have benefited from this source of cheap labour that has had the effect of keeping wages down, so that many low-waged workers have to receive additional welfare benefits. There is also, of course, an unfortunate social cost, which is the high unemployment rate largely of our own young people who then have to live on benefits. Thus the costs of unskilled and unemployed labour are shifted from big-business to the state, that is, onto the tax-payers. So, if and when we leave the EU, we should immediately stop the immigration of unskilled workers. But we need to go further, and that means persuading those immigrants already settled here *to return home.*

I suggest that we should start by offering a repatriation allowance of something like £10,000 per adult, and £3,000 per child for returnees during an offer period of about three years. Returnees should have their passports revoked, and their fingerprints and DNA identity recorded, so that they cannot return to Britain. I think that some enterprising people would take up such an offer which would allow them to start a business back amongst their compatriots. I have often wondered why immigrants who have benefitted from the training and skills which they have acquired in Britain do not seem to feel that they should return to their country of origin in order to help that country to develop. Perhaps we are too generous and tolerant, so that we allow selfish immigrants to settle here, who prefer to live in Britain rather than help their own people. They would surely feel happier amongst people in their own culture.

An interesting suggestion to help prevent children being born to poor mothers with mental health problems, or drug and alcohol addiction, has been made by Helen Rumbelow in an article in *The Times* of 14th June 2014. Some of these unfortunate women have had eleven to fourteen children taken into care. The cost of fostering each child is about £30,000 per annum, and the cost of an adoption procedure about £35,000, and this can take two years. So each of these children can cost about £100,000 till adopted. The emotional cost to the mother alone, having repetitive pregnancies, and after the births, having the children taken away from her in the inevitable, Court care-proceedings, is incalculable. This innovative suggestion to reduce all this suffering and cost, is to pay the mother a monthly stipend for having one of the safe, reversible and long-acting (three to five years) contraceptive implants, in the hope and expectation that the mother will be able, with support and therapy, to break out of the vicious circle of repetitive pregnancies, and turn her life around. In the present context, this sort of arrangement may make only a small contribution to reduction of the national birth rate, but should surely be tried because it has the additional potential for helping a group of sad and long-suffering women. The scheme could perhaps be extended to some immigrant mothers. It has the advantage of being voluntary, and giving mothers the control of their reproductive system so that they can better plan their life, as many Western women now do.

Another measure, which is long overdue is, for us to be *much tougher on immigrant criminals,* and indeed, on all professional criminals. I suggest that any immigrant who is convicted of a crime, no matter how trivial, in the first twenty years of settlement in Britain, should be deported along with his family. We are entitled to make our own laws, and the horrendous crime epidemic calls out for stern measures. We have had to submit to the laws of the EU and their version of human rights, which has been far too liberal. Surely the law-abiding natives have rights to a life of freedom from the noxious and destructive activities of foreign, criminal gangsters. The EU laws have over-ruled our own laws and we have stuck to the letter of those laws, unlike other European countries that often cherry-pick in practice the ones that suit them. A good example is the rule about asylum-seekers being accepted in the first country in which they land. The notorious Sangatte camp in France, which encouraged immigrants to travel to Britain through the Channel tunnel, is a well-known example of European countries ignoring that rule at our expense. The process of immigrant invasion into Britain has also been encouraged by our 'human-rights' lawyers, whose efforts have so often defeated Home Office attempts to deport even the worst terrorists. We need, by means of these suggested tactics, to make it clear to potential immigrant settlers that Britain has changed from being a benefits paradise, to being a very unwelcoming country which is overpopulated. Every effort to deter more immigrants, to persuade those already here to return to their land of origin, and every innovative idea that might contribute to the reduction of the birth-rate should be tried.

By these and other measures the population tide can be turned and British culture repaired and revitalised. I don't pretend to have all the answers and everyone should have their suggestions heard. All we need is the *political will* to reclaim our own way of life. Hopefully UKIP and its rising influence will push the other parties into taking strong measures to reduce the population, and to stop the suicidal takeover of our culture. When this part of the Great Project has shown that it can be effective, it will enable us to restore our real liberal values, which would be easily done once the community is rid of foreign domination, and infestation with foreign, criminal gangs. Difficult problems require tough and effective actions to solve them.

The crime epidemic is out of control, although to see the official statistics one would think that crime is falling and of no real importance. We all know how statistics can be falsified, and that if any organisation's top management presses down hard on its employees to produce unrealistic targets, the first thing that happens is that the figures get massaged. The police can be seen nightly on the popular reality TV programmes dealing with many serious criminals in car and helicopter chases that must cost a great deal of money, and yet the convicted criminals get off lightly and are soon free to carry on their nefarious trades. Many are bailed and then 'disappear'. There can be no doubt that if a criminal carries on offending despite being caught and punished frequently, then there is something wrong with the system that is supposed to be preventing crime. The lawyers say that the best deterrence is the certainty of being caught, but that is only half the solution: being convicted must be accompanied by a penalty that can be seen to be effective. I would recommend readers interested in crime and punishment to read a well-researched book published in 2007 by an experienced probation officer, David Fraser: *A Land Fit For Criminals*.[35] It has been largely ignored by our 'Criminal Injustice' system, with dire results. It must surely be the case that the British system of justice is comprehensively flawed, when serious crimes are so often repeated by the criminals. If they receive mild penalties they clearly view these as just an expense of their trade. Effective deterrence of serious crimes requires severe punishment. The police do their job of catching the criminals and the ' Criminal Injustice' system just undermines their work. I watched a TV programme (01.09.2014) showing police catching several criminals coursing deer with a vehicle and dogs at night. The police had several cars with armed officers on the ground and a helicopter tracking the vehicles below. The criminals were

---

35   Fraser, David, (2007).

convicted on several counts, including causing cruelty to animals. They were given short prison sentences of a few weeks, *suspended* for about a year, with small fines. So this successful police action, probably costing tens of thousands of pounds, was clearly useless from a deterrent point of view. Another TV programme: *Armed and Dangerous: Caught on Camera* (25.09.2014) stated that there are an estimated eight thousand gangs of professional criminals operating in Britain at a cost to the economy of £1 million every day! We were shown armed gangs crashing cars into jewellery shops, criminals on motor cycles snatching mobile phones and bags from unsuspecting pedestrians on pavements, and drug dealers openly plying their trade – activities common in some areas of London. It was noticeable that most of the criminals were black or brown men. The penalties handed down to the convicted criminals were clearly not going to deter them from carrying on their trades.

The Home Office needs a *radical overhaul* because it has failed, over several decades, to control our borders. The Ministry of Justice needs the same treatment, because it also has failed to tackle effectively its main task of protecting the public from criminals. It should have two strategies for this task, namely a thorough programme of education and after-care support aimed at stopping youth offenders from taking up a criminal career, and *much heavier* prison sentences for the small proportion of serious professional criminals. The sentencing policy laid down by Parliament needs to be much tougher, so that these recidivists are at least taken off the streets for ten years or so, with parole being allowed only after 90% of the sentence has been served. And if ten years does not produce much better results, fifteen years should be tried. Tougher sentences would send a clear message to others thinking of taking up a career of crime, and thus act as a real deterrent. Community sentences should also be toughened, and these should be accompanied by a certain prison sentence for non-compliance.

The cautions which are now being given to so many offenders should be used only for the most trivial crimes, and second offences should automatically be punished by the Courts. All offences against women and children should be taken seriously by the police and the Crown Prosecution Service. Antisocial behaviour should not be tolerated, and firm action taken against offenders, as this form of crime afflicts people who are underprivileged in the main, and makes their lives a misery.

The police service needs to be less elitist, and to take more care of the problems of the poor and vulnerable. A comprehensive inquiry into drug abuse and its criminal aspects should be undertaken, with thorough research into the various ways in which other countries are dealing with this important problem. In general a 'zero tolerance' policy should be maintained in most areas of police work.

If hardened criminals had been given ten-year prison sentences, with no parole until nine years had been served, they would at least be unable to repeat the crime for that period, and I doubt they would want to repeat their crimes on discharge. In addition, such sentences would deter others from committing the same offences. The primary duty of Governments is to protect their citizens, and for decades, our Governments have failed to do so. Unfortunately it appears that our politicians are more determined to cut the costs of providing the required number of prison places than to cut down the serious crime rate. The man in the street wants the criminals taken off the streets, and doesn't care much whether they get wonderful, educational and rehabilitative programmes or not. Personally, I think that they should, but they should have to work hard, as so many law-abiding people have to, and earn their keep. Short prison sentences are not effective because there is not enough time for educational programmes to be able to produce any beneficial results. Community sentences should be severe also, and prison should follow if these are avoided by the convicted criminal. People charged with serious offences should not be given bail, because many such offenders disappear before trial. And young offenders should be targeted with effective remedial programmes, as soon as they begin their criminal careers, in an effort to head them off before they become repeat offenders.

A disturbing aspect of the 'Criminal Injustice' System is the matter of falsification of the crime statistics. H.M. Inspectorate of Constabularies revealed that an internal report in 2012-2013 concluded: 'Wiltshire Police have intentionally or inadvertently manipulated the recording of sex offences, and thereby improved the perception of performance.' The report estimated that the number of rapes not recorded was about fifty in that year, and that about thirty serious sex offences had been dealt with by 'community resolution orders' (apologising!), including rape and sexual activity with a child. *Mail Online* (26.09.2014) revealed, from Freedom of Information inquiries in the previous month, that people arrested for suspicion of rape, child rape, creating child pornography, child abduction, and sexually abusing a mentally ill patient, had escaped prosecution by just apologising. In thirty police forces across England and Wales 'resolution orders' were used in the cases of thirty rapes, including twenty-one against children, and seventy-five for sexually assaulting young children. In all, 284 cases of sexual assaults were dealt with by just 'apologising'.

Now most of us know, I hope, that managers under pressure to achieve unrealistic targets will, of course, manipulate the statistics, in other words cheat. But the above stories suggest a worse possibility than that – namely, that there must be a suspicion of paedophiles operating at senior level in some of our police forces to allow people to get off scot-free with sexual abuse of children, as well as with serious sexual assaults on women. Even if that suspicion turns out to be wrong, at the very least the statistics reveal a very lax approach to so-called criminal justice. How many more reports like the Jay Report on the Rotherham scandal must we collect before child and female victims of serious, sexual assaults are given any form of justice? There is something very wrong indeed with the state of

Britain. Slowly but surely our relatively fair, gentle and harmonious culture is being throttled from above. Our political establishment is beyond the pale, and our so-called representative democracy needs to be replaced so that the will of the citizens is sovereign.

The current Cameron Government is trying to modify the benefits system so that immigrants cannot demand, as they still do, immediate housing and access to our free public services. Immigrants should have to work and pay income tax for at least five years before having the rights to any free public services. I also think that British citizenship should not be offered until the applicant has worked and paid tax for ten years. Criminals who are deported should have their passports revoked and their fingerprints and DNA identity recorded, so that they cannot return through our border controls, as many currently do several times.

In a 'multicultural society' there will always be fault-lines between all the major cultural groups, as is clearly seen in Britain in 2014. Major differences of opinion, behaviour, moral codes and racial identity will be sources of conflict from time to time, despite periods of apparent harmony. Mutual suspicions are easily aroused, and feelings of unfairness and discrimination are all too often felt on both sides of a dispute. We had a perfect example of this in Birmingham, where the so-called 'Operation Trojan Horse' episode erupted in June 2014 over the attempt of militant Muslims to take over control of several state-funded schools, and to pursue an aggressive and organised campaign of Islamisation. After a damning report by an OFSTED investigation, several Muslim governors were dismissed and replaced by new people. Whatever were the rights and wrongs of this strongly-disputed matter, the importance from a cultural point of view is that *bad feelings were aroused on both sides*, and the deep suspicions that surfaced will undoubtedly persist in the local communities. It cannot be denied that many problems have been caused by the Muslims in Britain since they arrived here, many exceedingly serious, and the terrorist threat from the fundamentalists amongst them presents the police and security services with a large and very expensive continuing operation, which looks likely to have to be maintained for decades. We should therefore stop all appeasement and positive discrimination tactics, and make it crystal clear that any attempts from the Muslims, or any immigrants, to demand special advantages will be turned down. They must obey British law *or leave the country*, and all convicted criminals and their families should be deported. Personally I am now so averse to any Muslim immigrants settling in Britain that I would do everything possible to get them all to leave our country, short of compulsion. Many of them have no intention of integrating into our culture, and indeed, wish to take-over our country and turn it into an Islamic state. We need to let them know unmistakeably that this is not *their* country, it is Britain, and they must conform to all our laws and customs or leave. If English people work or settle in Saudi Arabia they have to abide by their customs and laws, and we should do the same here. Offence is not the unique privilege of our invading immigrants, and I want them to know that *the natives' offence is greater than theirs*. They have come here without the invitation of the natives, and many have caused great offence by their provocative behaviour and all their cultural obscenities. If this opinion invites the starry-eyed liberals to call me 'racist' I shall take that as a compliment, as I have always done when anyone stoops to the use of abuse. I class myself as a 'Ghandi racist': Mahatma Ghandi was, I'm sure, a hero of the liberals when he campaigned for the British to leave India, and I want no more for my country than he did for his. It is one of the social paradoxes of this century that, soon after all the colonised peoples of the British Empire won their freedom from being dominated by the British, they started leaving their freed countries to head for Britain in droves, to colonise us. Now what does that phenomenon tell us? Perhaps the liberal academics will be good enough to explain that peculiar state of affairs.

We should insist that all state-funded schools should work to the same rules and curriculum. This should apply rigorously in the subject of religious education, which should be of a comparative and factual nature, and not favour any particular creed. *Religious practices should be banned from all state schools.* No 'faith' schools should be part of the state system. The proper place for religious indoctrination and practice is in private places of worship. As Richard Dawkins wrote in his book *The God Delusion*: 'It is not an exaggeration to say that the troubles in Northern Ireland would disappear in a generation if segregated schooling were abolished'. This throwaway line, with which I would hesitantly like to agree, is perhaps one of the best suggestions in the book, although I fear his timeline may be a trifle optimistic. However, the evidence in Britain is against this optimistic idea, given that we now have had hundreds of second generation immigrants, born in Britain and educated in our state schools, who have gone to Syria to fight for the IS barbarians. Culture has a profound effect on people because it is acquired in the first years of life, and if it is strongly reinforced throughout child development in family and community, it can produce unexpected extremism, as we are now seeing.

As far as religion is concerned, I think that we should disestablish the Church of England. I do not think that this would harm the C. of E. but would probably strengthen it. It is now a very benign Christian sect in Britain and, despite my atheism, I think it does much good in the pastoral and moral sense. It has come to terms with Darwinian evolution and undoubtedly helps many people to live happy lives. But I do not think that it should have a special place in our political constitution because it still has some adherents (as in most religions) who think they should tell others how to live their lives. The debate about whether we should all have the legal right to have an assisted suicide if we wish, is a typical example: religious views were clearly expressed in the House of Lords in 2014, but are not relevant to those without any faith. I think that *the autonomy of the individual should be respected absolutely*, providing only that one's actions should not cause anyone else physical harm. I wish to die when and how it suits me, if and when I find my life is not worth living, and I strongly object to anyone else's insisting that I should suffer for their strange beliefs.

If and when we have left the EU, one of the early tasks should be to *adopt a new written constitution* with a Bill of Rights, and to publish these important documents to make them freely available to the public. We do still have the 1215 Magna Carta and the 1689 Bill of Rights, but these documents are not freely available, and in any case need updating! Any other democratic organisation, such as a club or committee usually has a written constitution, the obvious reason being that everyone involved should have a clear set of rules that enable the organisation to function without the danger of power falling into some tyrant's hands. The much-lauded, unwritten constitution of Britain, which is largely hidden from the population and is the arcane province of lawyers and politicians, is a sign that it probably is of most benefit to members of the establishment. A written constitution should be freely available to the public so that the Government can easily be held to account for transgressing articles by the electorate, as in Switzerland. In that country, under its political system of Direct Democracy, the electorate have modified their written constitution so many times that in effect *it has been written by the population*. Thus their constitution gives the Swiss population the set of constitutional rules that *they* want, not what those in power want. Our politicians are always talking about transparency, but they are strangely reluctant to give us a new written constitution. I wonder why? One would think that the present situation, in which power is being devolved to Scotland and the other countries of the United Kingdom, including England and the regions, would be just the opportunity to provide us with a written constitution, after a thorough public debate. A further improvement in our archaic form of Government should be the long overdue *abolition of the House of Lords,* and its replacement with an elected second chamber.

At the time of writing (29.08.2014), the news of Douglas Carswell's defection from the Tory Party has dropped a bombshell into Britain's political scene. He intends to resign as an MP and fight the ensuing by-election on the UKIP ticket. He has a substantial personal following in his constituency, and if he wins, as he may well do, he will be the first UKIP Member of Parliament before the next general election. He says, which is true, that the Tory Party leader, Prime Minister David Cameron, has no intention of letting the country vote for leaving the EU. Speculation amongst political commentators has already begun as to whether other Eurosceptic MPs will follow suit. I have no doubt that their decisions will be based on their estimation of the probability of their being able to get re-elected, whether as Conservative or as UKIP members. In other words, personal survival in a good job will be uppermost in their minds, rather than what is best for their constituents. From my viewpoint, we need UKIP's momentum to be maintained, so that we can have an early referendum and hopefully an early exit from the EU. The more MPs who defect to UKIP from the other parties before the general election of May 2014 the better, no matter what their motivation.

The referendum in Scotland (September 2014) presented us with an interesting example of the consequences of the preceding campaigns and has stimulated a fairly long, public debate on the merits and possible drawbacks of Scotland becoming an independent country by leaving the United Kingdom. It seems that this debate has had the unintended, but not surprising, effect of rousing the Scottish nation to become greatly involved in a political decision, and of stimulating a great deal of national pride. This is a wonderful example of what happens when the people are given the chance of making an important decision, which they know will affect their own lives and that of their children and grandchildren. My hope is that this lesson will be learned by the people of the rest of the UK, and that the benefits of using this basic tool of Direct Democracy will stimulate an appetite for more referendums. Of course, as with the Scottish referendum, the Government must accept that the results are mandatory, and not just consultative exercises that they can ignore.

There is another *absolutely vital part* of the Great Project, which should involve a serious attempt to deal with the underlying problems of the third-world countries that are losing so many of their emigrating young people. We cannot expect to solve our problem of illegal mass immigration by just trying to defend our borders, especially since the invasions are organised on an industrial scale by the criminals making fortunes. The loss of these vigorous young men and women from third-world countries constitutes a *serious brain-drain* for those countries. The causes, of course, are the lack of opportunities in their own, usually badly-run and corrupt countries, beset by famine, diseases and warfare. The consequential and natural desire is for them to move elsewhere in order to better their life chances. Western countries have encouraged this brain-drain in order to exploit these young people as cheap labour, and I have already said that I think this is immoral on our part. Western countries have, however, assuaged their guilt by sending state and publically-raised funds as development aid. Billions of pounds and dollars have been transferred in the last few decades to African and Asian countries with what seem to be very poor results. Much of the transferred money is confiscated by the ruling establishments of those badly-run countries in order to enrich themselves, and much of the rest has been used to buy arms and fund armies that oppress their poor people, and keep the tyrannical politicians in power. We appear to be just throwing good money after bad. After decades of giving large sums of aid to African countries we are still seeing daily TV appeals for money to bring clean water and food to save starving children from death.

A new way of helping underdeveloped countries is clearly needed. I suggest that we should use *an adoption scheme*. Countries needing aid for development could be given help only if we are made equal partners in the use of the aid money. Instead of giving the money to despots, we could send groups of experts to assist the management of aid projects in coordinated development schemes. We could train a civil service so that the assisted country could begin to manage its own affairs with a more reliable, dedicated and less corruptible government, based on a proper democratic system. We could set up schools and universities to train teachers, doctors, nurses, engineers and other professionals and tradesmen. Factory-made prefabricated housing could be a cheap and quick way of improving the living standards of the population. Some will say that this is just a new version of the old British Empire. But call it what you will, the idea is of *a voluntary partnership* that is dedicated to developing the expertise, the organisation and the infrastructure that a backward country needs in order to reach the point of having the *critical mass of skilled human capital* which is necessary for continuing and sustainable, independent success.

We should start with the most likely country to be successful because lessons will need to be learnt, and success breeds success. It might well be that other European countries would wish to emulate our example, and obviously, previous colonial experience and a common language would make it easier to work together. The control of finance and the elimination of corruption would be an initial major objective, whilst the adopted country could determine, with our help, which projects they should prioritise, and the expected time-frame for each component of a master plan. We should give all our training staff a preparatory sensitivity training course to ensure that they are made aware of the need to respect, as far as possible, the different culture of the adopted country, and to work as partners with the aim of preparing the adopted country's workers to take over as soon as possible. An important part of the project would be to establish an effective education system, including especially *girls and women*. Educated women are more likely to help to stabilise a country, and if given equal power would, with contraceptive knowledge, skills and facilities, plan smaller families. For those people sceptical of such a coordinated development project I would ask them to look at what we and our allies have already done in Afghanistan, where the military have trained new Afghan police and military forces to set up schools and a military college. But we probably have not done enough to ensure that this country will not slip back into the old ways, and the military campaign was our primary objective, and was forced on the Afghans for our own reasons. The attempt of the Americans and Britain to prepare Iraq for democratic government, along with training their army, has not been successful, but was not done thoroughly enough. I am suggesting a voluntary enterprise consisting of an equal partnership, and a comprehensive plan agreed by both parties before the start. The idea is that aid should be *targeted to one country* as a pilot scheme, with the objective of setting up a modern system of Government with all its supporting institutions, so that value for money, and effectiveness, is monitored from the beginning. We should also encourage our young people to join a national volunteer force to help with the work in the adopted country, and as part of their own social education.

I think this approach would be a much more focussed way of delivering aid and a much better use of our aid funds. It might well be that some of the present, settled immigrants in Britain, who are already trained and skilled, would seize the opportunity to return to their country of origin where they should be able rapidly to prosper. It is essential that the third-world countries should make much more rapid and *sustainable* progress for their own welfare, and we must deal with the root causes of the mass migrations which are doing so much damage to them and us. A better example than the Afghanistan military exercise is the way

Britain and other countries are helping to fight the Ebola epidemic. The British military expedition force based on *HMS Argus* were able, *within eight weeks*, to build a hundred-bed Ebola Treatment Unit in virgin jungle, and to train Norwegian nurses to deal with the essential hygiene and corpse disposal methods. This humanitarian exercise was clearly much more effective than just sending money or food, which we have been doing for the last sixty years or so. The intention would be to repeat this sort of fine achievement across the country, and as an example of what could be done within a comprehensive master plan.

If we don't tackle more effectively the corruption and the poverty of the third-world countries, we shall suffer a rapid and total destabilisation of British and European culture, which has taken hundreds of years to evolve. If the past and present aid continues to be given in its *ad hoc* fashion, through a number of uncoordinated organisations, with frequent crises, corruption and warfare using up all the aid money, the undeveloped countries will just keep falling further behind. The gross income and wealth inequality gap between rich Western countries and the undeveloped countries must be closed, if we are not all going to suffer the current, destructive, mass migrations. The scheme outlined here should be able to harness the productive enthusiasm and hard work of the native young people in the adopted countries, who are the greatest resource which is going to waste at present. The past and present *ad hoc* aid to African countries *may be making things worse*. The result of this approach, as is explicit in many of the adverts, is to save more children from starvation and an early death, which appeals to the compassionate European public. The motivation is irreproachable, but the *consequences are surely disastrous,* because more children survive into the same poverty as afflicts their parents, so that the problems are worse ten or twenty years down the line. The population rises, the local farmers are put out of business, and vigorous young men either join terrorist groups or leave the country to travel to Europe. This wasteful and failed process indicates, that to bring these African countries into the 21st Century, *we need a comprehensive plan* to tackle, at one and the same time, *all the problems*, both political and structural. That requires a well-planned and *coordinated plan focused on one country at a time,* that has a realistic time-table for success. If other European countries were to do the same, the competitive spur would help, because national pride would be at stake. The successful example (so far) of the military campaign in Afghanistan, as opposed to what happened in the Iraq campaign, gives some support for this idea. Although the Afghanistan example was primarily aimed at the military containment of Taliban influence, it also had a fairly large effort aimed at building a democratic state with all the public services, infrastructure and political governance. Unfortunately, the Taliban have not been defeated and will undoubtedly try to make a come-back.

The example of the British military effort to help Sierra Leone cope with the Ebola crisis, shows what can be done by a disciplined force. No doubt, when the buildings are operational, the local natives will be trained to run the hospital, and to carry out decontamination and efficient burial practices. We must take a similar positive approach to get at the root causes of mass migrations, alongside the expensive protective and security measures at home that are currently failing to stem the immigration tide. Alongside this attempt to give more effective help to the poor countries, we must also be much more radical in stopping their young men from leaving their homelands and trying to enter Britain illegally. The large numbers that are arriving still in Calais must be returned to their own countries, partly to stop the problems in Calais, and also to deter others from leaving their home. I suggest that Britain and France should co-operate in a joint operation *to return the migrants* to the embarkation ports and beaches in Libya and Tunisia. Our military forces should help the French forces to round them up in Calais and return them directly in small naval ships, and leave them at their starting points with a few supplies. If they have given a lot of money to the gangsters who are organising their journeys across the Mediterranean Sea, they will not be likely to try again, and the word would soon get around that the expensive and dangerous migration trips are futile.

I am not suggesting that I have the answers to all these formidable problems which beset us in Europe and Britain, but I hope that my feeble efforts will stimulate others to tackle the problems before it is too late. All empires in history have risen and fallen, and I fear that the recent ending of the British Empire has been accompanied by the usual terminal state of psychological decline, with apathy and moral chaos rife in the governing classes helping to speed up the process. However, if the People's Army can free themselves from their slavery and take control of their own destiny, there is still hope. If we don't do it, nobody else is going to do it for us.

The BBC inquiries into the Saville sexual abuse scandal should be expedited and published. At present it looks as if these inquiries are being 'kicked into the long grass', that is, hushed up until after the 2015 general election. All the senior managers who were in post during Saville's reign of abuse should be removed, if any are still employed in that sorry organisation. The same goes for the senior managers who were involved in giving this sexual predator freedom of access to some NHS hospitals.

The BBC and its Trust *should be abolished* and a more vigorous and truly independent body formed to regulate its successor, so that its programmes are really impartial and politically unbiased. The BBC is run by people who seem to think it is their right to destroy our moral code, to promote the multicultural society, and to portray all abnormal sexual activities as part of alternative and desirable life-styles. An example of the biased material that they put out as a 'debate' was the *Question Time* programme on

15 December 2014. The audience was stuffed, as usual, with pro-immigration people, and the UKIP leader, Nigel Farage, was abused by the self-styled comedian, Russell Brand, to the point that a panel member intervened to try to stop his tirade. David Dimbleby then said it was his job to control the speakers, as indeed it was, but he had failed completely to act firmly as the Chairman, as he often does.

I think the BBC's performance over the last few decades indicates that it is past reform, and it should be disbanded and a private company set up on a five-year renewable contract (similar to the train operating companies). The new company should be *tasked to uphold decent moral standards and British cultural values*, such as were evident when Lord Reith was the Director-General. It should have a special duty in these respects, and it should not try to emulate the trashy programmes of the commercial channels, even if this means its viewer ratings are lower than those of the other channels.

I realise that many of my suggestions will be heavily criticised, particularly by the unrealistic liberals and, of course, the BBC. My motivation is to protect our culture and our country, and to those momentous ends, the means may have to be severe. The ends in this formidable problem seem to me to justify some unpleasant means, if benign ones prove to be insufficient. Some immigrant people would be disadvantaged and their innocent children upset. However, many of them had much worse pain and dangers to overcome in travelling to Britain, and some distress in being sent back to their countries of origin is probably an inevitable and unavoidable result of being repatriated. If they entered our country illegally or have been convicted of any criminal offence here, then it is difficult to have much sympathy for their plight.

I will explore the moral questions involved in my suggestions in the next chapter, in an effort to answer some expected criticisms.

§

CHAPTER EIGHTEEN

MORALITY

THE BRITISH PEOPLE have long been thought to have been a tolerant nation, with a benevolent and welcoming attitude towards mankind in general, and a culture that was once admired the world over. Of course this statement is a generalisation, and our history also has been marked with many wars and grand mistakes. The British Empire was, like all empires, largely exploitative of its colonised subjects, and grew wealthy on its commercial activities. In modern times, liberal opinion has concentrated on this aspect of its history and neglected the benefits that it also produced, again like similar empires. The Romans covered the known world with roads; the British covered their empire with railways, to say nothing of spreading the English language, both of which have made a great contribution to facilitating world-wide communication and trade.

In recent decades the British, along with other European nations, have drastically altered their attitude to warfare and colonisation, and have adopted a much more benevolent ethical stance towards all other nations and peoples. Again this is a generalisation, and this ethical political policy is not always put into practice. The nation has drastically reduced its armed forces, perhaps largely due to financial constraints rather than to a more benevolent attitude towards other nations. However, in general, along with the other developed democratic Western nations, we now believe in free world trade as a more ethical way of interacting with other poorer countries. This can still be seen to be an exploitative relationship in reality, but at least the practice of fair trading is gradually growing.

Social contract theory

The moral philosophy which endeavours to inform the motivations and actions of both individual citizens and nation states in the modern world is enshrined in the constitutions of Western democracies, and in global organisations such as the United Nations with its Universal Declaration of Human Rights. However, professional philosophers have, since the time of the ancient Greeks, argued about what is moral or good behaviour. Even today there are many divergent views on the subject of what we should do in various situations, particularly in the legal and political areas of human activity. One attractive modern philosophical approach to justice, is that of John Rawls, whose political philosophy stems from what is called 'social contract theory', based on the objective of fairness and impartiality. He suggests that we should think and act 'under a veil of ignorance', meaning that we should devise a rule of justice as if it applies to everyone, no matter what their religion, race, talents, age, gender, disability, wealth, or position in society. This approach has an obvious tendency to egalitarianism, but does not necessarily impose full equality. It would, however, if applied, suggest that one group of powerful people should not be able to pass a law which would benefit themselves, but disadvantage another group.

It is not my intent to discuss moral philosophy in general, but to give some account of the moral justification for the measures proposed above. Many liberals will take an instant dislike of the suggested measures, and some will consider them outrageously immoral. We are faced in the Western democracies, however, with a most serious and increasing problem, which threatens to overwhelm our culture. Not only is that problem out of control, but our politicians do not really want to solve it, because they and their cronies, from the time of our first Parliaments, have been motivated by holding on to power and enriching themselves. The ordinary natives of Britain are therefore going to suffer continuing misery and eventual domination by alien cultural groups in the current circumstances, or, if they rebel, the horrors of civil war. Under Rawls's veil of ignorance, we must think not only of ourselves, but of all Britons, including our descendants, and what will befall them when we have shuffled off this mortal coil. We should not keep our feelings, hopes and fears concentrated only on ourselves when, as we do every day, we think of the chaotic and terror-ridden world that appears to us to be the legacy that our generation is going to leave to our children and grandchildren.

But you may rightly say, under a veil of ignorance we have to consider what will be the plight of the immigrants and their descendants if the suggested measures were to be implemented? I have tried to think of measures that would reduce the immigrant proportion of the population, but would use as many incentives as possible, and as little coercion as possible. If these measures do not work and civil war results, as history and the current horrific wars in Israel/Palestine, Syria, Iraq and Ukraine indicate is highly likely, then the immigrants will suffer with the natives. The option of doing nothing seems to me to be a recipe for total disaster. 'It is necessary only for the good man to do nothing for evil to triumph.' – as Edmund Burke is believed to have said.

Jeremy Bentham's 'greatest happiness principle'

My former realistic liberal instincts to welcome foreign visitors and settlers has been totally extinguished over the last 50 years or so. If there is any immoral behaviour or attitude in this sorry affair of cultural suicide, it is surely that of the establishment cabal that has *discriminated against its own population* with no concern for the plight of its long-suffering poor natives. I do not think it is immoral to air my opinion, nor to make suggestions for a project of national cultural revival. The suffering of some of the immigrants in Britain that would be caused by the suggested measures is likely to be less than that which has been visited upon our people, and especially upon the poorest in society. I recognise that some suffering will be caused if my suggestions or similar ones were to be implemented, but that is an unintended and unavoidable consequence. If rioting and civil strife breaks out the immigrants will suffer a worse fate, along with us all. The alternative of carrying on allowing our native population rapidly and inevitably to become a minority in our own country is to my way of thinking totally unacceptable, and it may be that civil war will explode before that point is reached.

More immigrants from Africa and Syria

The moral aspect of our current politics is highlighted in an article by Yvette Cooper, the Labour Shadow Home Secretary, in the *Independent* newspaper (online) on 29.10.2014. I will quote her argument at length, because it illustrates what is wrong with our present political system, and the difficulties that we face. She says: 'The Home Office announced this week that Ministers have decided to support a massive downgrade of rescue help for immigrants travelling in overcrowded rickety boats across the Mediterranean, because they think that rescuing people whose lives are at risk is a 'pull factor', encouraging more to travel. So to deter others it's OK to let more drown. This lack of humanity is appalling. How has our politics come to this? Failure of enforcement is no excuse for abandoning our values. It's quite possible for Britain to support strong border controls and enforcement and still help those in desperate need.' She later says: 'The arms race led by UKIP is so destructive and is making things worse.' She objects to UKIP's poster campaign touring Rotherham depicting an abused child and says: 'UKIP's campaign doesn't call for justice or reform, only for UKIP votes. Too often what we get (sic) from UKIP – no answers, just division and exploitation. No shame, and no limits to how low they will stoop. No qualms about joining up with a Polish MEP whose party trivialises the Holocaust – even at a time when we are facing a big increase in anti-Semitic attacks. Farage is no fool and no fruitcake. He knows what he is doing, who he is manipulating and who he is exploiting. It will poison our politics and pull apart our country if everyone gets dragged into his game.' 'Playing divisive politics in pursuit of votes is not just immoral. It won't solve the problems of the country and is something Labour will not do.'

This somewhat churlish outburst needs to be put into context. It was published the day before an election of the Police and Crime Commissioner for Rotherham, following the fall from grace of the previous Labour Commissioner, who was implicated in the child-abuse scandal mentioned on pages 74-75. It seems that Ms Cooper was fearing a UKIP victory, and was making a last-ditch attempt to rubbish the political opposition. The outburst also appears to be motivated by a desire to keep power amongst the three traditional parties, all of which are trying desperately to prevent any further advancement of UKIP. It is amusing and ironic for Ms Cooper to accuse Mr Farage of 'playing divisive politics in pursuit of votes', which 'is immoral', and of 'poisoning our politics and pulling apart the country', which of course is just what the three other parties are always doing. Furthermore, Ms Cooper has been a long-standing supporter of the Labour Party, and a member of Gordon Brown's Government, and must know that many of the problems in Britain caused by mass immigration were and are a direct result of the undemocratic gerrymandering of the 'New Labour' Government of Tony Blair and Gordon Brown. But she still apparently wants to help more African illegal immigrants travel safely to Britain, and not to do so is to show an 'appalling lack of humanity'. I wonder whether Ms Cooper's strong feeling of humanity might impel her to arrange for a free travel service for the immigrants by hiring a cruise ship to ply directly between the Northern African ports and Britain. She thinks that 'it's quite possible for Britain to support strong border

controls and enforcement and still help those in desperate need.'
However, she does not tell us how those somewhat contradictory
aims could be achieved.

It is not my intention here to protect the reputation of
UKIP or Mr Farage, but to consider the morality of the current
Government's policy concerning the withdrawal of rescue help
for the immigrants travelling across the Mediterranean Sea. This
policy has a lot in common with my suggestion that we should
deal with illegal immigrants trying to cross the English Channel
from Calais, by returning them to their embarkation ports (via
a free-return-travel service), in order to discourage them from
travelling to Britain.

Philosophers, when investigating 'what is the right thing to do?'
often use a simplified 'thought experiment' to try to understand
the issues. We have in the present context the opposing views of
those who wish to deter the immigrants from travelling to Britain,
at risk of drowning, and those who think that we should rescue
them to prevent any being drowned, but at the cost of encouraging
more to travel. A simplified thought experiment, which puts the
action and its consequences closer together in time, may shed
some light on the problem. Imagine a heavily overloaded lifeboat
full of women and children in the cold Atlantic Ocean, with
several men swimming and trying to get into the boat, which
will surely capsize and drown everybody. What is the right thing
to do? Let the swimming men climb into the boat and cause *all*
to be drowned, or push the men away and cause them *only* to
drown? This scenario is not just a fanciful thought experiment;
it almost certainly has occurred several times at sea, and probably
did so when the Titanic sank.

The current problem is not quite so simple, but certainly has
some resemblance to the thought experiment. The immigrants
are *choosing* to travel in rickety overloaded boats, in order to
try to enter Britain *illegally*. If we help them by having a rescue

service because we don't want them to drown, this will certainly encourage more to come, some of whom will also drown. If a continual stream of immigrants reaches Calais, as it surely will, we then have the problem of letting them into Britain, which will not sink and drown us, but will certainly cause our already overpopulated island to have so many serious problems with our public services that, sooner or later, civil commotion will erupt. These problems will not affect liberal-minded people like Ms Cooper, who live in leafy suburbs or in city centre mansions, but will certainly cause horrendous problems for the poor underprivileged citizens that Ms Cooper and her Labour colleagues think that they represent. Whilst all humane people would not want to see innocent people drown, there are situations in real life where no simple solution exists, and where one must choose between two unpleasant choices. Just because the inevitable unpleasant consequences of more illegal immigrants entering Britain are separated from the time of their embarkation, does not excuse the favoured choice made by this liberal-minded and emotional politician, who is acting in a way that makes her feel virtuous, whilst she is scoring cheap political points over her more rational opponents. If, as is likely, the withdrawal of the rescue services, and my suggested *return* service, quickly reduces the number of people willing to hazard their lives in overloaded rickety boats, the number drowning in future might be smaller than it is currently. Sometimes the game is 'lose-lose', and one has to make a difficult choice – as any experienced politician must surely know.

For those politicians and liberal-minded commentators who think that my comments above indicate a callous and appalling attitude towards poor African economic migrants, I would remind them that politicians in Government have to make similar hard decisions all the time, based often on cost-benefit analysis. For a simple example, if a dangerous stretch of road could be reconstructed so that one life per ten years is likely to be saved, but the cost is such that the available money could be better spent elsewhere, then the rational decision is to spend the money on the alternative project. To take another real-life example, if the death of 453 British soldiers, and the horrendous wounding of another a thousand or so soldiers, has enabled our military forces to help in clearing Afghanistan of the Taliban, in order to protect Britain from terrorist attacks by Al-Qaeda, and to help the Afghan people into the 21st Century, then our politicians seem to think that the thirteen years of military effort was 'worth it'. Some of us may disagree, but one must realise that these decisions are extremely difficult to make, because sometimes *there are no easy options*, predictions are unreliable, and, of course, the decision-makers are dealing with other people's lives. I think that such decisions must be taken in as rational a fashion as possible, and not wholly under the influence of an emotional impulse. In the case of Ms Cooper and the drowning immigrants, I think she is hoist with her own petard, because she wants to portray her political opponents as being callous and appallingly inhumane, when in fact she is showing herself to be trying to score the cheap political points that she ascribes to her opponents.

My main moral standpoint in this book is based on the fact that we are in grave danger, across the globe as well as in Britain, of ignoring mounting population pressures on the one hand, and of pursuing utopian liberal policies which are making the inevitable catastrophes more imminent and worse on the other hand. If this prediction proves to be accurate, the modern technology which has produced weapons of mass destruction, and which is in the hands of tyrannical dictators, may be unleashed upon the helpless innocent victims, mainly women and children who always suffer from military conflicts. But even if that worst scenario is avoided, we are already involved in the ancient and horrendous curse of inter-faith wars and cultural terrorism. Many of those people who are scornful and sceptical of such doom-laden predictions are currently (2014) getting on with their pleasures and happy lives with little care for the Syrians, Palestinians, Iraqis, Yasidis and Ukrainians who are already suffering in such horrific conditions, with much ineffectual hand-wringing and word-slinging from the 'international community' as the only comfort to relieve their soul-crushing misery. The suggestions I have made seem to me to be the minimal sort of action that we need to take, to save our Western culture from extinction, and the moral justification for this Great Project is based on Bentham's utilitarian objective of 'the greater good for the greater number' in a situation *that does not lend itself to a quick-fix with no pain.*

There can be no doubt that there are too many people on the earth at the moment, and we have the frightening knowledge that the world population is growing at an increasing rate, and everybody wants and expects to improve their standard of living. This amounts to a totally unsustainable situation, if we are to have some hope of dealing successfully with all the problems caused by the inequalities of wealth and life chances, between the haves and the have-nots. Violence and wars are already being fought over territory and natural resources, and as the global population grows these vital human essentials are shrinking. The mass migrations that this book has tried to investigate are a symptom of the underlying problem of the rich people and rich countries taking their unfair share of wealth and resources, at the expense of the poverty of the world's powerless poor who produce much of the wealth. The thing that has changed recently (for the good) is that the poor now have access to more knowledge, owing to the advent of efficient and cheap information technology. For the first time they are beginning to know how poor they really are, and how rich the wealthy are, and they are therefore no longer willing to continue their lives in uncomplaining poverty. Even in Britain, one of the richest countries in the world, the unequal distribution of wealth is alarming and the inequality-gap is growing. The recent, frequent scandals involving establishment figures have opened the eyes of ordinary people, who have now lost all trust in 'the great and the good'. People are now beginning to realise, despite the relentless propaganda, that the nation is in a worse state than the one which described our troops in the World War I cliché as: 'Lions led by donkeys.' This should now be altered to fit the modern state of Britain: 'Honest labourers led by political criminals.' The establishment criminals should be dismissed once and for all, and the honest labourers should take power into their own hands, where it belongs. We shall never abolish poverty while the wealth that the people create is syphoned off by the governing elite. How many more billionaires do we need whilst our poor people wait for a few drops of 'trickle-down' wealth?

The immoral system called 'representative democracy' must, if we are to complete the long historical struggle for freedom, fairness and justice, be swept away and replaced by our version of the Swiss system of Direct Democracy. Representative democracy divides the nation into two opposing groups, those who want to pay less tax, and those who want to have more hand-outs. Governments, as somebody has said, take money from one half of the nation and hand it out to the other half. He forgot to say that the governing classes take their big cut in the process.

So my last words are: **read up on Direct Democracy**, and vote UKIP in the May 2015 general election in order to send a strong message to the politicians that we have had enough of their devious and self-serving behaviour, and we want to start immediately with a referendum on the EU issue, so that we can run our own country and revitalise our much-loved British culture. Only in this way can we finally begin the process of throwing off the chains of the power establishment, and achieve real and lasting freedom. Perhaps, just perhaps, we have time to prevent the suicide of our culture by standing up for our own way of life, and rejecting the 'multicultural society' that we never asked for and do not want. We must be resolute in the face of many difficulties, including an expected liberal torrent of abuse aimed at weakening our campaign. We have everything to gain and nothing to lose.

§

CHAPTER NINETEEN

LATE NEWS

THE BBC DAILY POLITICS SHOW. *01.09.2014* : a discussion took place about the measures needed to deal with the returning jihadist Muslim young men who have been fighting in Syria for the Islamic State (IS). What interested me was the fact that the Lib-Dem and Labour politicians on the show were so concerned that political correctness (PC) should not now be allowed to stifle debate about the indoctrination and radicalisation of young men in the Muslim community in Britain. It was amazing to hear such a clear belief in free speech, despite the sensitive nature of the topic, when these same politicians have for so long been part of the establishment that has totally suppressed free speech on such topics, on the grounds that it would give offence to Muslims and promote social disharmony. The serious current threat of terrorist acts which may be committed on our streets by these 'home-grown terrorists' has suddenly changed some people's minds. Why they couldn't have seen the inevitability of this sort of problem coming to our country over the last few years I cannot imagine, especially since we have already had the atrocity of the London bombing in 2005, and several other plots prevented by the security services. And how these politicians and other utopian liberals in the establishment could not have seen the inevitability of severe social problems developing below the radar as a result of the suppression of free speech, I also cannot imagine. No wonder the electorate has detached itself from this dysfunctional group of starry-eyed and passionate believers in the 'benefits' of mass immigration and the so-called 'multicultural society'.

I doubt that they can see the irony of their new viewpoint and attitude to open debate. I also doubt that they realise yet that their previous views have been a major cause of our having imported these serious and inevitable problems into the country, and I am sure they will be in denial of any guilt or responsibility. If anyone has the courage to accuse them of gross culpability, they will doubtless fall back on the defensive cliché of the 'small minority' of terrorists so loved by the utopian liberals when their plans for a wonderful society show any signs of serious problems.

I'm pinning my hopes on the common sense and perceptiveness of the electorate to see through this faint (and probably temporary) change of heart, and to realise that no real change of elitist arrogance is likely to happen. The politicians will still know that they are right, and that a few sticking-plaster changes to the law will bring harmony and happiness to us all in their splendid creation of the 'multicultural society'. You may have noticed how many top posts are now occupied by the enterprising immigrant Asians, mostly of course Muslims, who have benefitted from positive discrimination. Whoever rules this dysfunctional society in future will find it very difficult to govern because there are now so many different and substantial groups ('communities') in our country, that most policies will cause serious offence to one group or another, and we shall have many more street protests and riots for the police to manage. We have lost our national unity, which was so easily mustered in two world wars, for a mess of cultural pottage.

It seems that our politicians are now becoming aware, at last, that Muslims across the world are causing the greatest threat to Western democracies since the Middle Ages. Their new awareness is the result of the horrendous barbarities being committed in Iraq and Syria by the Islamic State (IS), and its stated object of producing another Caliphate (or Muslim Empire). These vicious terrorists have been killing Yasidi Christians and anybody else who will not convert to Islam, and have now beheaded the second American journalist James Foley and have flaunted these barbaric acts on video. They have beheaded two British hostages and aid workers, David Haines, and Alan Henning. It is believed that the man committing the atrocities in these videos is a 'British' man, presumably one of our 'home-grown terrorists'. No wonder many English natives now think that the word 'British' has no real cultural meaning. These Muslims clearly are adopting a tactic of spreading terror to intimidate any opposition forces, and seem to be trying to get the Western forces involved in a ground war, which they can then portray as an anti-Muslim religious war. Our politicians are now realising with horror that many of the estimated five hundred or more 'British' Muslims who have joined this jihadist war will be returning to Britain, and no doubt, will be spreading their evil ideology in our Muslim 'community'. None of the establishment intellectuals who have so fiercely pursued their utopian project has expressed any sorrow or apology for the enormous damage they have wreaked on our culture. We do not yet know what horrors we and our children and grandchildren will suffer in the years to come.

It is noteworthy that many Muslims in Britain are now explaining that the IS terrorists are not *true* Muslims, and that the Muslims in Britain are moderates, who detest what the terrorists are doing in Iraq and Syria in the name of their faith. I do not doubt the truth of their (new) protests, but wonder why they did not protest in similar fashion after the London bombings and other terrorist plots. Indeed, many Muslim leaders in the past made statements of support for the jihadists. I think that they have at last realised that their previous comments and silences, which went unchallenged because of the atmosphere created by the PC-induced campaign against 'racism', were not wise, and they are now feeling more threatened because of the change of English opinion which is currently being more openly expressed. However, they still have not told us why, and how, their 'moderate' Muslim communities manage to spawn the British-educated young men (and women) who wish to join in the barbaric IS jihad. If they are unable to understand and stop this process of terrorist indoctrination in their communities, it will only serve to make me, and many others, feel that we should try to get rid of all of them. It surely is up to the new 'moderate' Muslims to investigate and deal with a problem that arises so easily as an offshoot of their faith. The problem is going to be protracted, like the war in Syria and Iraq, and to an outsider it seems that for a so-called 'peaceful religion', Islam is paradoxically riven with tribal conflict of a very barbaric and horrific nature.

05.09.2014.

At the moment we are witnessing a serious invasion of immigrants at the port of Calais, where some 2,500 young (mainly African) men are desperately trying to get to Britain illegally by any means possible. The Mayor of Calais is crying out for help, but it seems that neither the British nor French politicians are taking much notice of this frightful scenario, which requires *urgent and effective attention*. The politicians are having NATO meetings at Cardiff, where they are preoccupied with the IS threat in Iraq and Syria, and the conflict in Ukraine. In my view these two threats pale into insignificance for Britain at this particular moment because the massive Calais invasion is happening now, and will continue at a frightening pace unless effective and urgent action is not taken.

I feel strongly that this latter problem, which has been festering for decades and has now reached intolerable proportions, must be dealt with in a manner that will **send a clear signal to all potential migrants in Africa and Syria that they will not be allowed to enter Europe illegally by any route, and any attempts will be dealt with severely,** as outlined previously.

My suggested course of action will, of course, set up a roar of protest from the Liberal and Labour intelligentsia (including

Yvette Cooper). But surely most ordinary people will realise that Britain and Europe cannot allow a large proportion of the population of Africa and the Middle East to enter our territory illegally, or even legally. We cannot be expected to put up with the current situation, which is causing chaos in Calais, and seriously interfering with our continental trade, to say nothing of the problems which past illegal immigration has caused to Britain.

If international law would be transgressed by my suggested actions, then so be it. This problem is unprecedented, and we all know that the law is very slow to catch up with fast-moving criminal events. Urgent action should be taken to *change* international law, if it needs changing, to meet this serious problem. In the meantime we should take firm and urgent action, because delay is going to cause even more tragedy than occurs now, when some migrants drown crossing the Mediterranean Sea. NATO must act, and act now. This organisation is good at talking and holding expensive conferences, but this problem now requires concerted and effective action.

29.10.2014.
On the BBC Andrew Marr show on 26.10.2014 Michael Fallon, the Defence Secretary said 'some British towns are being swamped by immigrants, and residents are under siege. Foreigners and immigrants need to be under some form of restraint or they risk dominating the local population.' His mild comments were immediately condemned by his Lib-Dem cabinet colleague Ed Davey, the Environment Secretary, who said he disagreed with Fallon's language. He said: 'When we talk about immigration we need to be responsible in the words that we use'. So we must add a few more words to the banned lexicon, according to this self-appointed editor with his Liberal sensitivities: 'swamping', 'siege', 'dominating', and possibly 'restraint' are now not to be used in

relation to the mass immigrant invasion. Perhaps 'invasion' will also cause Mr Davy to have a Lib–Dem fit of the vapours. I suggest that some enterprising person might soon issue an English 'banned words' dictionary, which would be better formulated online, as it will doubtless need updating every week with additional terms. My sympathy goes to Mr Fallon, who said what he meant in plain English, but who will soon have to recant for his 'crime'. It is a good thing that the English language has so many words in its lexicon, otherwise we would soon all be tongue-tied. What nonsense these liberals keep spouting, and what arrogance to think that they know what we should all be thinking, saying and doing to bring about universal happiness. The only good that can come of this depressing PC phenomenon and the suppression of free speech, is that the Lib–Dems will surely get wiped out at the next general election.

09.11.2014.

The *Sunday Times* reports that Tony Blair had a secret contract signed in November 2010 between his company, Tony Blair Associates, and a Saudi oil company, for £41,000 and 2% commission on any deals he brokered. He was to find new sources of investment for PetroSaudi and to promote that company to Chinese political leaders and other contacts of his. As the newspaper comments, this poses questions about conflicts of interests, between this role and that of being a UN Special Envoy for the Middle East. My comment is: no wonder this avaricious man quit the British Parliament in a hurry. His whole career as a Labour politician, 'fighting for the working classes', seems to have been a hypocritical exercise. Any interested observer might reasonably conclude that his true objective has been to make as many useful contacts across the world as possible in order to enrich himself. He is a prime example of the self-serving leaders in our establishment whom we must get rid of as soon as possible.

05.11.2014.

The *Daily Telegraph* reported that David Cameron said: 'I want to see an Asian Prime Minister, but not yet.' He made the remarks at an award dinner in central London where Sajid Javid, the Culture Secretary, topped a power list of the most influential Asians in the UK. Mr Cameron went on to say: 'In Britain there are still too few people from ethnic minorities in top positions. The absence is glaring in the boardrooms of the FTSE 250, in the chambers of the Houses of Parliament, football managers' benches, on High-Court judges' benches, and in our fighter jets, our naval ships, our armed battalions around the world, and I am clear this has to change, not to tick boxes, not to fill quotas, but to realise our full potential'.

So there you have it, straight from the horse's mouth. Who says we are not committing cultural suicide, when our own PM is offering the top Government job to an immigrant? And note the 'not yet'. In other words, he wants to hold onto the top job until he has finished his work of colonising the country for the benefit of himself and his cronies. As for not ticking boxes and not filling quotas, that was just what he was doing. One has to wonder why the political establishment is determined to discriminate so blatantly against British natives. I think we must recall again Cicero's wise question: 'Who benefits?' Our PM was surely just wooing the 'British Asians', because he is desperate to win the upcoming general election in May 2015. And note that Mr Javid, who is a British-born son of an immigrant father who is said to have come here with nothing, has already managed to achieve a wealth of about £20 million, apparently from working in the City of London. That sounds like a wonderful achievement, but in effect he acquired this money from other British people, as do all the financial experts working in the City. They don't 'make money', as they like to say, in fact they don't make anything. They provide a simple service manipulating *our* money and, in the process, take a large percentage for themselves. And, of course, our Prime Minister is anxious to welcome Mr Javid into the club of rich politicians who are supposed to be looking after all of us. Remember that fatuous saying of George Osborne, another wealthy Tory, at the beginning of this Parliament's campaign to deal with the financial crisis: 'We're all in this together'? That was intended to get us all to think that the pain of cuts and austerity was going to be equally shared, so how come the rich have got much richer and the poor have got much poorer? The politicians' skilled use of words and slogans is part of their essential obfuscatory toolbox for maintaining the tyranny of control over the voters.

How can we ever trust this lot of charlatans again? The British people must be very naïve indeed if they think that the wealth gap between the rich and the poor is going to close up again, when as previously mentioned, the poverty at the bottom is *caused by the greedy people at the top* stealing an ever-growing proportion of the nation's wealth – which is produced not by them, but by us.

24.11.2014.
Ch.4 TV: The 'Dispatches' programme revealed the truth about the *industrial organisation* of the illegal immigration from Calais into Britain. About 2,500 immigrants, mainly from Africa and the Middle East, are camped around the port, and gangsters are providing different methods of travel according to the price charged. At the top end of their menu a gangster living in London provides a taxi service for about £5,000 and *within twenty-four hours* the immigrant customer is sitting happily in a London café. At the lower price end, immigrants stow away under lorries, with the very real danger of being run over and killed. There is even a white British man who provides a *free service* via his camper van, which has a secret compartment for the stowaway. He does

this because he 'feels sorry for them'. He is aware of the danger that he may be sent to prison if he is caught, and clearly is a very sincere, if somewhat oversensitive, man. There is no doubt that the French and British authorities are failing in their duty to stop this desperate human trafficking.

14.12.2014.

We now know that more aid workers and Yasidi civilians have been beheaded by the barbaric Muslim extremists in Syria and Iraq. We also have had some of the returned, British, 'home-grown' jihadists convicted by our courts. The prison sentences handed down to these young men not surprisingly upset their parents, who had informed the police of their return. The parents 'felt betrayed' by the police and the justice system, and said that these prison sentences would naturally deter other parents of returnees from informing the police. These events illustrate the difficulties that multiculturalism is sure to throw up. The parents feel betrayed by the police and the legal system; no doubt the jihadist young men feel betrayed by their parents; and the natives feel that the jihadists brought up in Britain have betrayed their country. And all of these people are only experiencing *natural human feelings*. What is the right thing to do? Whatever the authorities do, with the best of intentions, someone is going to feel very aggrieved. There is no easy solution in this situation and it will not be the last example of the problems that our 'multicultural society' will produce. The reason we have such modern predicaments is clear – we have many different cultural groups, but we do not now live in a 'society' that depends on mutual trust between all law-abiding citizens and an accepted code of behaviour. Cultural conflict and rioting, such as that being currently witnessed throughout the USA over white police behaviour following a black man's death, is certain to be our normal lot in future.

14.12.2014.

We had an example today of the behaviour of a major BBC interviewer on the Sunday Politics show, namely Andrew Neil. He interviewed the Secretary for Work and Pensions, Ian Duncan Smith, who clearly had a medical problem with his throat and speech, as Mr Neil acknowledged. IDS was harangued mercilessly for about thirty minutes. Mr Neil's technique was, as it often is on that show, to read aggressively from his prepared notes, a large number of questions at his victim, and, as soon as the victim begins to answer, fire out his next question or argue over the reply, so that a listener cannot hear it. The questions were about the roll-out of the Universal Credit, which Mr Neil rubbished from beginning to end of the interview. He did not attempt to listen to the replies because he was busy reading his notes and disputing as IDS spoke. In addition, two graphs prepared for, or by, the BBC were shown to illustrate increases in the 'nominal' cost of the benefits – which IDS repeatedly disputed in 'real' terms. Apart from being unable to hear all that IDS was saying, the amount of financial information left me confused half way through the interview. I would guess that most ordinary viewers would have gained little from this poor performance. The aggressive and grossly impolite manner in which an indisposed politician was treated is typical of this ill-mannered example of BBC interviewing technique. It is important that politicians should be thoroughly questioned, but the viewer wants to hear the politician, not the BBC celebrity bully. I have no desire to defend a Tory Minister, and IDS was well able to fight his corner in an unruffled manner, but this sort of biased and loutish public broadcasting is yet another reason for the BBC to be broken up and replaced by a more civilised and expert private company, with a proper oversight from a regulator responsive to the public.

17.12.2014.

We learned today that Julie Phillips, a fan at a Middlesbrough football match, tore up a copy of the Koran, and has been convicted of causing 'racially aggravated harassment, alarm or distress' and has been banned from all football matches in England and Wales for three years by Teesside Magistrates Court. She has also lost her job with Middlesbrough Council.

By all accounts Ms Phillips has repeated such disturbances several times at football matches, often under the influence of alcohol, and it may be that most people would think that she has earned the additional permanent ban from the Middleborough Riverside Stadium. My concern however is not that the law against public disorder is unwarranted or unnecessary, but that there should be a *special offence* of 'racially aggravated harassment'. We know that all cultures and religious groups have a number of alcoholic, eccentric, mentally unbalanced or frankly psychotic nuisances, who have to be restrained at times. But what bothers me is the gradual constraint which is being put on perfectly normal citizens on the grounds of 'racial offence'. We are entitled to question why some religious groups are *thought to be so easily offended*. The Koran after all is a book, albeit highly valued by Muslims. I have thousands of books which are my most prized possessions, but if someone were to tear up a copy of, say, Charles Darwin's 'The Origin of Species', in front of me to indicate their hatred of his theory of evolution or of me, I would naturally consider him to be a bigot, or possibly mentally disturbed. A book is a book, and if one loses a book it is nearly always possible to replace it with only little inconvenience. So why are Muslims thought by the British establishment to be so easily offended? Before answering that question we should note that there seem to be very few cases of religious offence being caused to Christians, or perhaps they are just more tolerant. One would have thought that people in a host culture would be more easily offended than immigrants, who are, after all, the guests in the host country, and usually guests go out of their way not to offend their hosts. It also seems to me, as previously mentioned, that servile, establishment attempts to try to appease the immigrants, especially the Muslims who are causing us much more serious problems than tearing up a few books, are guaranteed to make the Muslims *ultrasensitive* to insults on the one hand, and to use *manufactured offence* as a tool to bully us into more special treatment on the other hand.

We have, for some time, been warned by our security services that the likelihood of a bomb attack or similar atrocity is high, and the public need to be vigilant, although there is no actual evidence of an imminent attack. In the last few days, our soldiers have been told not to wear uniform when off duty, in case they become the target of an extremist determined *to carry out a beheading on our streets*. This news was swiftly followed by a similar warning to all our police officers. Not much comment was made about these frightening possibilities, and it looks likely that we shall passively accept yet another sad step into the abyss of cultural decline. Unfortunately the human tendency is to accommodate easily and unconsciously to successive small potential threats, especially when our own daily experience does not actually reinforce the warnings. Even when reinforcement occurs by hearing of an actual event somewhere else, as with the appalling death of Fusilier Lee Rigby on 22.05.2013, most people quickly forget. We all live largely in a little familiar bubble of our own, which is so reassuring that we think that nothing will happen to ourselves. How often do we see, on TV, people reacting to a murder or other tragic event in their neighbourhood by saying: 'I never thought it would happen in our street.'

So, little by little, our culture has been, and still is being, slowly and relentlessly destroyed. Most naturally tolerant and friendly British natives are sleepwalking into a multicultural Armageddon. According to a child expert on TV, our young schoolchildren now need to be *taught* that some of the things that they think are normal, such as stealing, are crimes. At a time when we should be helping other countries and cultures to behave in a more civilised fashion, the opposite is happening in Britain; our hitherto relatively civilised culture is being dragged backwards into the Middle Ages.

Our self-serving establishment liberals have given us a new meaning of the phrase: 'assisted suicide'. Cultural suicide looks to be a dead certainty as the colonisation of Britain proceeds apace. Unless that is, the British natives wake up and vote for UKIP and decimate the three traditional parties at the next election. Winston Churchill must be groaning in his grave.

§

CHAPTER TWENTY

DISCLAIMERS

I MUST FIRST EMPHASISE that I do not hate anyone, (with the exception of Tony Blair and his cronies, for reasons given elsewhere in the book). Nor do I ever wish to harm anyone, whether foreign or not. I have spent most of my life helping other people, as I would expect any civilised person to do. It is, nevertheless, sometimes necessary to cause someone pain or harm in order to achieve some overriding good, as in the practice of medicine, psychiatry and of course politics.

I also want to make it clear that most of the psychological traits and behaviours which I have mentioned as being inherited or culturally acquired, and described as being attributes of foreigners, are *common to all foreigners*, including British natives when they are abroad. In other words 'foreigners' are not people of any particular racial or cultural group, but are to be assumed to be any people in a country different from their own, when mentioned in the book. People of all races and cultures tend to be much the same psychologically. Nevertheless, cultural differences can be very different indeed (as the barbaric IS terrorists exhibit only too well). Even slight and subtle cultural differences, such as is seen between people of different socio-economic classes, can be enough to cause friction, dislike, or even hatred. Humans have a strong universal tendency to be happiest with people like themselves, as is obvious in ordinary social life. Our choice of mate and firm friends usually is based on this tendency. That does not however prevent some people of different races or cultures from finding compatible foreign friends, or deciding to marry across cultural boundaries.

I do not object to foreigners settling legally in Britain, either temporarily or permanently, *in small numbers*. Many skilled foreigners, such as professionals and scientists, have made substantial contributions to our culture and economy in the past and no doubt will in the future. Many people will make strong friendships with foreigners. I do, however, object strongly to having our country invaded with *huge numbers* of poor foreigners whose motivation is to avail themselves of all the benefits and public services that our politicians have made freely available without our consent. I also object strongly to masses of foreigners, such as the Muslims, arriving with deeply alien cultures and religions, and thus contaminating and threatening our own culture. My relationships with individual foreigners has always been, and is now, based entirely on their individual characters, interests, values and personalities, as with my compatriots.

I have not consulted any other person or any organisation in writing this book, and it is based solely on my own opinions. I have no doubt that I have made mistakes as to facts and that many of my opinions will give some readers offence. I have quoted in the book the opinion of the philosopher John Stuart Mill, which I also passionately hold: 'Free speech or expression has no meaning if you are not allowed to *offend* other people who have different views. The only constraint should be that one's words should not cause actual bodily harm'. I hope that any opposition to my views will be expressed in a civilised manner. I shall ignore, as I always have done, all abuse as being a sign of a total lack of reasoned argument and good manners.

I have made recommendations for certain books, which I hope will be of interest to readers wanting more information. I have no personal contact with their authors, nor do I have any pecuniary interest in the sale of those books.

I have had no contact with UKIP relating to this book, and none of my opinions have been approved by them, nor has that organisation seen any draft of the book before publication. I am an ordinary member of UKIP, and have recommended that readers should vote for that political party solely because I think that it is the most democratic party, and is the only one that would trust the electorate in an early referendum on the crucial matter of membership of the European Union. Nevertheless, as with all politicians, the UKIP hierarchy should not be trusted naively because, no doubt, their success will in time go to their heads as it does to all the others. They should be assessed, as with all politicians, on what they do and not on what they say they will do. Personally I am hoping that they will move towards Direct Democracy because that is my own ultimate objective for our country.

§

BIBLIOGRAPHY

Bryson, Bill (1996): *Notes From a Small Island*. London, Black Swan Books. A picture of Britain in the early 1970s, wittily described by an American Anglophile.

Fraser, David (2007): *A Land Fit For Criminals: An Insider's View of Crime, Punishment and Justice in England and Wales*. Sussex, England, Book Guild Publishing. A devastating and thoroughly researched account, by an experienced probation officer and criminal intelligence analyst, of the corrupt British Criminal Justice system and the false government propaganda.

Hitchens, Peter (2002): *The Abolition of Britain: The British Cultural Revolution from Lady Chatterley to Tony Blair*. London, Quartet Books. A sustained and powerful attack on the cultural decline of a once great nation.

Lorenz, Konrad (1966): *On Aggression: London*, Methuen & Co Ltd. A fascinating book on the evolution of aggression in vertebrates by the father of modern ethology. He ends by making some suggestions as to how the aggressive drive of humans might be channelled into benign activities.

Malthus, Thomas (1798): *An Essay on the Principle of Population*. Oxford World's Classics, Oxford University Press, (2014 reprint). The book that inspired Charles Darwin by its emphasis on the danger of overpopulation and competition.

Marsh, John (2012): *The Liberal Delusion: The Roots of Our Current Moral Crisis*. Bury St Edmonds, England, Arena Books. This important book explores the idea that Western liberal society is based on the mistaken view that human nature is fundamentally good, as promoted in the Enlightenment by Rousseau. This view overturned the Biblical one of a flawed nature. The liberal understanding of human nature has now been contradicted by scientific discoveries based on evolutionary psychology and genetics.

Orwell, George (1945): *Animal Farm: A Fairy Story*. London, Penguin Modern Classics, (2013 reprint): A political allegory of a revolution that went wrong in Soviet Russia, with its savage attack on Stalin. Thought by many to be the most influential book of the 20th century.

Orwell, George (1949): *Nineteen Eighty-Four*. London, Penguin Modern Classics, (2013 reprint). A dystrophic masterpiece portraying a brutal tyranny, with many slogans and phrases which have passed into the language.

Phillips, Melanie (2008): *Londonistan: How Britain Has Created a Terror State Within*. London, Gibson Square. An alarming description of the British establishment's failure to deal effectively with the terror threat of religious radicalisation, and the attack on our culture by the Muslim programme of Islamisation.

Thomas, Hugh (1997): *The Slave Trade: The History of the Atlantic Slave Trade 1440-1870*. London, Picador, Macmillan Publishers Ltd. A scholarly and comprehensive account of one of our most shameful imperial enterprises, but including the well organised abolitionist movement of the Quakers.

Wade, Nicholas (2006): *Before The Dawn: Recovering the Lost History of Our Ancestors*. New York, The Penguin Press. A fine account of the recent discoveries in the biological and social sciences, including genetics, concerning human evolution.

Wilkinson, Richard & Pickett, Kate (2010): *The Spirit Level: Why Equality is Better for Everyone*. London, Penguin Books Ltd. A groundbreaking book based on years of research. It shows how almost everything in human affairs, from life expectancy to mental illness, violence to illiteracy, is affected not by how wealthy a society is, but how equal it is.

§

INDEX

B

Balkan   19, 92

Balkanisation   50, 135, 140

Bangladesh   17, 80, 101

Bangladeshi   74

Basque   13, 92

BBC Andrew Marr   318

BBC Daily Politics   114, 228, 314

BBC Daily Politics Show   114, 228, 314

BBC TV   47, 172, 259, 266

Belfast City Council   81

Belfast City Hall   43, 81

Bentham   305, 311

Bentham, Jeremy   305

Bible   23

Biblical   15, 22, 76, 136, 195, 331

Big Brother   160, 169

Bill of Rights   294

Birmingham   41, 83, 160, 239, 278, 291

Blair, Mr   189, 214, 222, 225, 331

Blair, Prime Minister   188, 213

Blair, Prime Minister Tony   213

Blair Government   57, 89, 151, 187-188, 197, 212, 222-223, 307

Blair New Labour Government   44, 151, 212, 307

Blakelock, PC Keith   35

Blunkett, David   232

Bolsover   180

Bombay Broadcasting Corporation   230

Border Agency   79, 85, 212

Border Control Agency   85, 212

Bradford   41, 83, 278

Brand, Russell   302

Bristol   233

Britain   65, 72, 77, 109, 126, 162, 233, 278

British Asians   320

British Civil Service   201

British Criminals   119, 158, 160, 287, 331

British Criminal Justice   35, 287, 331

British Cultural Revolution   331

British Empire   185, 193, 292, 297, 301, 303

British Government   12-13, 57, 76, 93, 182, 185, 207, 210, 218, 220, 228, 331

British Governments   18, 50, 188, 202, 220, 266

British Isles   47, 64, 173

British Muslims   108, 124, 126, 133, 197, 218, 229, 269, 292, 316, 322, 332

British National Party   128

British Nationality Act   185

British Parliament   182, 226, 319

British Parliamentary   220, 274

British Premier League   159

British Rail   34

British Union Jack   12

British-born   320

British-educated   316

Britons   18, 23, 41, 47, 63, 90, 107, 110, 146, 148, 159, 169, 180, 186, 195-196, 206-207, 223, 230, 234, 264, 278, 305

Brixton   41, 83, 145, 185, 278

Broadwater Farm Estate   35